EPISODE ONE: SISTER'S KEEPER

STORY
BILL JEMAS
MICHAEL COAST

SCRIPT
MICHAEL COAST
JEFF McCOMSEY

LAYOUTS
KURT TIEDE

PENCILS
FEDERICA MANFRED

COLORS
VLADIMIR POPOV

G ZHANG

LETTERS
DARRE   EZ
ELYSIA LIANG

EDITOR
ELYSIA LIANG

EPISODE TWO: LAST GENERATION

STORY
MICHAEL COAST
BILL JEMAS
JEFF McCOMSEY

SCRIPT
ED GAVAGAN
JEFF McCOMSEY

LAYOUTS
KURT TIEDE
JEFF McCOMSEY

PENCILS
FEDERICA MANFREDI

COLORS
VLADIMIR POPOV
MAXFLAN ARAUJO

COVER
CARLOS RENO

LETTERS
ELYSIA LIANG

EDITOR
ELYSIA LIANG

EPISODE THREE: YOU CAN'T GO HOME AGAIN

STORY
MICHAEL COAST
BILL JEMAS
JEFF McCOMSEY

SCRIPT
JEFF McCOMSEY
ED GAVAGAN

LAYOUTS
STAN CHOU

PENCILS
FEDERICA MANFREDI
NOVO MALGAPO
FERNANDO MELEK

COLORS
VLADIMIR POPOV
ROSS HUGHES
FRAN GAMBOA

COVER
APPLE QINGYANG ZHANG

LETTERS
ELYSIA LIANG

EDITOR
ELYSIA LIANG

EPISODE FOUR: BORN AGAINST

STORY
BILL JEMAS
STAN CHOU

SCRIPT
JEFF McCOMSEY
ELYSIA LIANG
ED GAVAGAN

LAYOUTS
STAN CHOU

PENCILS
FEDERICA MANFREDI
LEANDRO TONELLI
FERNANDO MELEK
NOVO MALGAPO

COLORS
VLADIMIR POPOV
ANDREA CELESTINI

COVER
CARLOS RENO

LETTERS
ELYSIA LIANG

EDITOR
ELYSIA LIANG

EPISODE FIVE: FALL

STORY
BILL JEMAS
STAN CHOU
MICHAEL COAST

SCRIPT
BILL JEMAS
MICHAEL COAST
ELYSIA LIANG
JEFF McCOMSEY

LAYOUTS
STAN CHOU
BENJAMIN SILBERSTEIN

PENCILS
FEDERICA MANFREDI
ADRIANO VICENTE
CLAUDIA BALBONI

COLORS
ANDREA CELESTINI
YLENIA DI NAPOLI

COVER
JEFF DEKAL

LETTERS
ELYSIA LIANG

EDITOR
ELYSIA LIANG

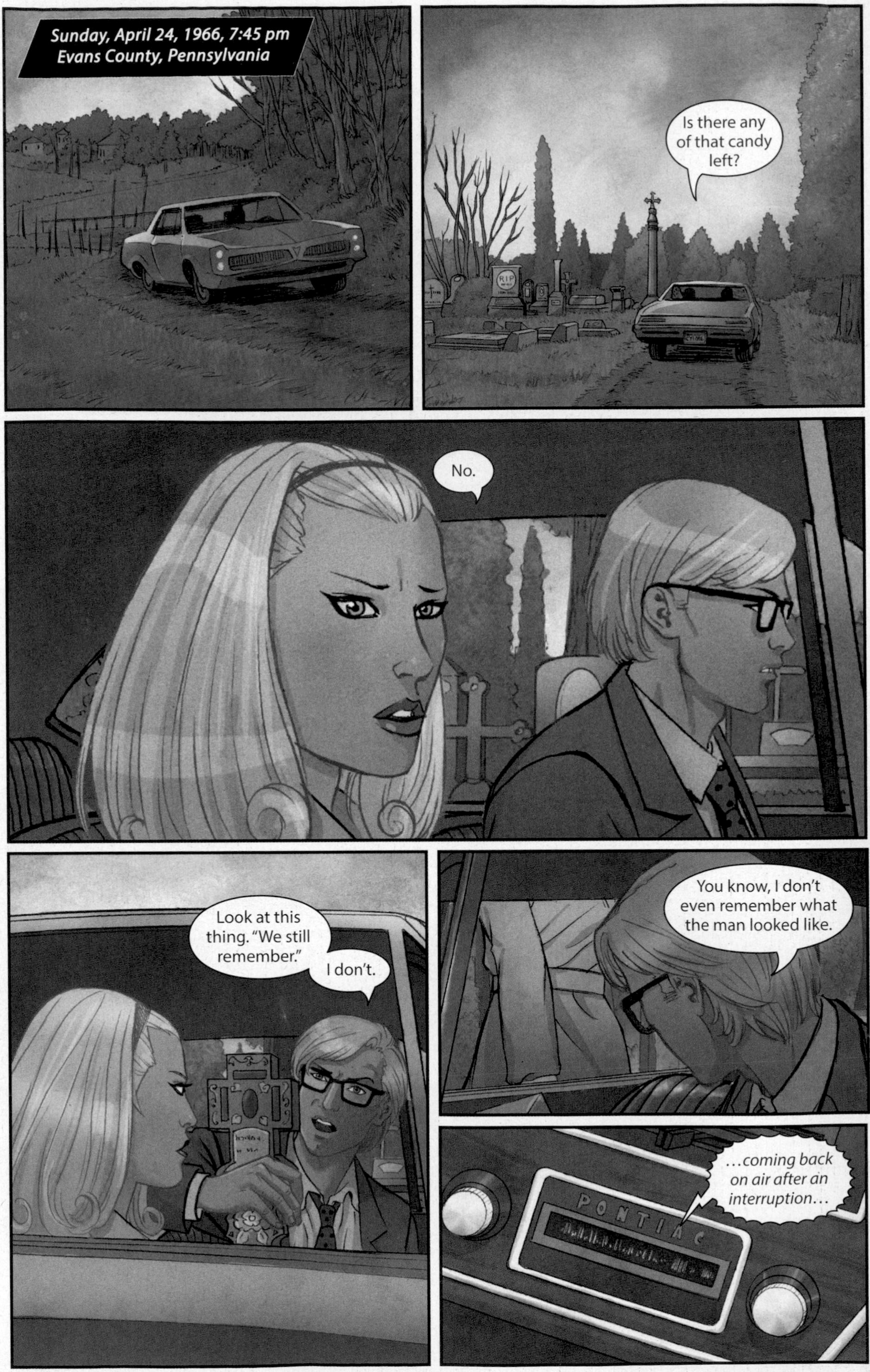
Sunday, April 24, 1966, 7:45 pm
Evans County, Pennsylvania
Is there any of that candy left?
No.
Look at this thing. "We still remember."
I don't.
You know, I don't even remember what the man looked like.
…coming back on air after an interruption…
PONTIAC

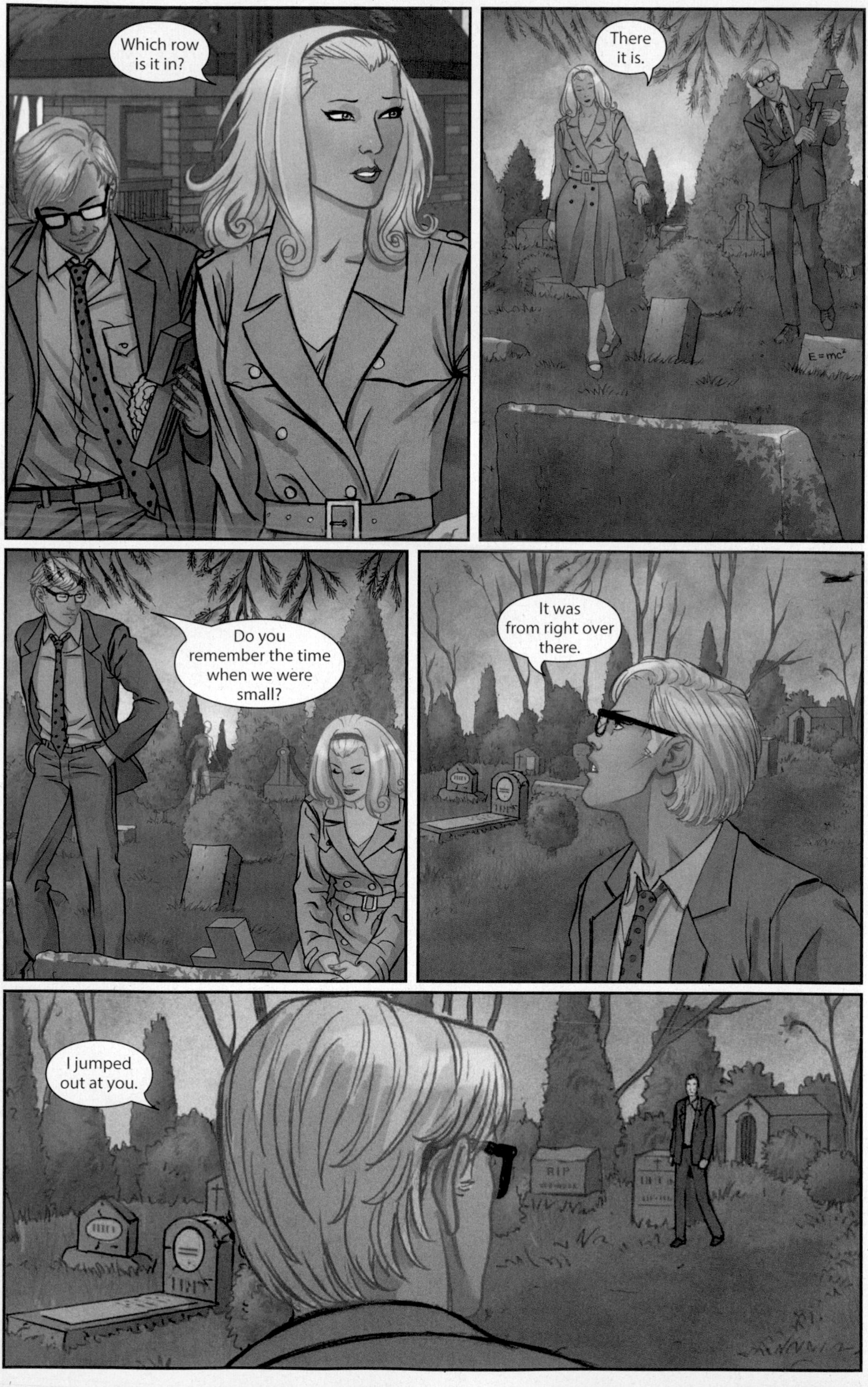
Which row is it in?
There it is.
E=mc²
Do you remember the time when we were small?
It was from right over there.
I jumped out at you.
RIP

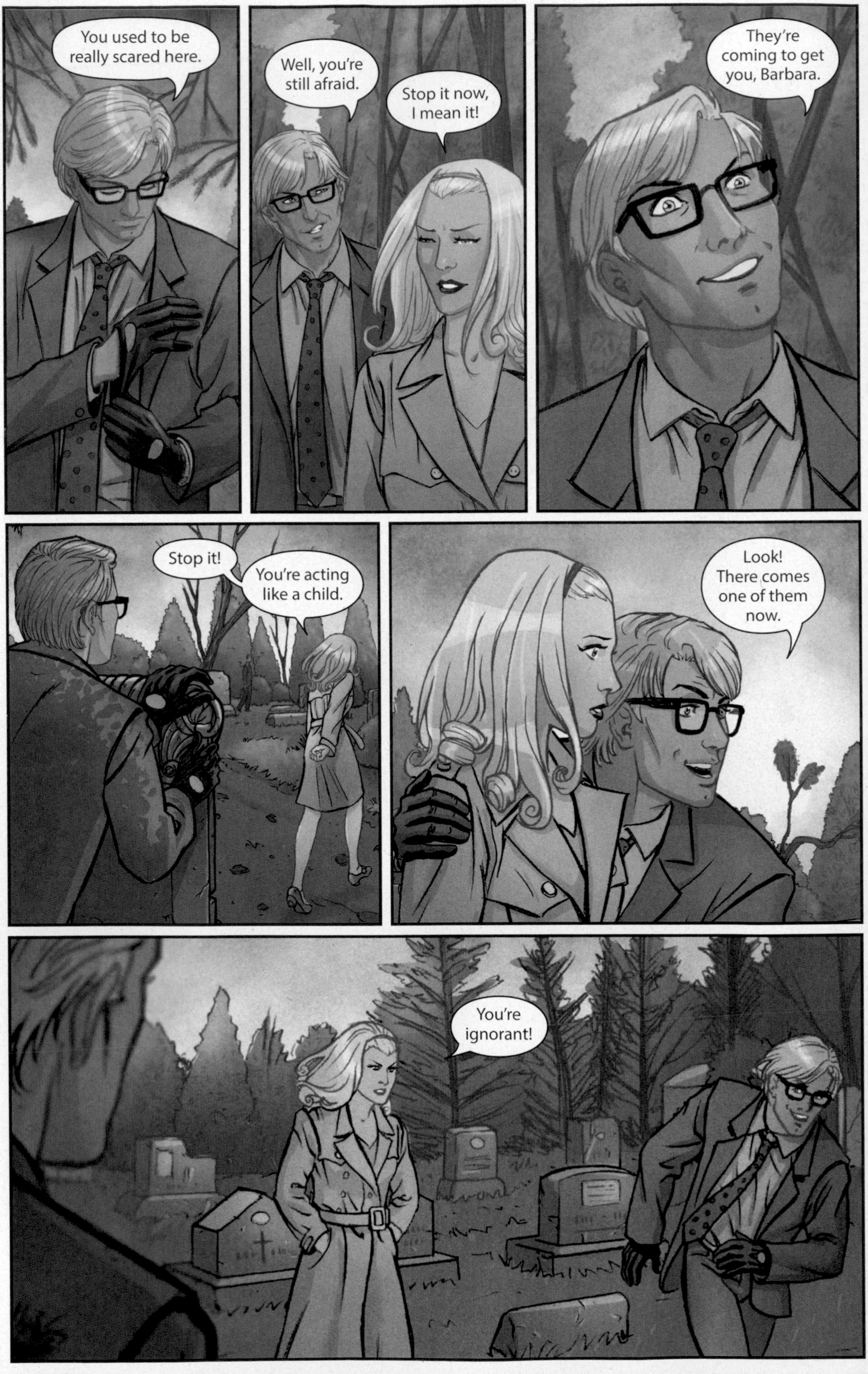

You used to be really scared here.
Well, you're still afraid.
Stop it now, I mean it!
They're coming to get you, Barbara.
Stop it!
You're acting like a child.
Look! There comes one of them now.
You're ignorant!

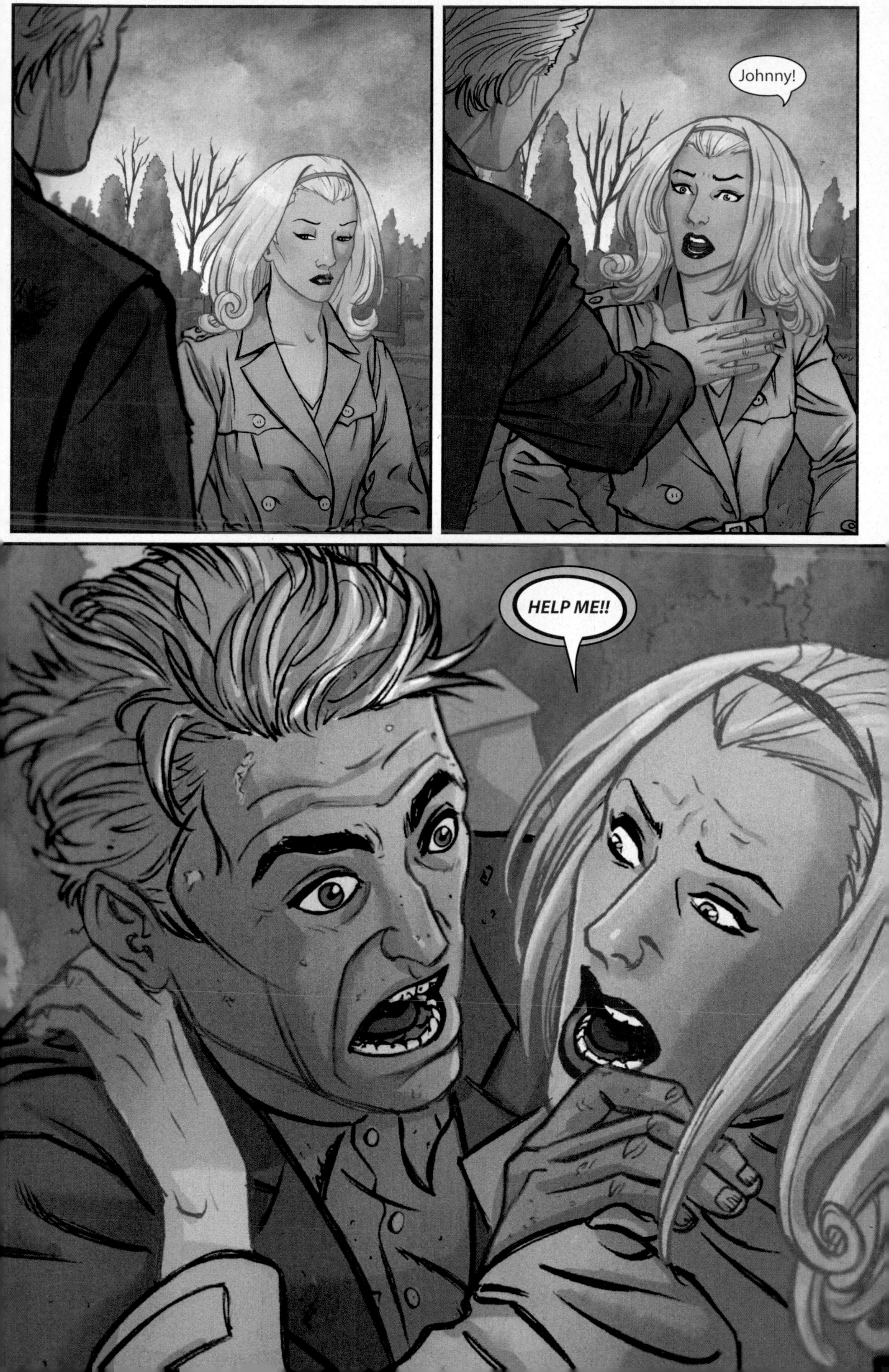
Johnny!
HELP ME!!

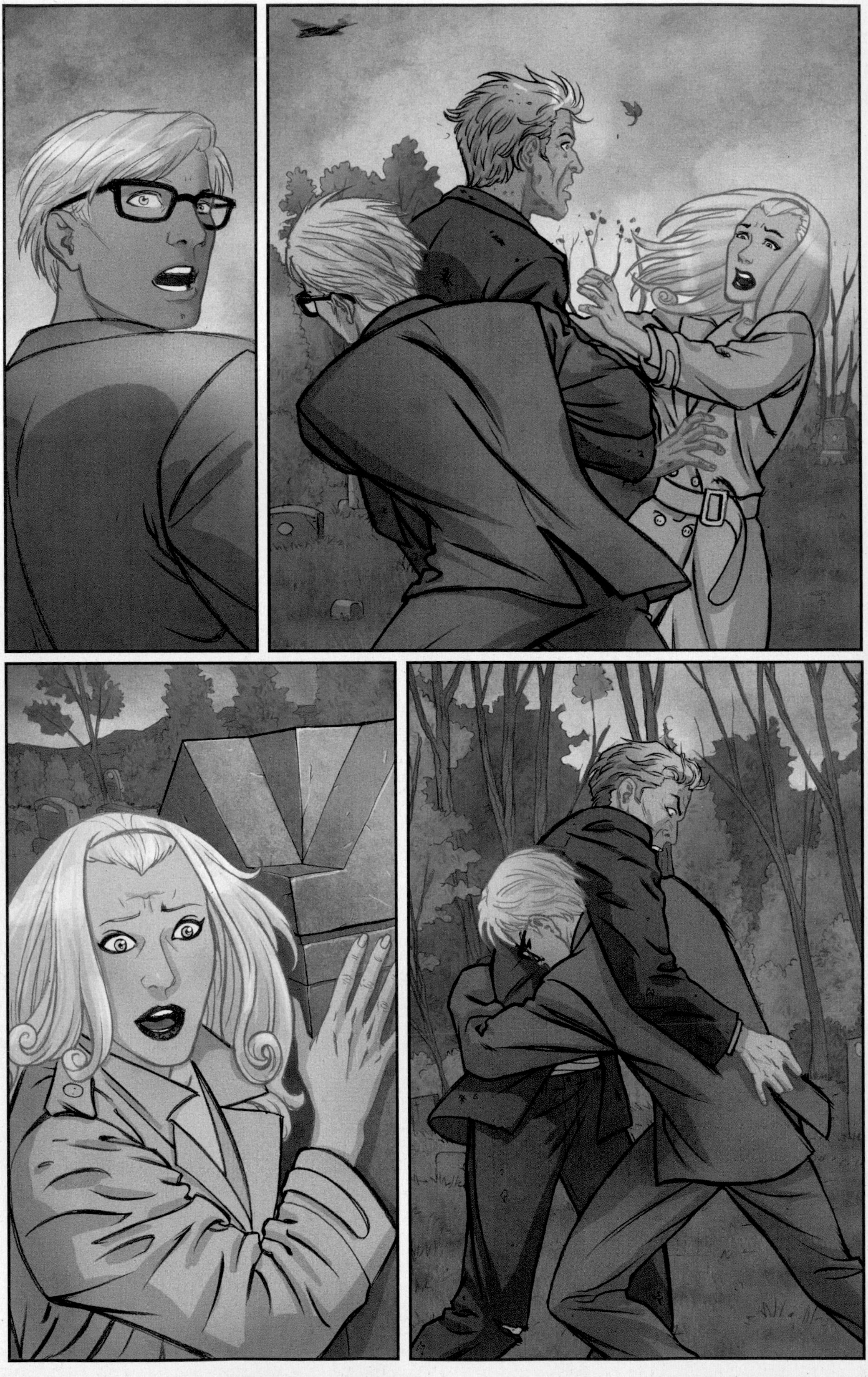

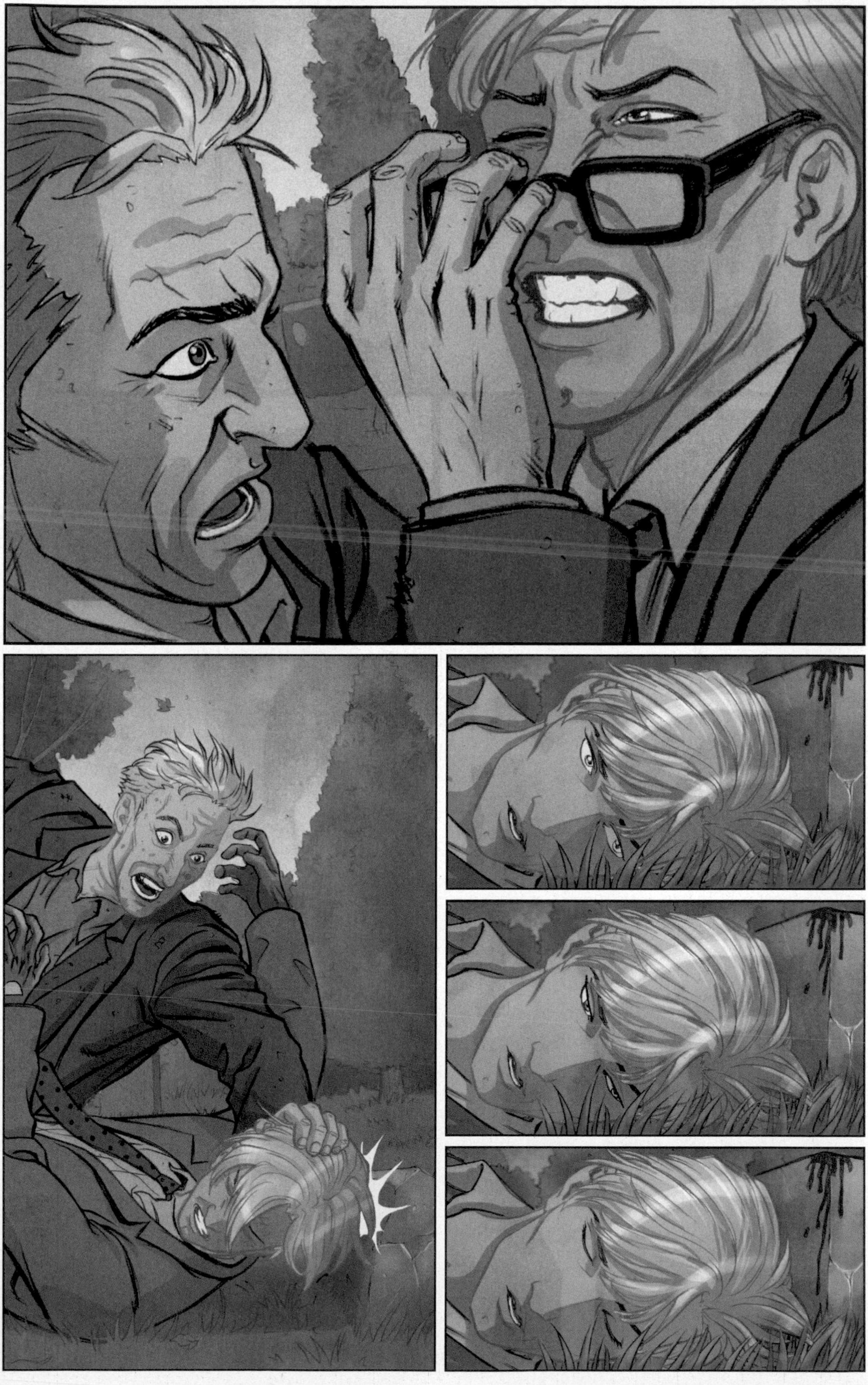

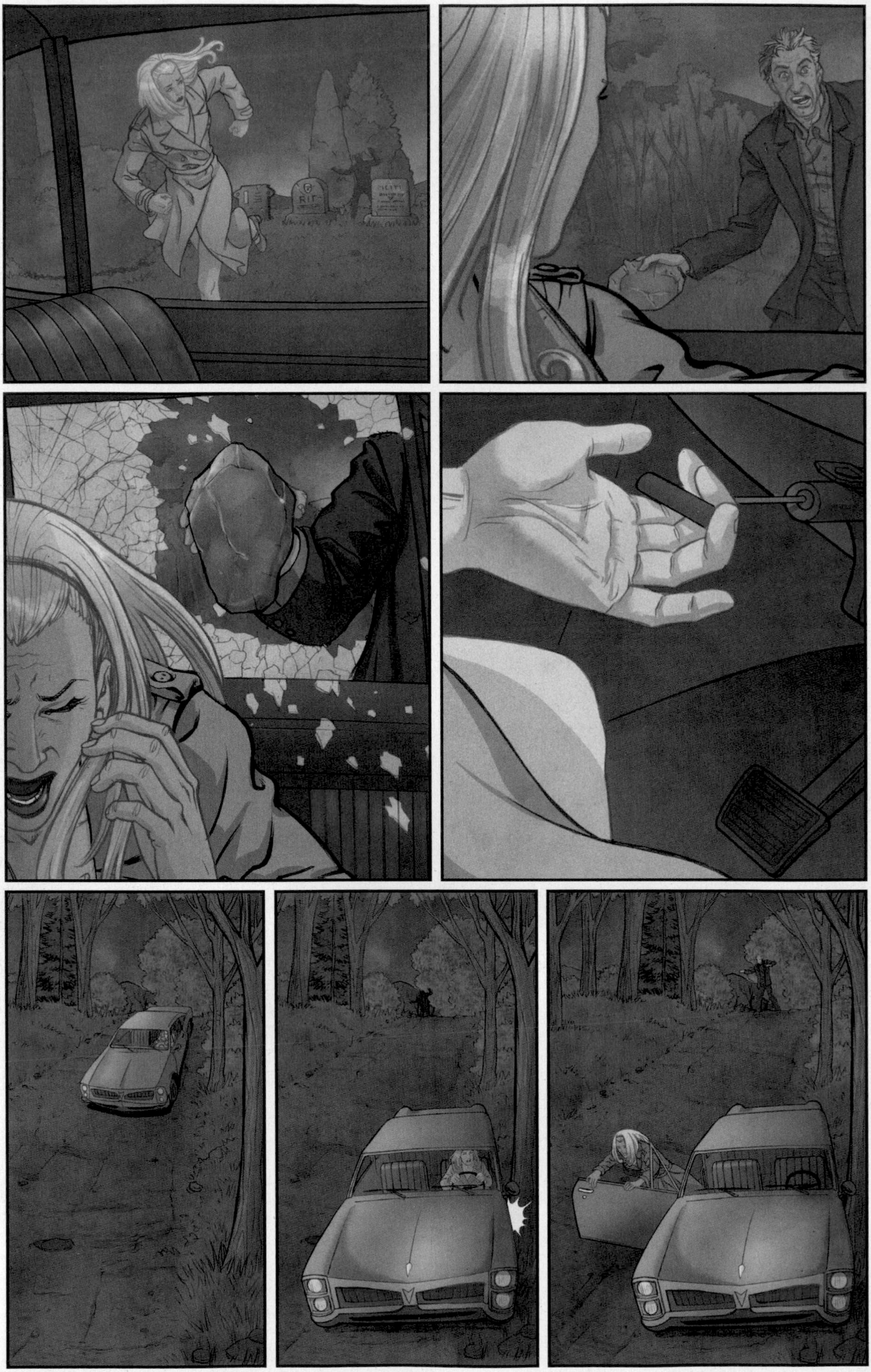

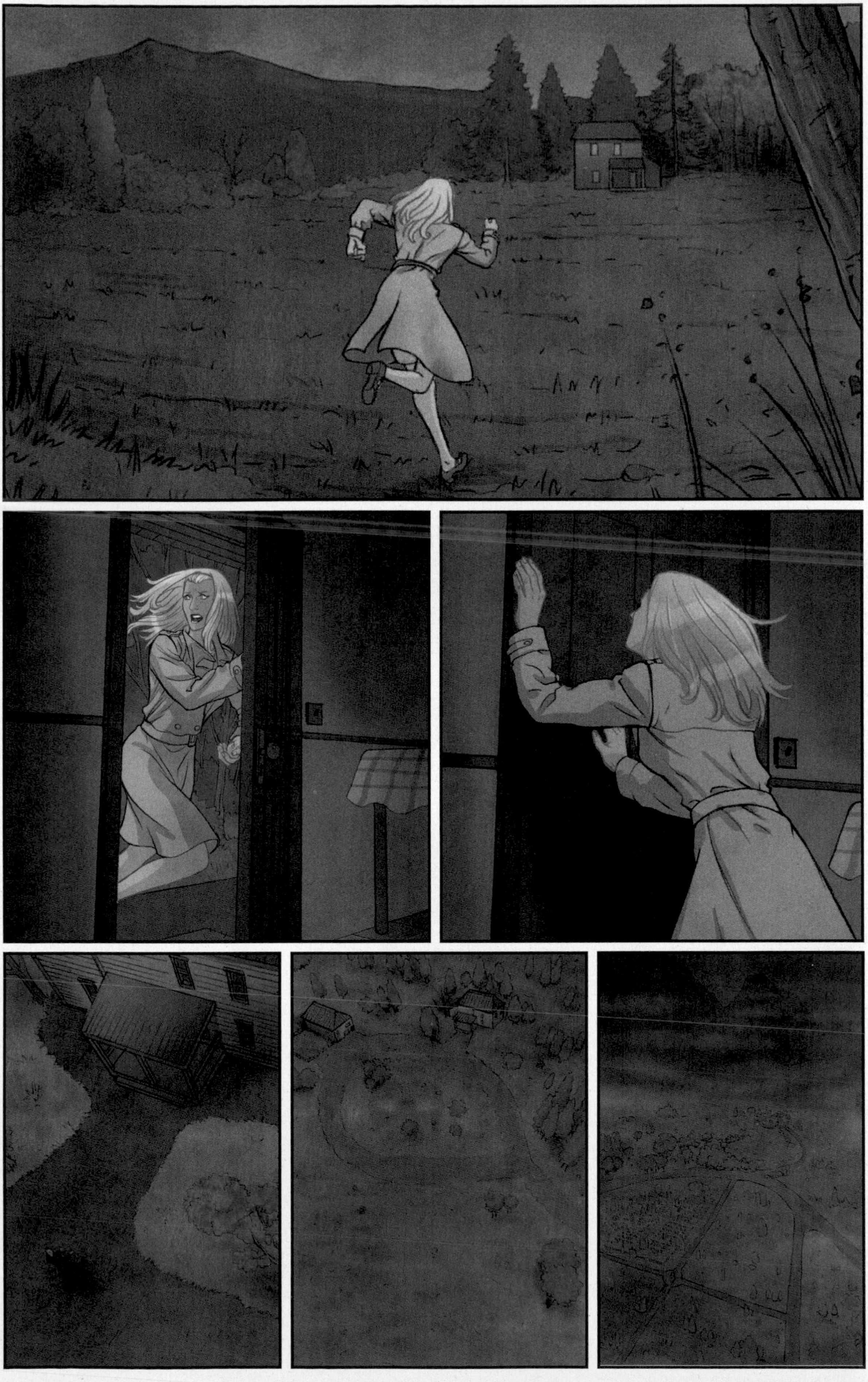

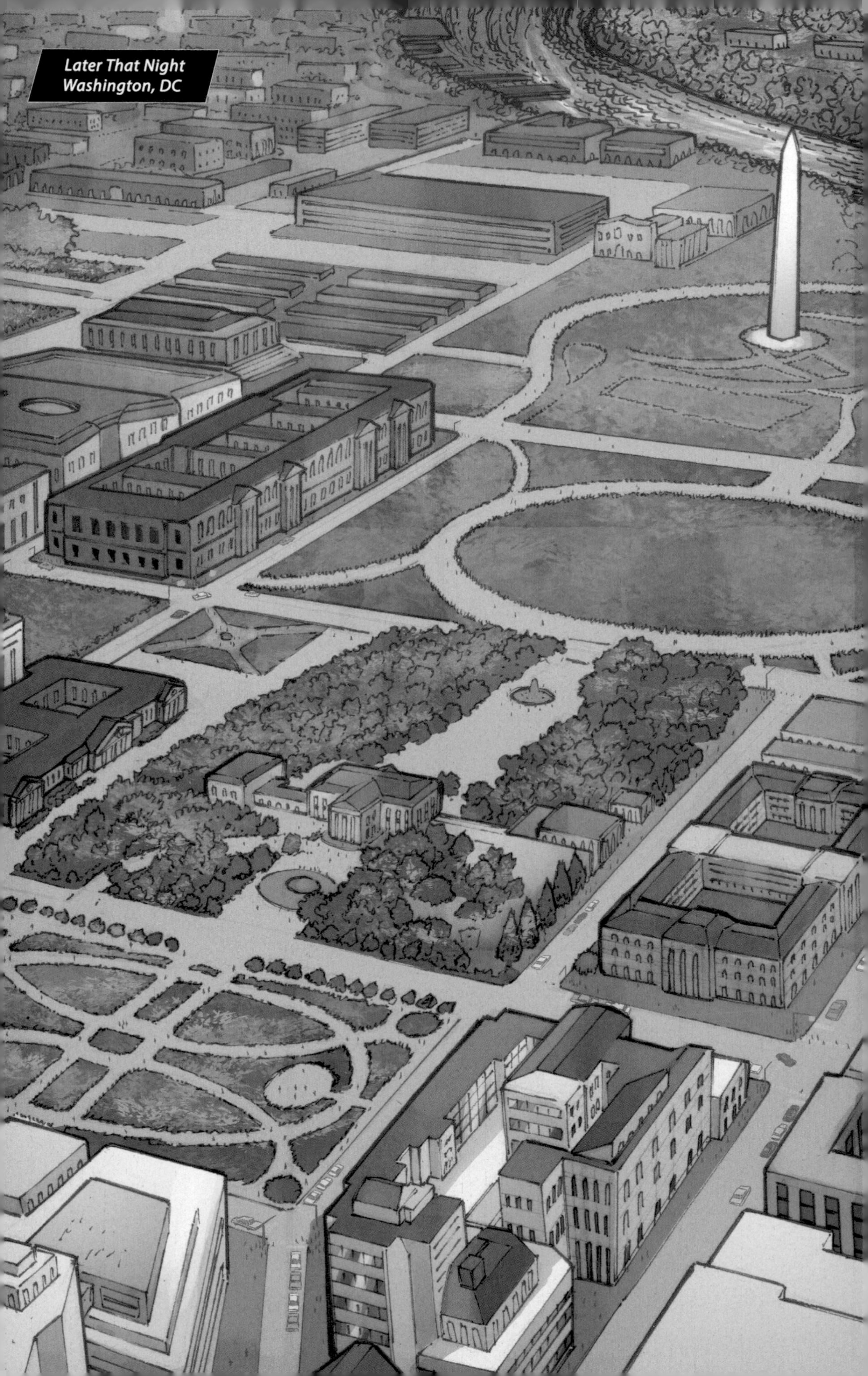
Later That Night
Washington, DC

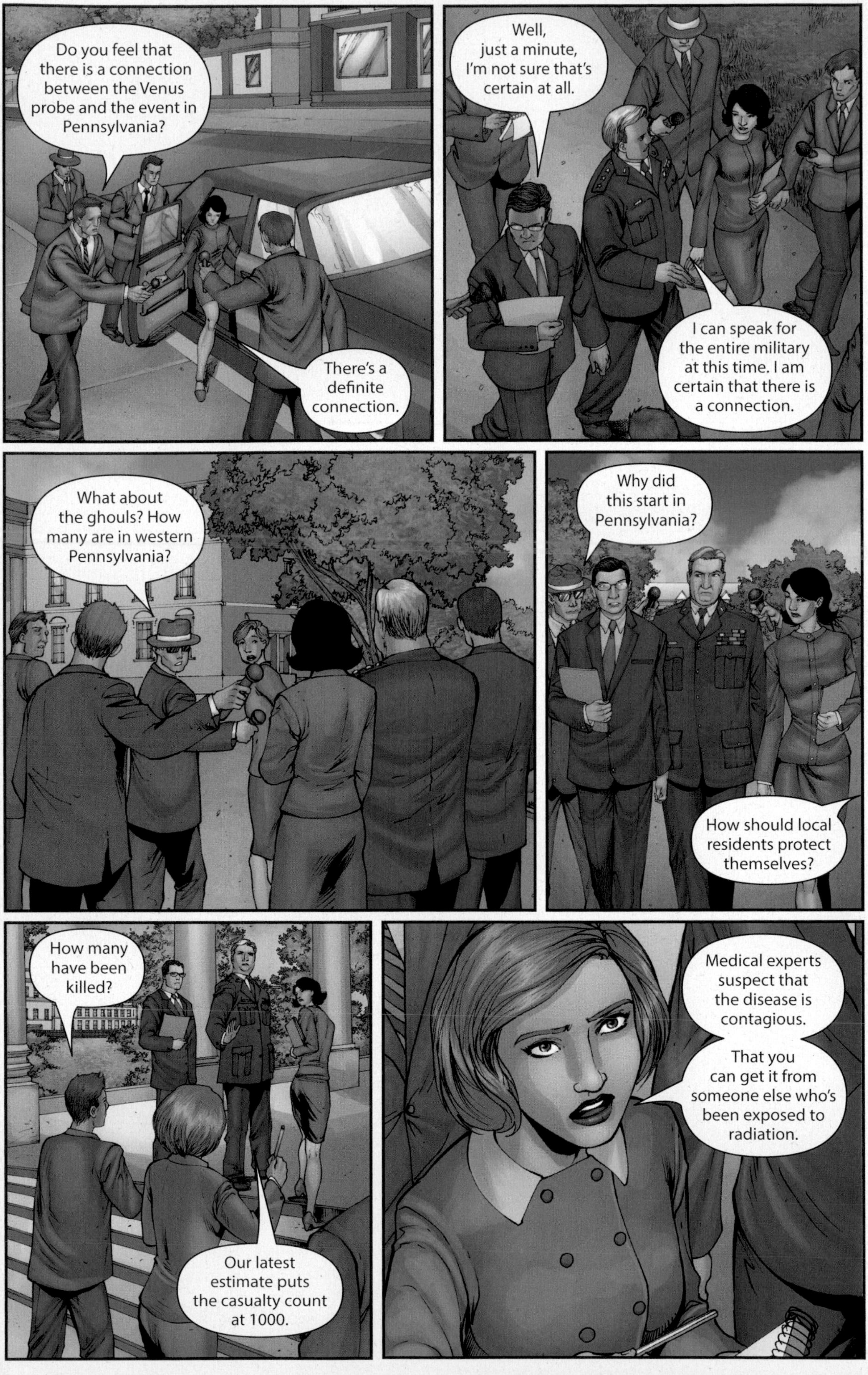
Do you feel that there is a connection between the Venus probe and the event in Pennsylvania?
There's a definite connection.
Well, just a minute, I'm not sure that's certain at all.
I can speak for the entire military at this time. I am certain that there is a connection.
What about the ghouls? How many are in western Pennsylvania?
Why did this start in Pennsylvania?
How should local residents protect themselves?
How many have been killed?
Our latest estimate puts the casualty count at 1000.
Medical experts suspect that the disease is contagious.
That you can get it from someone else who's been exposed to radiation.

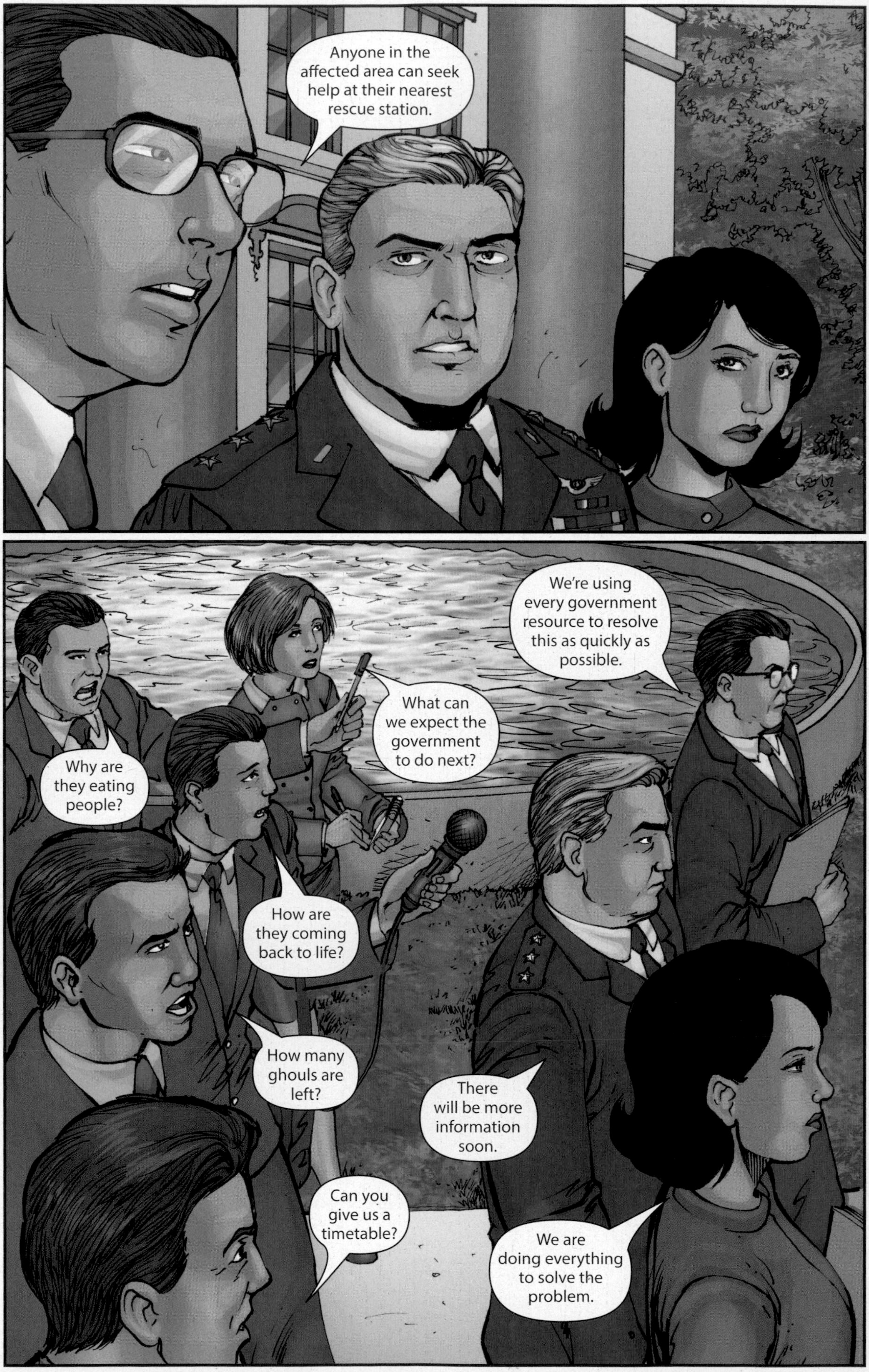
Anyone in the affected area can seek help at their nearest rescue station.
We're using every government resource to resolve this as quickly as possible.
What can we expect the government to do next?
Why are they eating people?
How are they coming back to life?
How many ghouls are left?
There will be more information soon.
Can you give us a timetable?
We are doing everything to solve the problem.

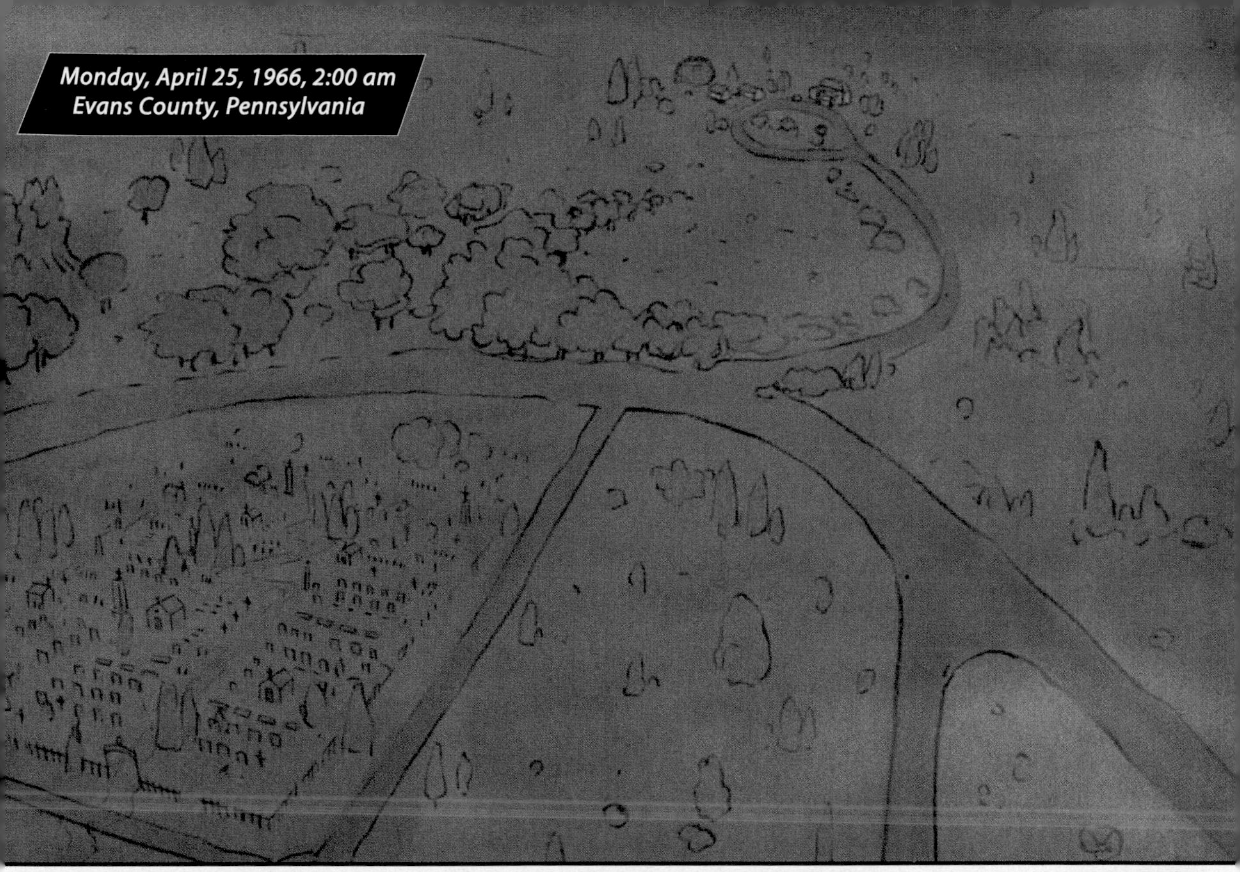
Monday, April 25, 1966, 2:00 am
Evans County, Pennsylvania

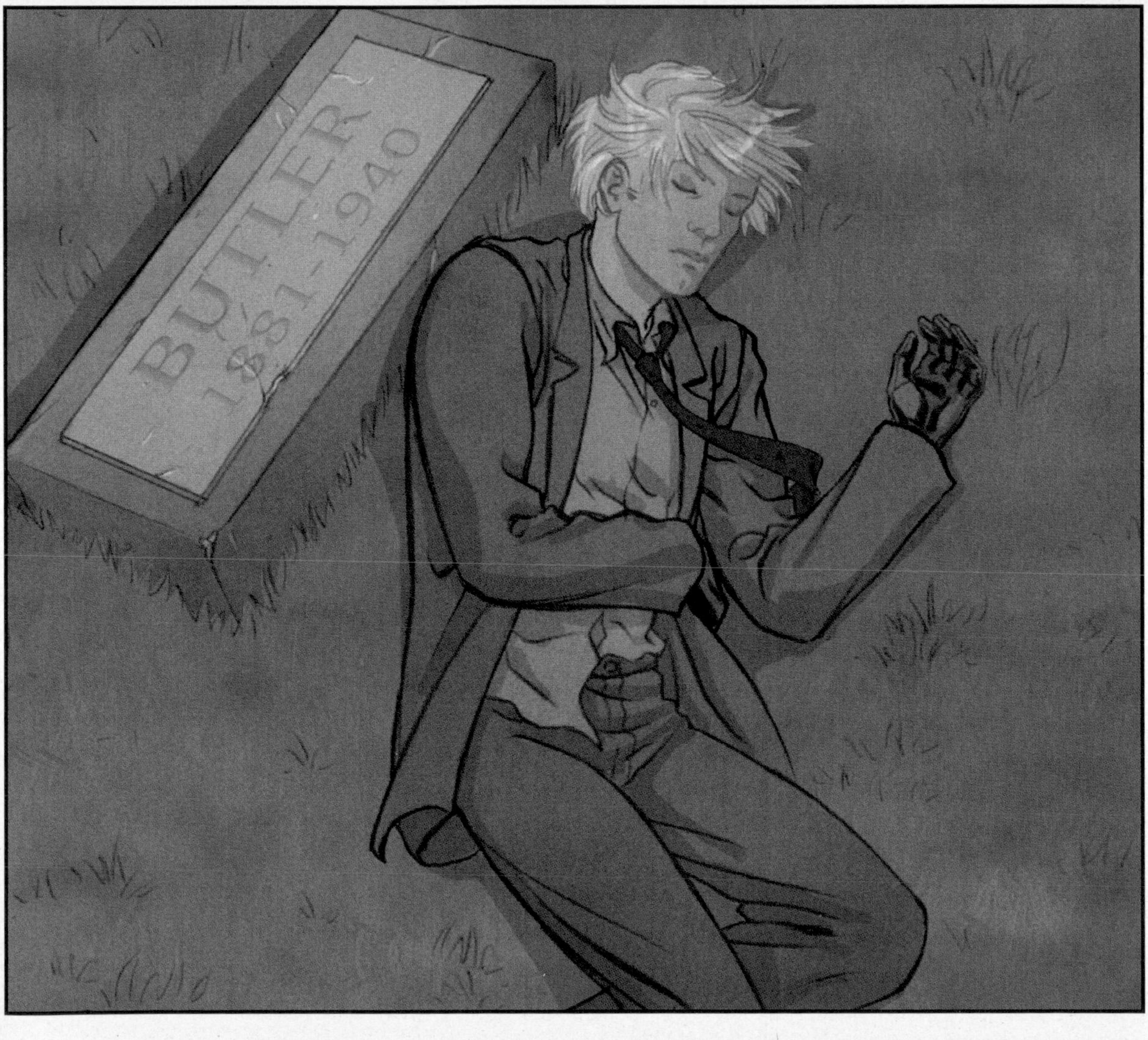
BUTLER
1881-1940

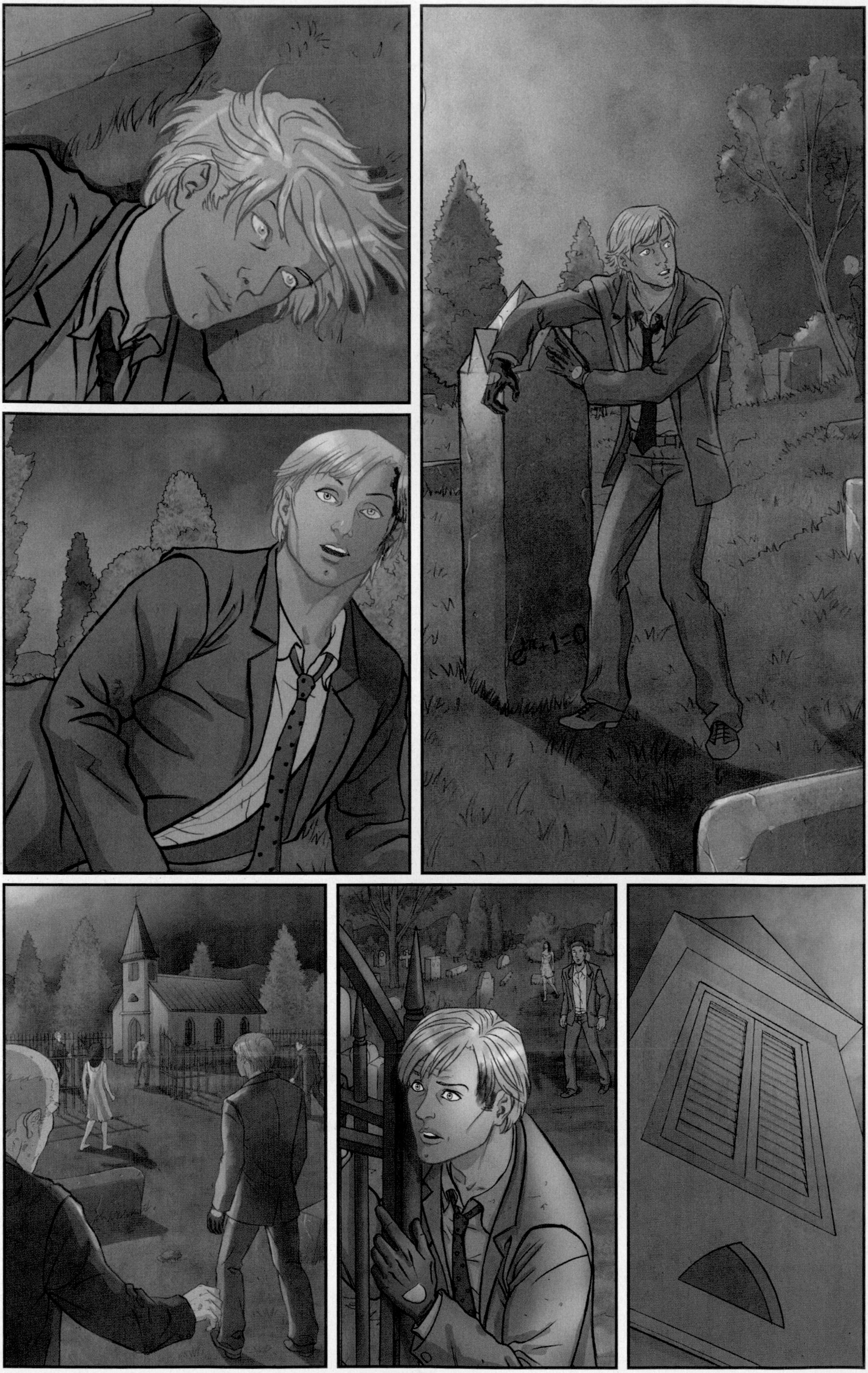
$e^{i\pi}+1=0$

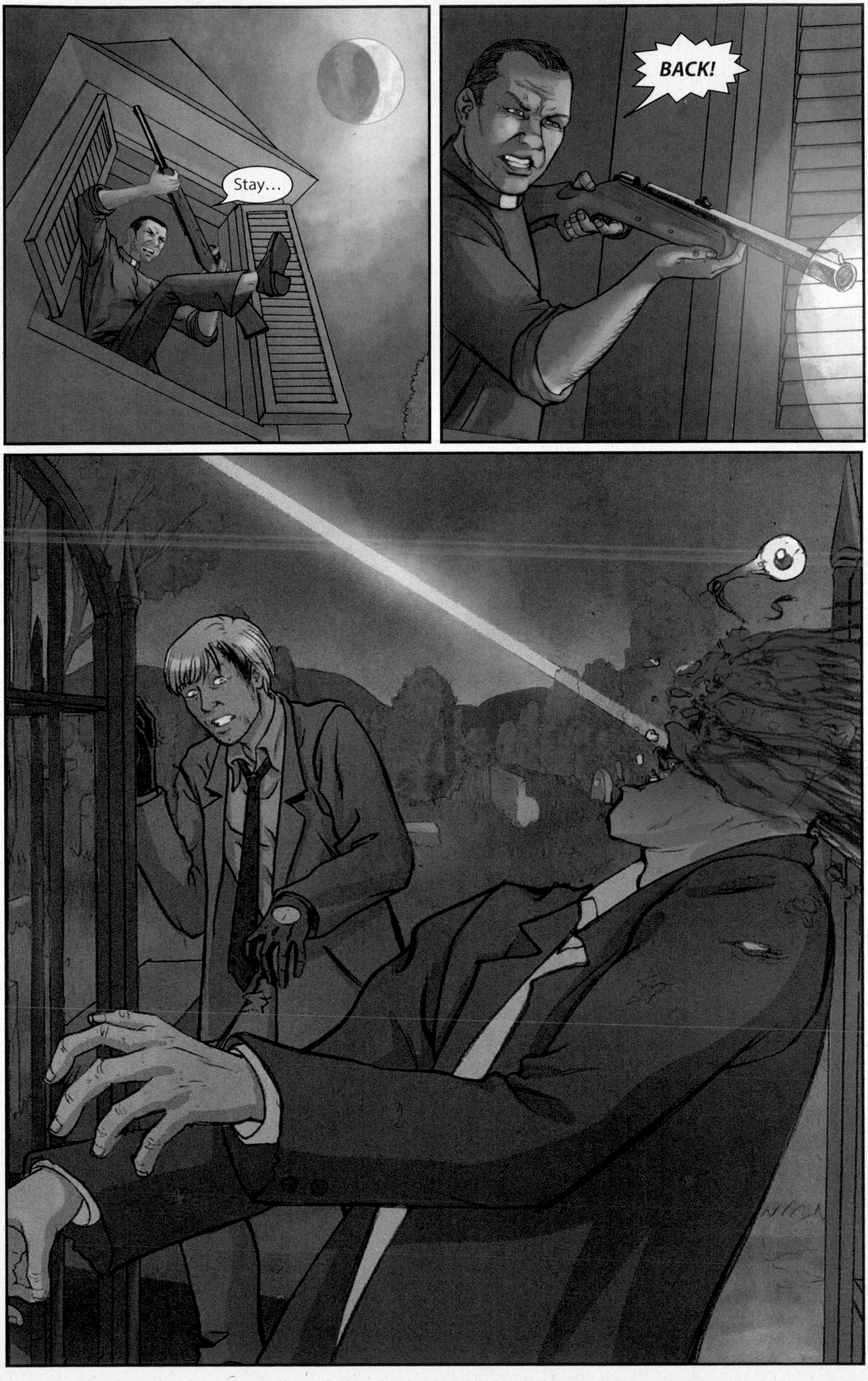
Stay…
BACK!

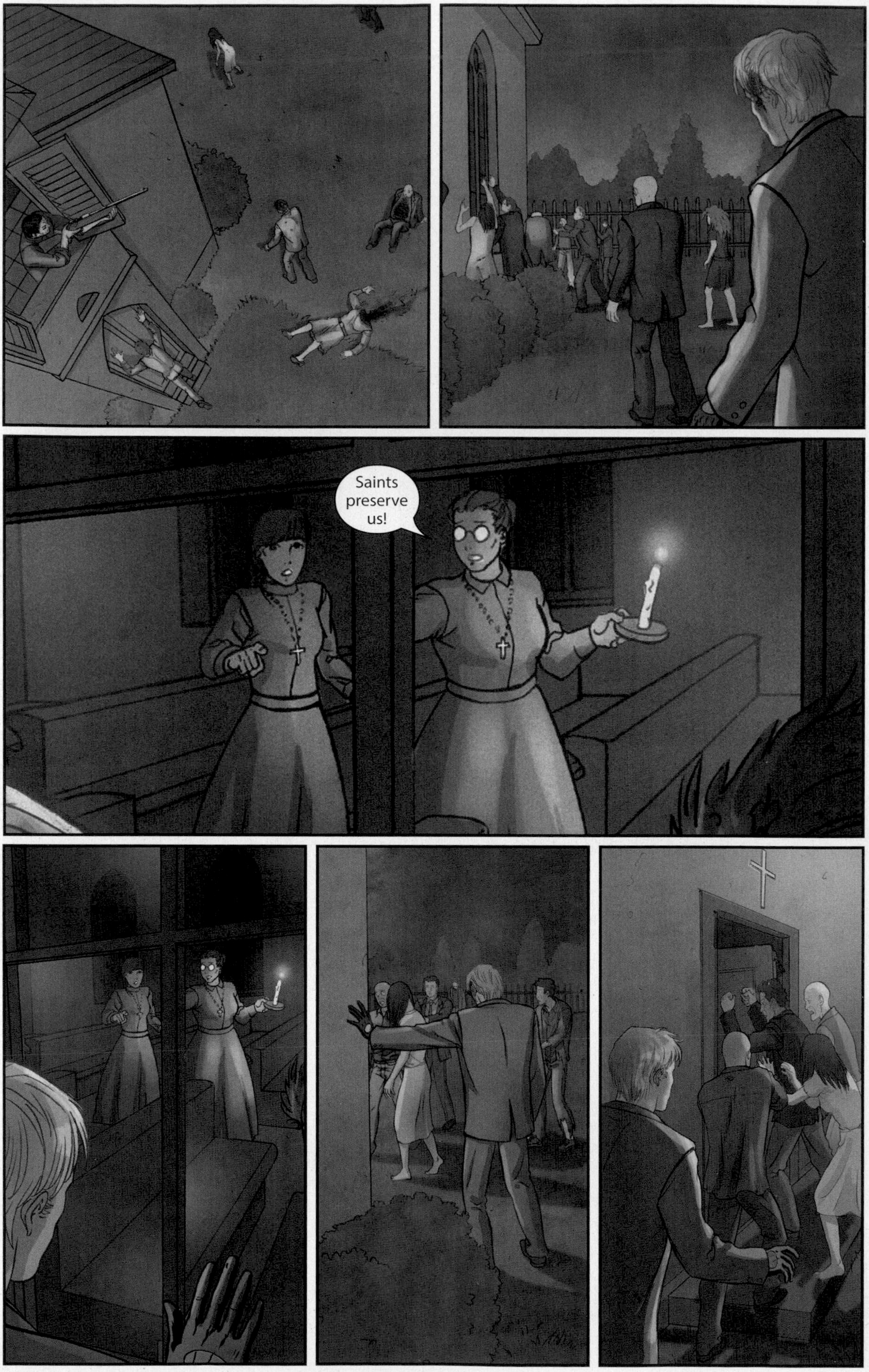
Saints preserve us!

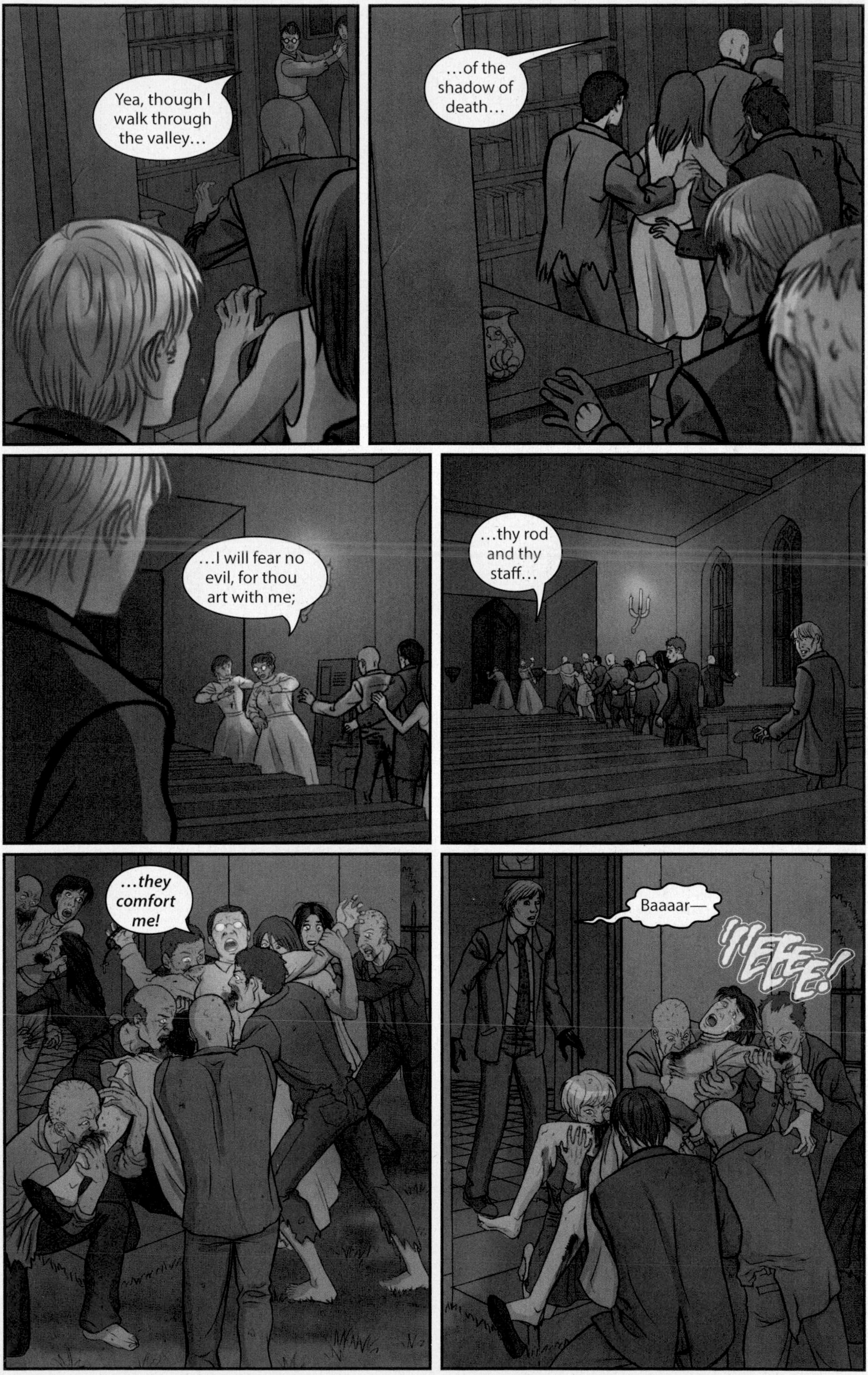

Yea, though I walk through the valley…
…of the shadow of death…
…I will fear no evil, for thou art with me;
…thy rod and thy staff…
…they comfort me!
Baaaar—
'EEEE!

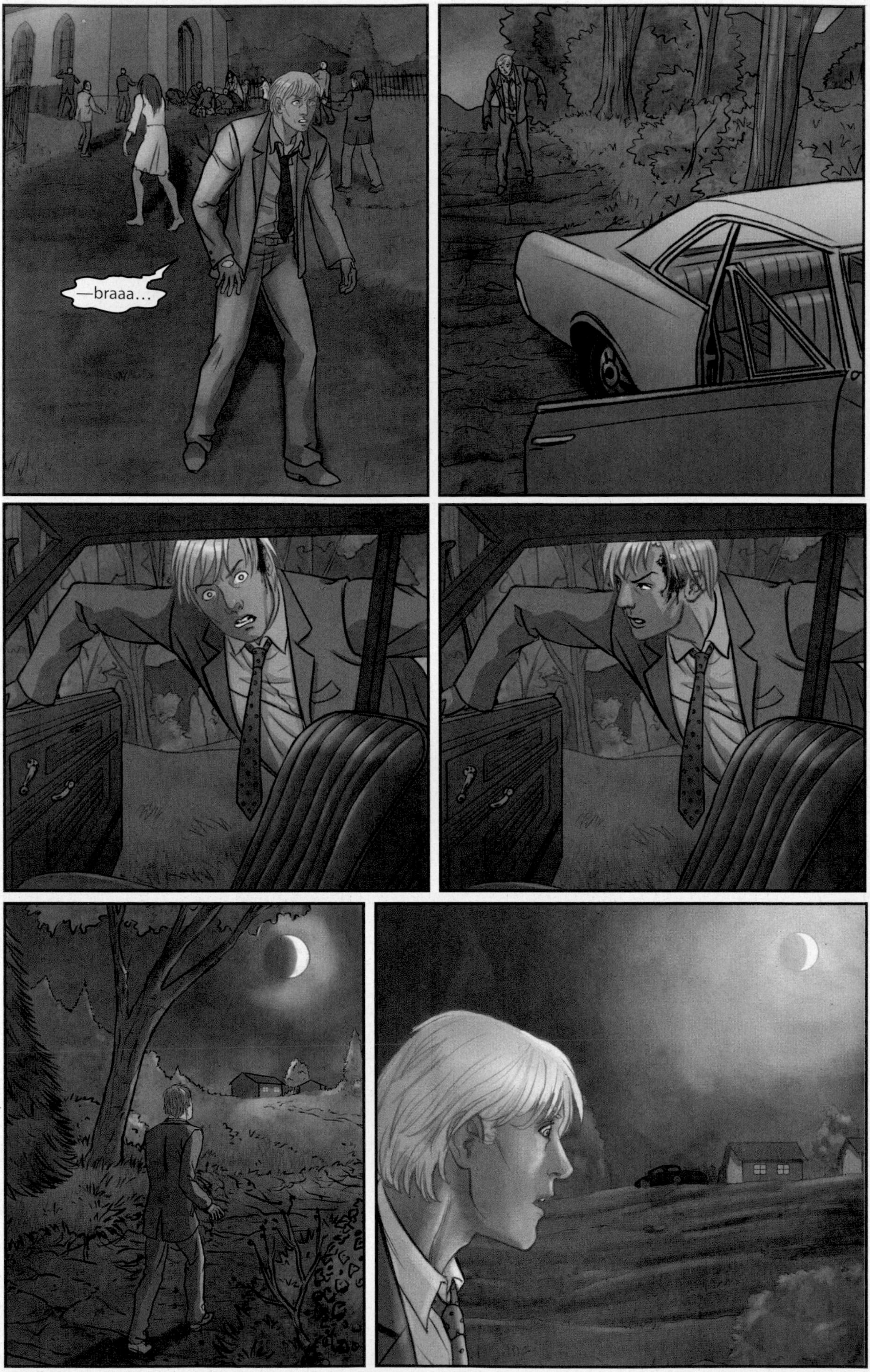
—braaa…

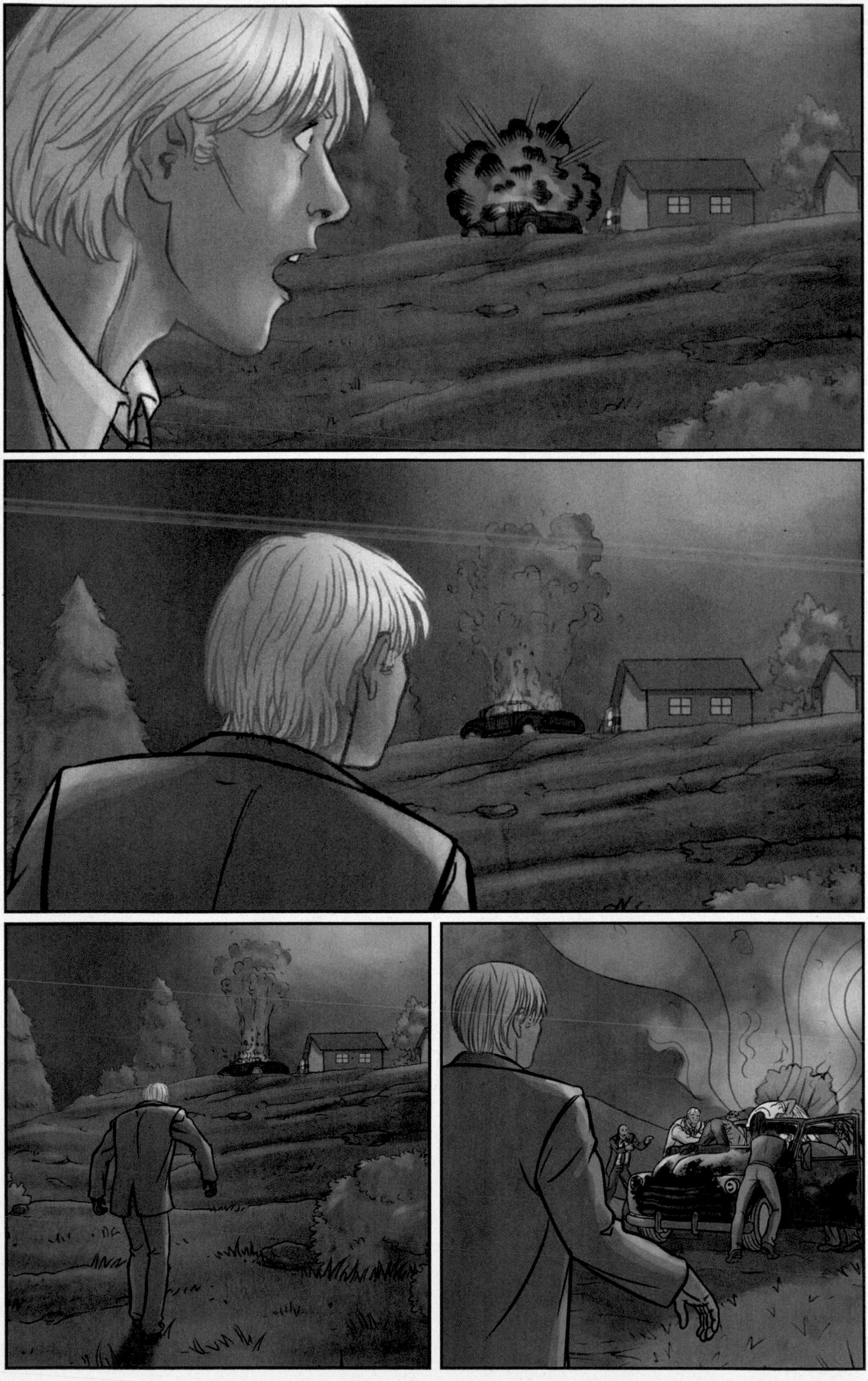

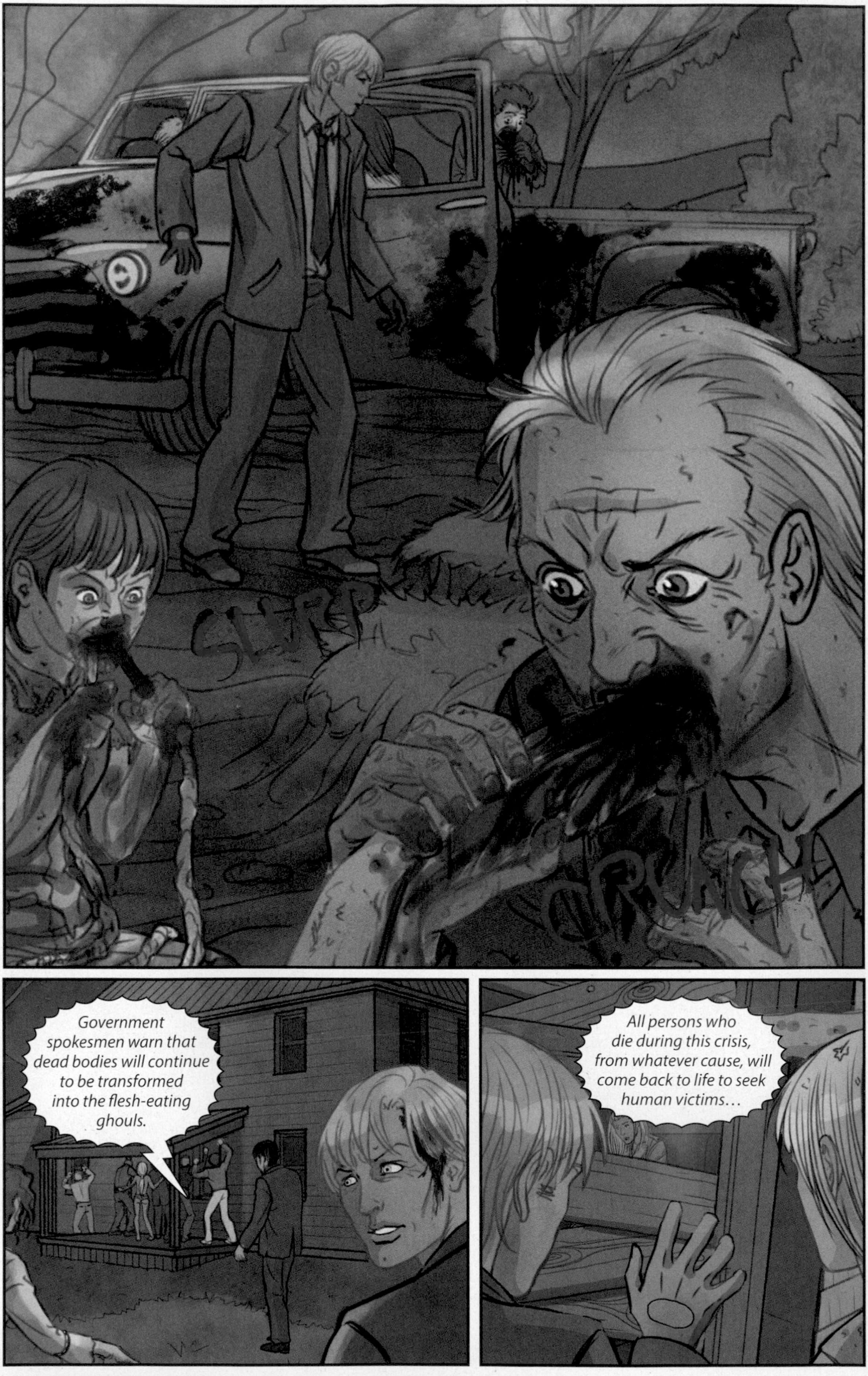
SLURP
CRUNCH
Government spokesmen warn that dead bodies will continue to be transformed into the flesh-eating ghouls.
All persons who die during this crisis, from whatever cause, will come back to life to seek human victims…

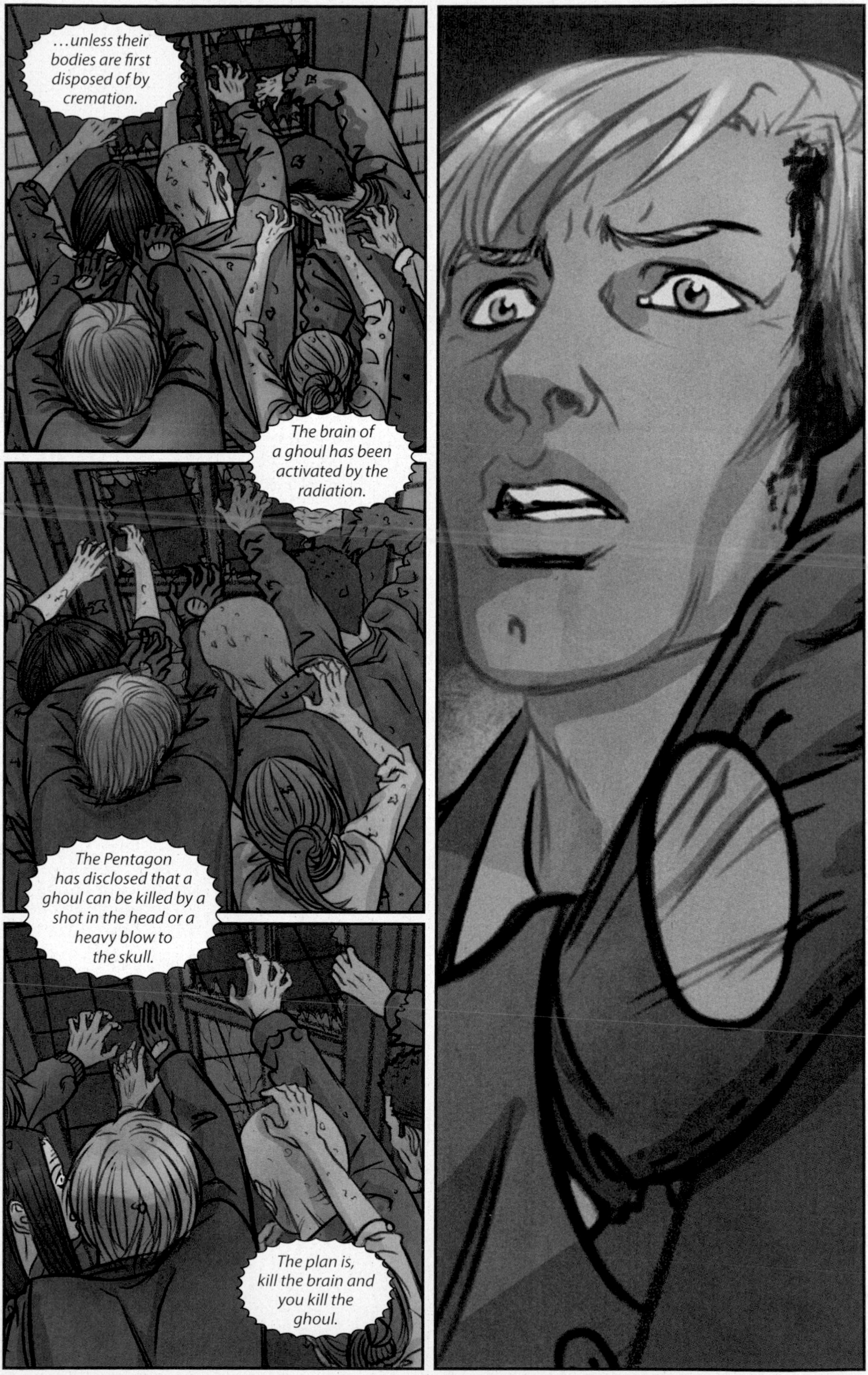
...unless their bodies are first disposed of by cremation.
The brain of a ghoul has been activated by the radiation.
The Pentagon has disclosed that a ghoul can be killed by a shot in the head or a heavy blow to the skull.
The plan is, kill the brain and you kill the ghoul.

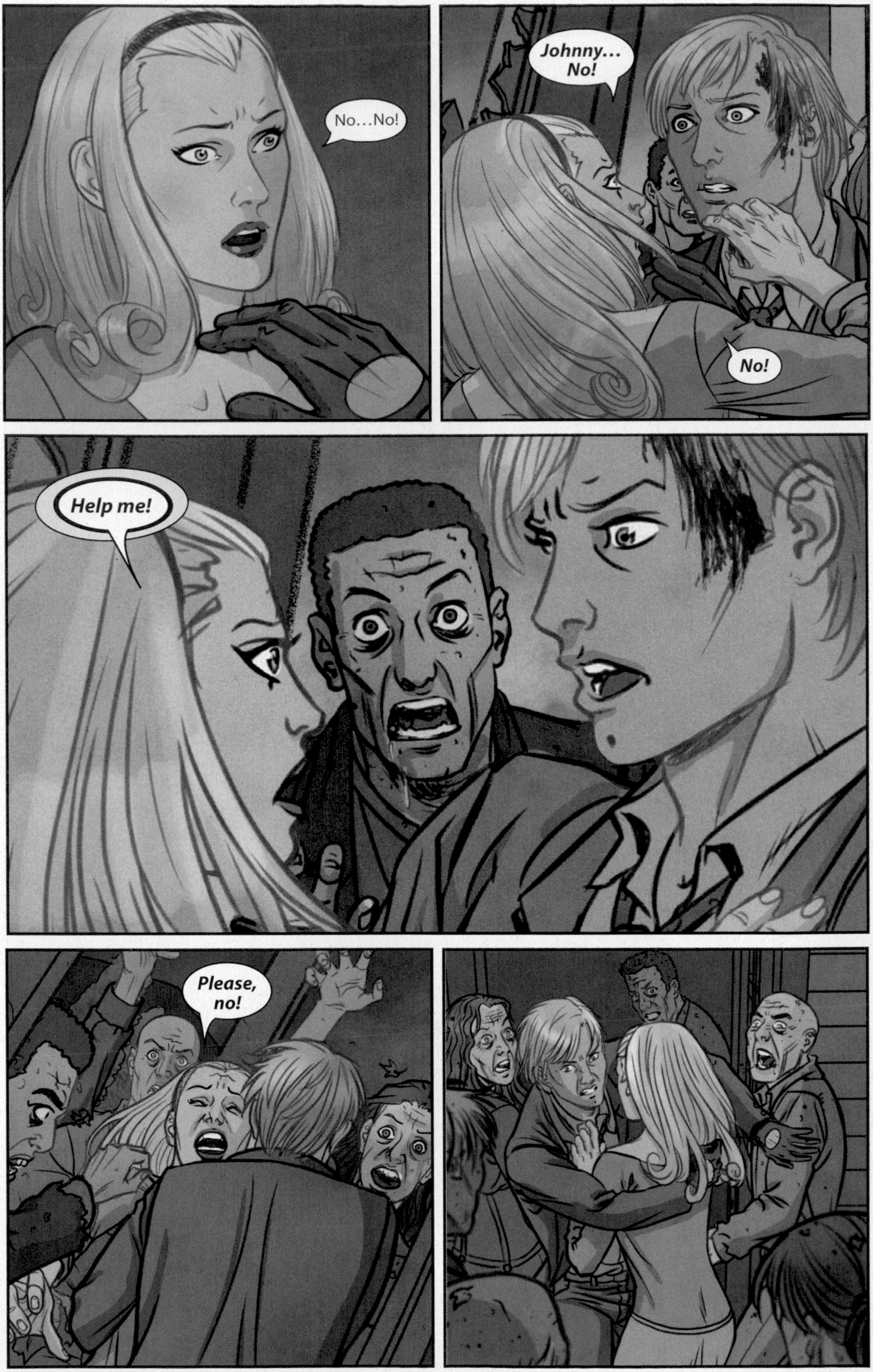
No...No!
Johnny...
No!
No!
Help me!
Please,
no!

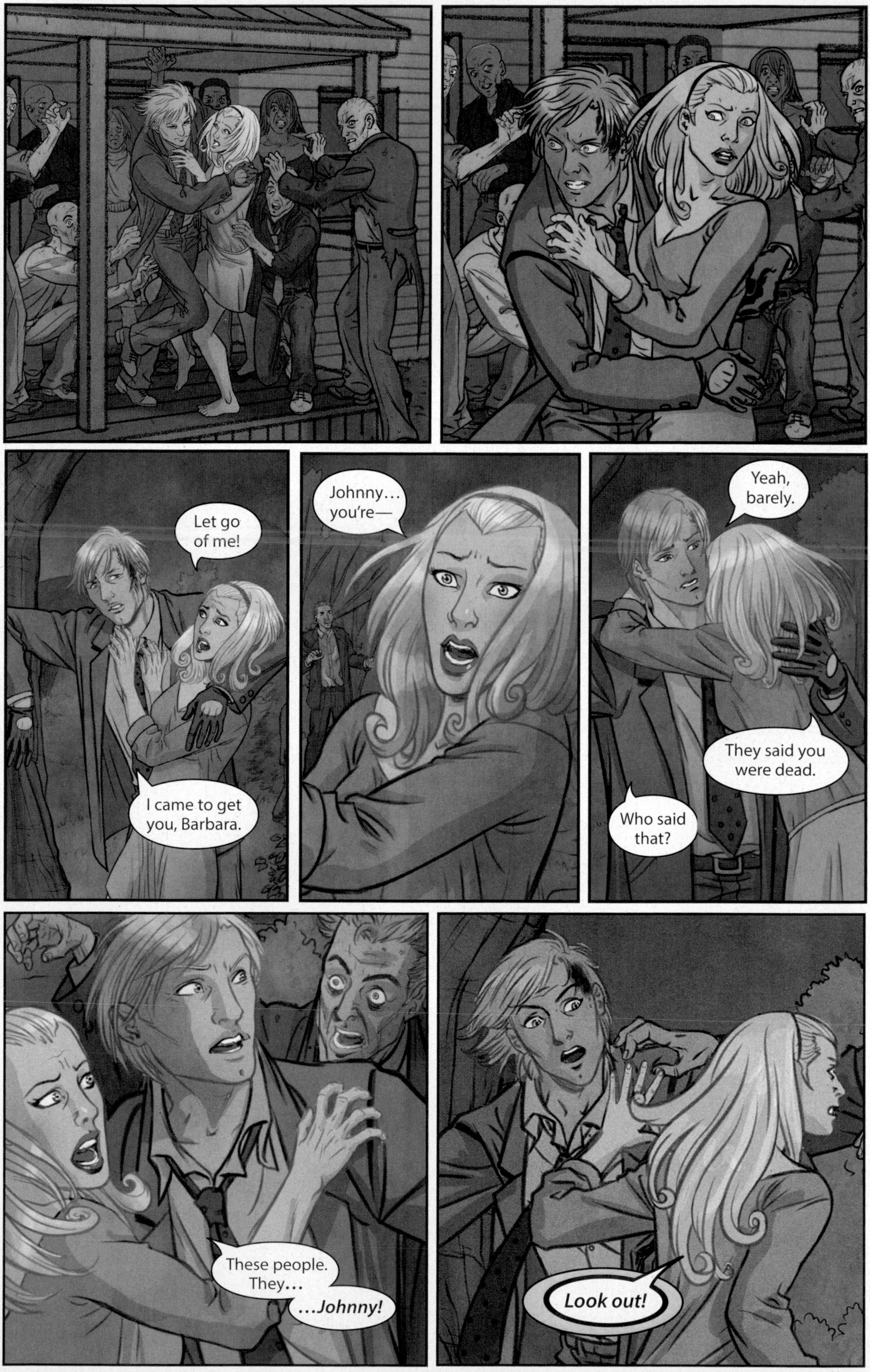
Let go of me!
I came to get you, Barbara.
Johnny… you're—
Yeah, barely.
They said you were dead.
Who said that?
These people. They…
…Johnny!
Look out!

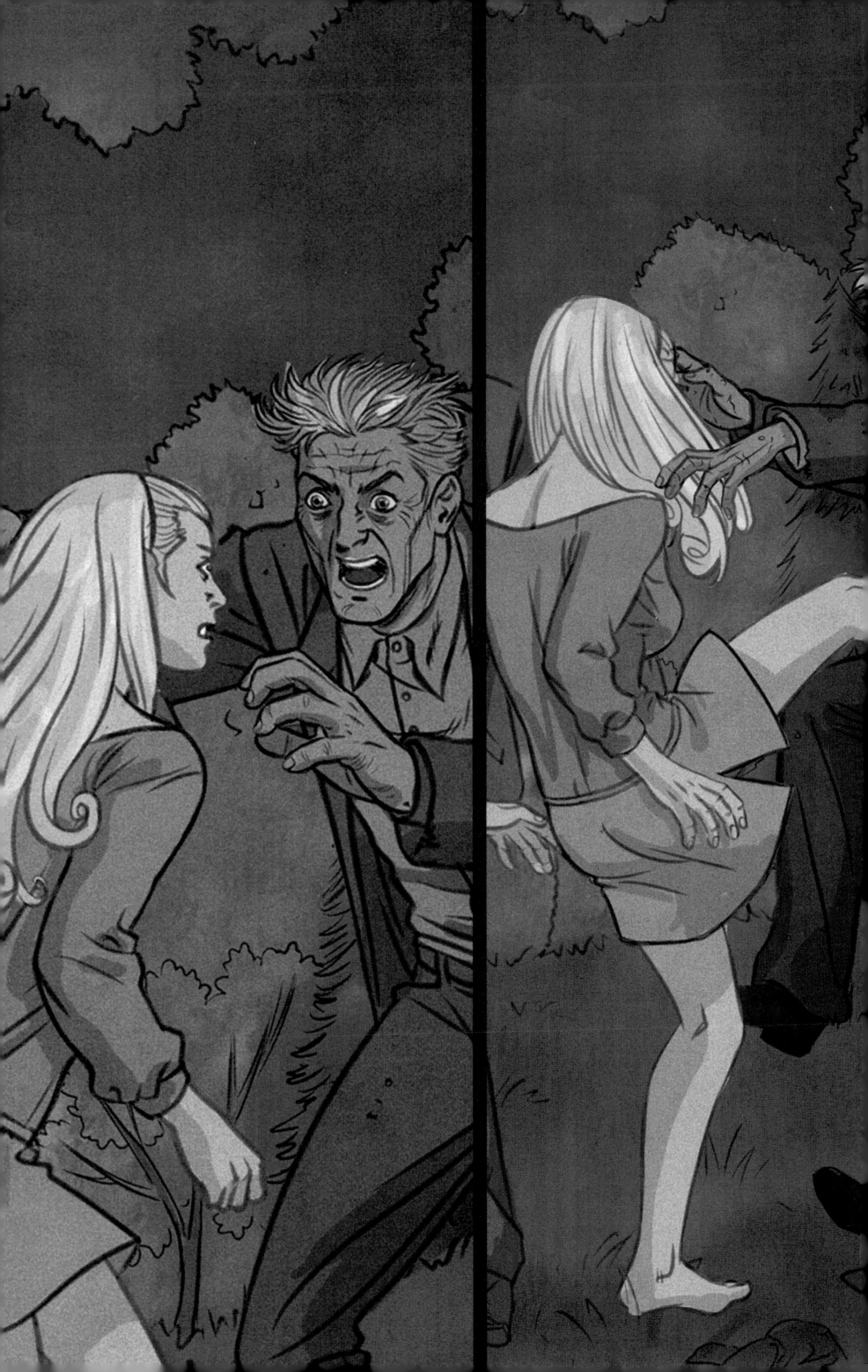

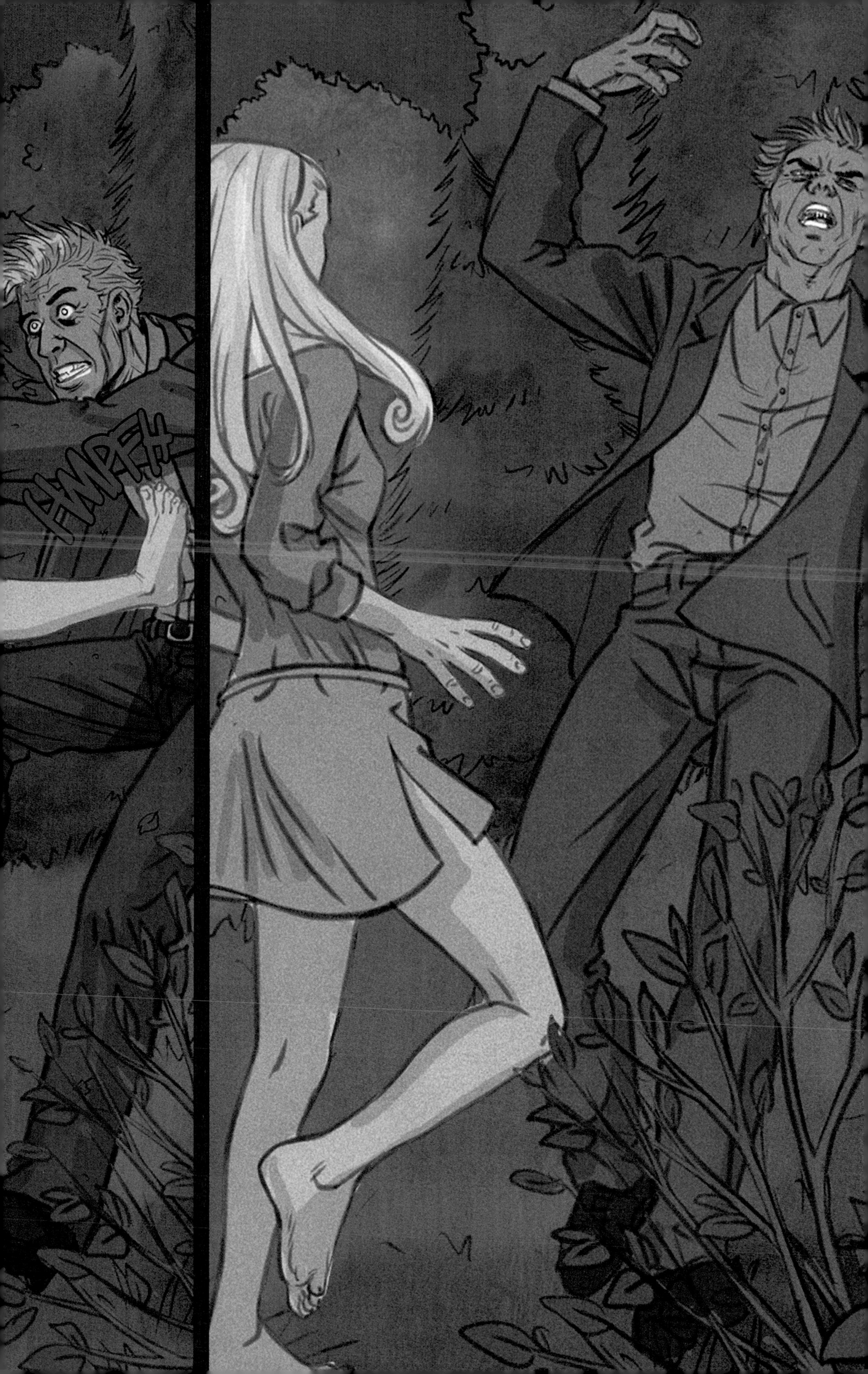
HMPFH

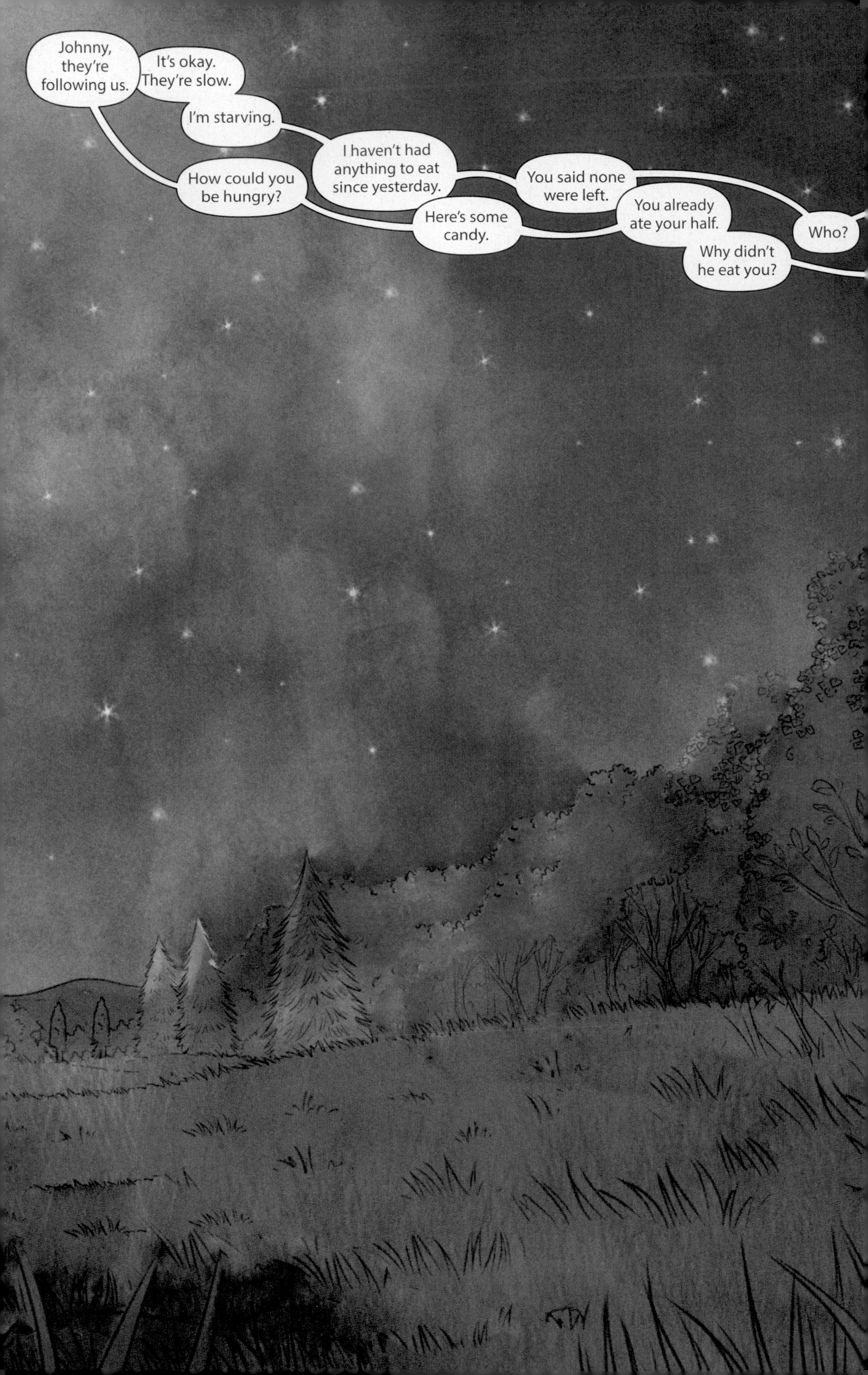
Johnny, they're following us.
It's okay. They're slow.
I'm starving.
How could you be hungry?
I haven't had anything to eat since yesterday.
Here's some candy.
You said none were left.
You already ate your half.
Why didn't he eat you?
Who?

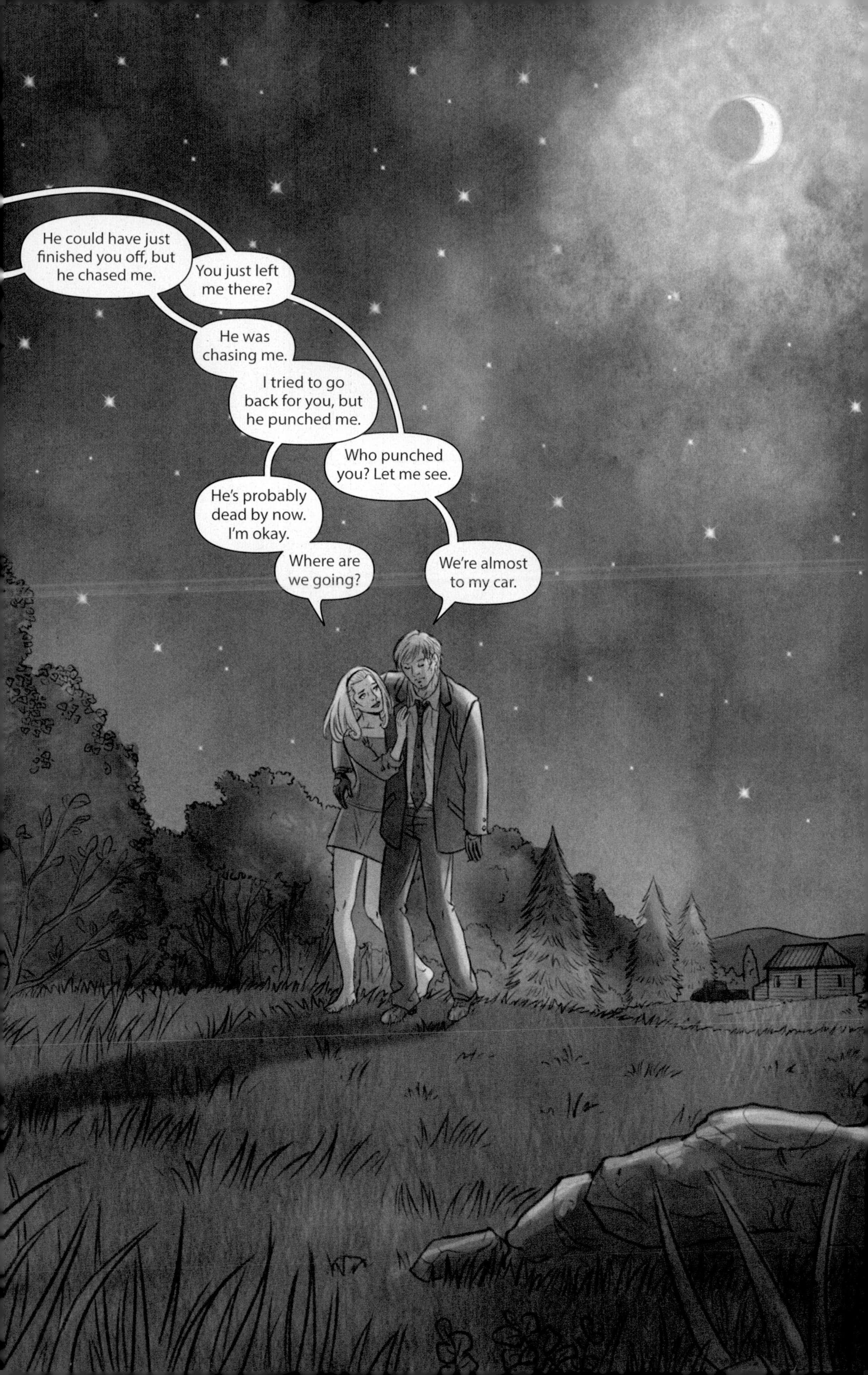
He could have just finished you off, but he chased me.
You just left me there?
He was chasing me.
I tried to go back for you, but he punched me.
Who punched you? Let me see.
He's probably dead by now. I'm okay.
Where are we going?
We're almost to my car.

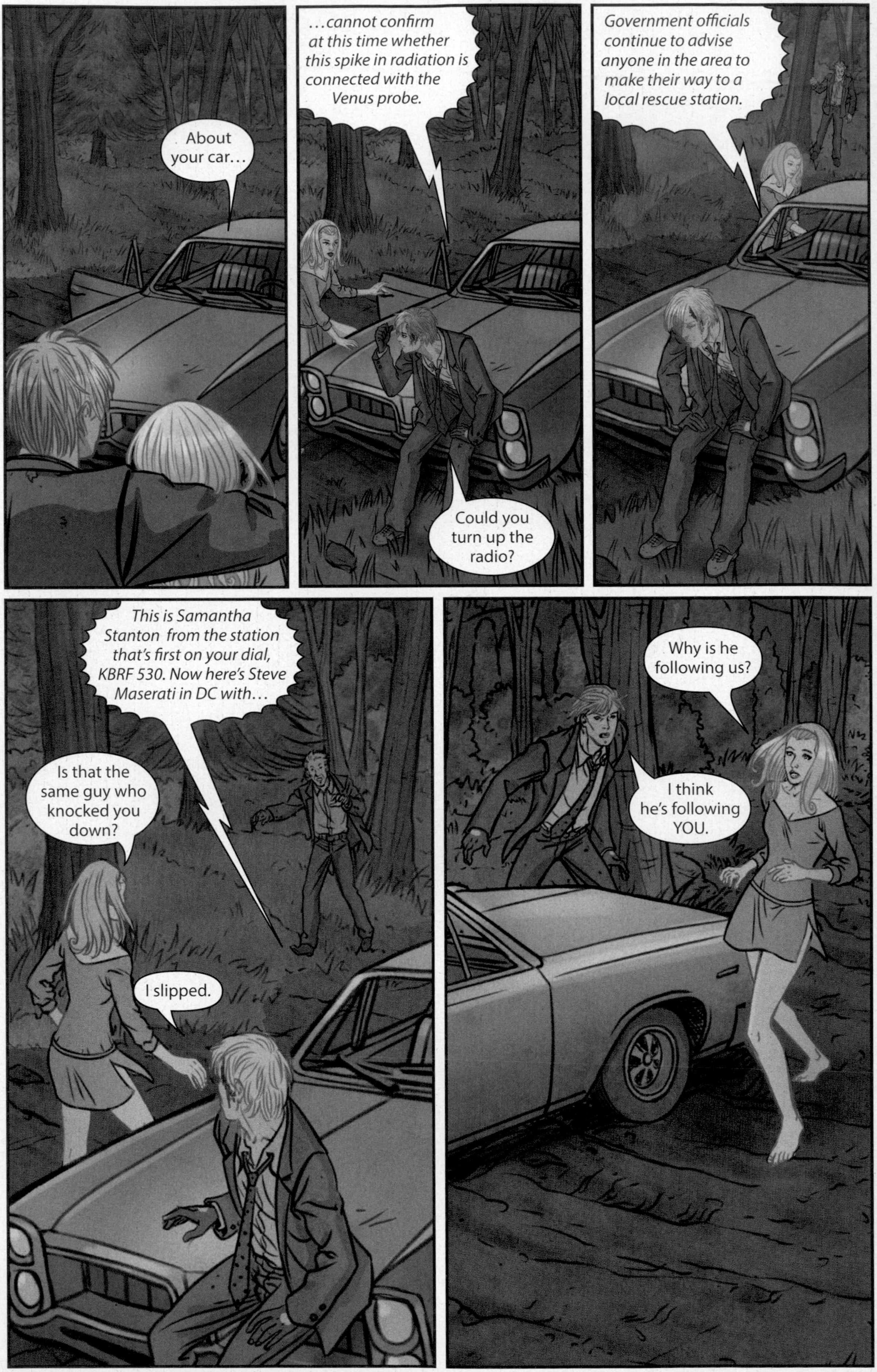
About your car…
…cannot confirm at this time whether this spike in radiation is connected with the Venus probe.
Could you turn up the radio?
Government officials continue to advise anyone in the area to make their way to a local rescue station.
This is Samantha Stanton from the station that's first on your dial, KBRF 530. Now here's Steve Maserati in DC with…
Is that the same guy who knocked you down?
I slipped.
Why is he following us?
I think he's following YOU.

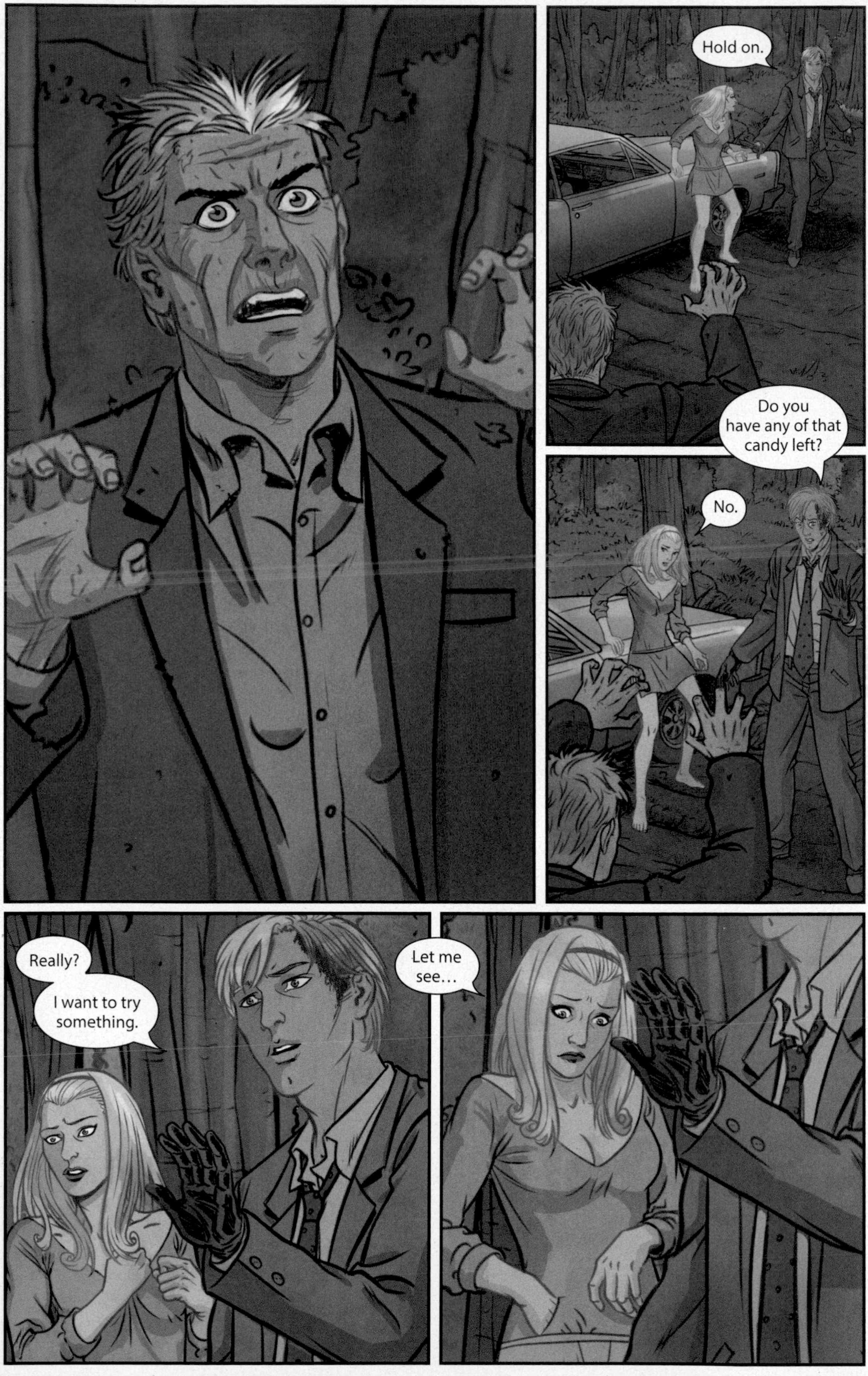
Hold on.
Do you have any of that candy left?
No.
Really?
I want to try something.
Let me see…

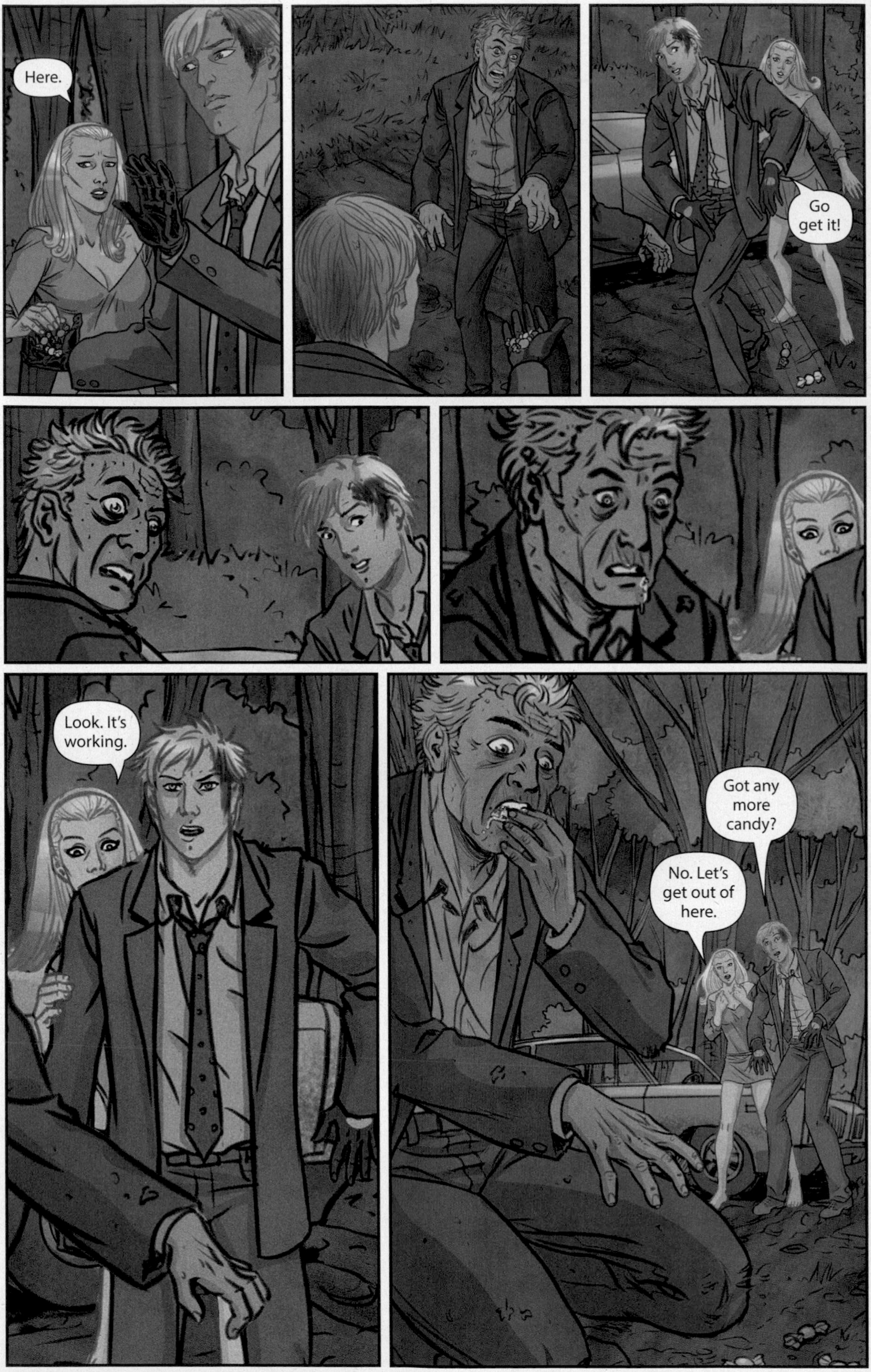
Here.
Go get it!
Look. It's working.
Got any more candy?
No. Let's get out of here.

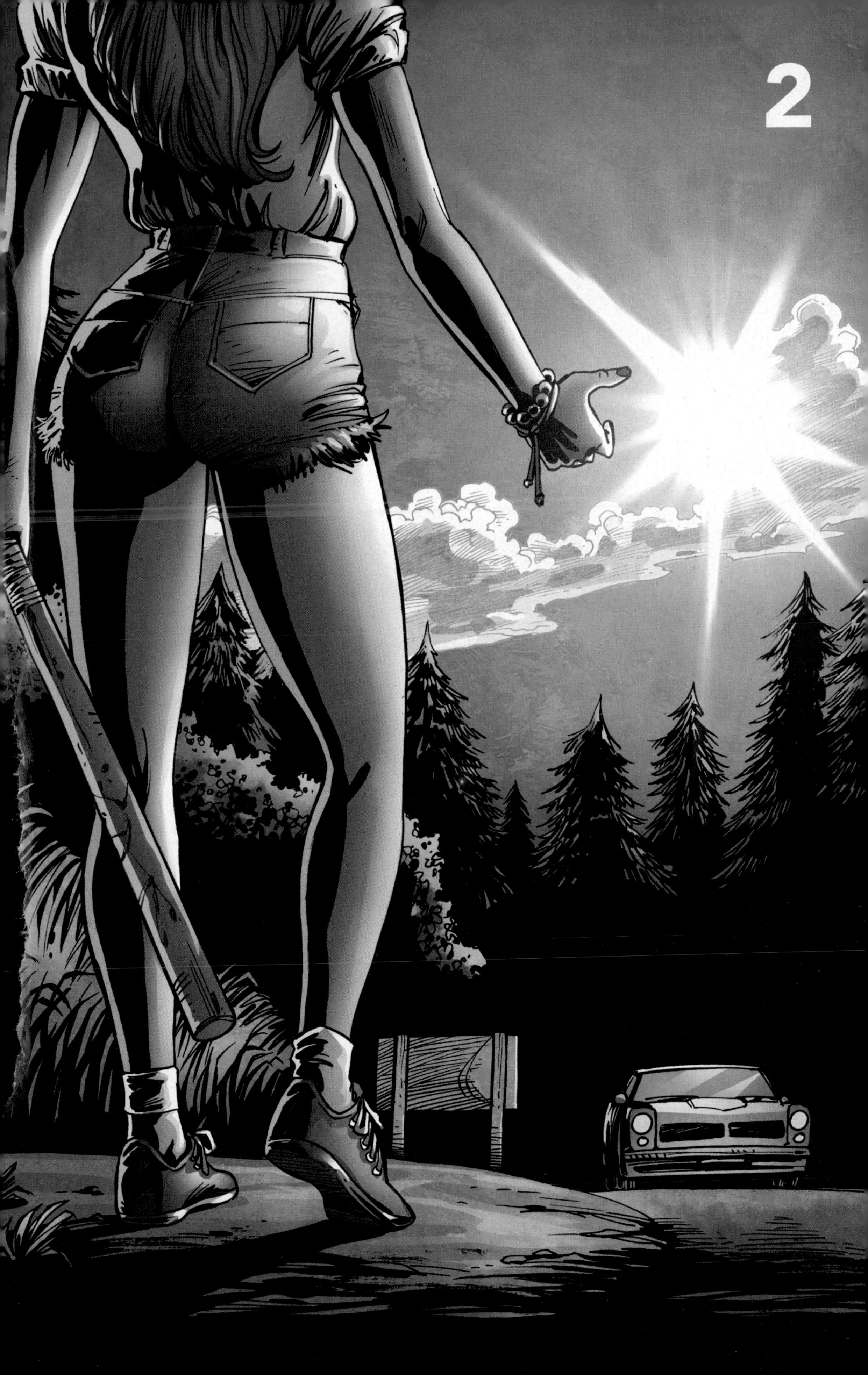

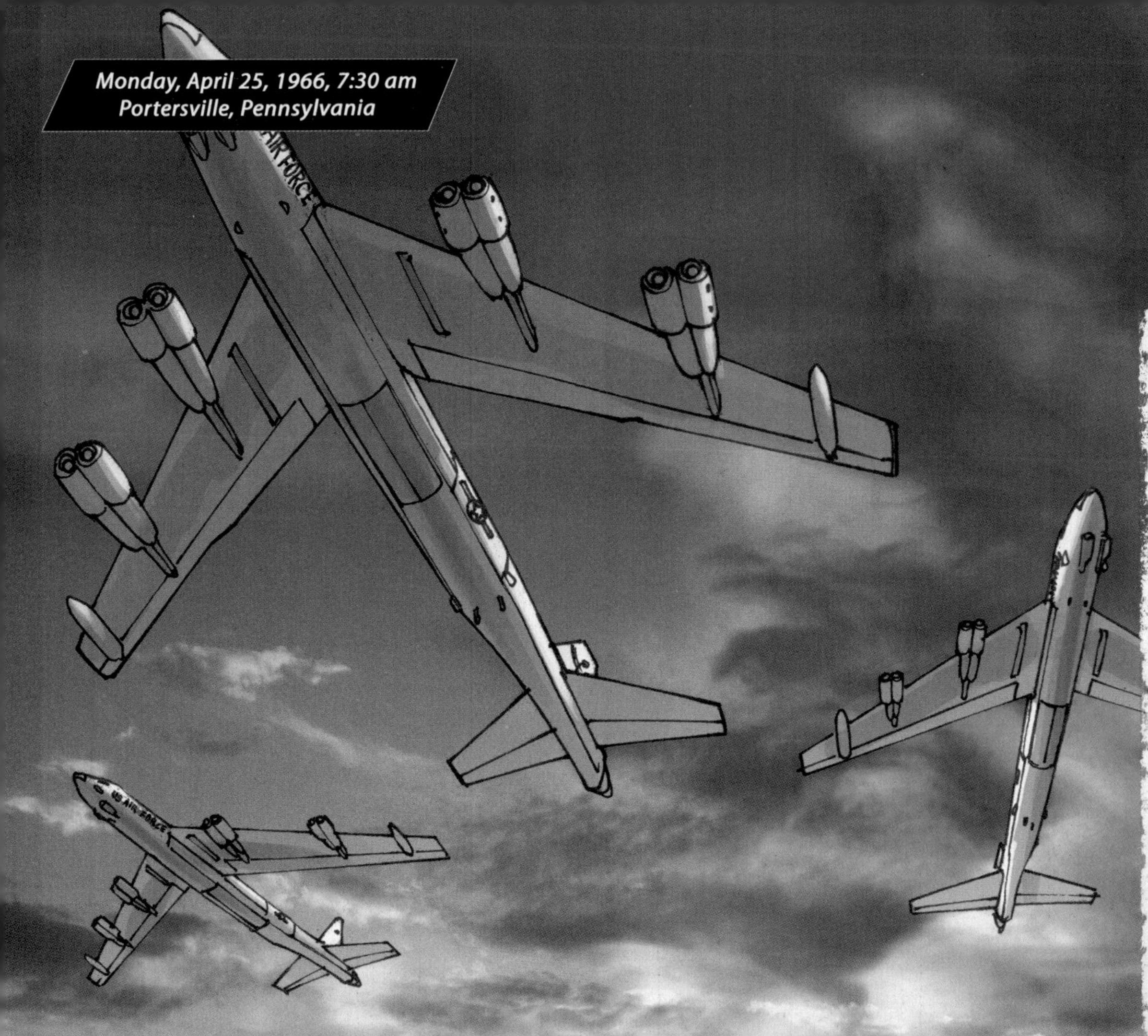

Monday, April 25, 1966, 7:30 am
Portersville, Pennsylvania

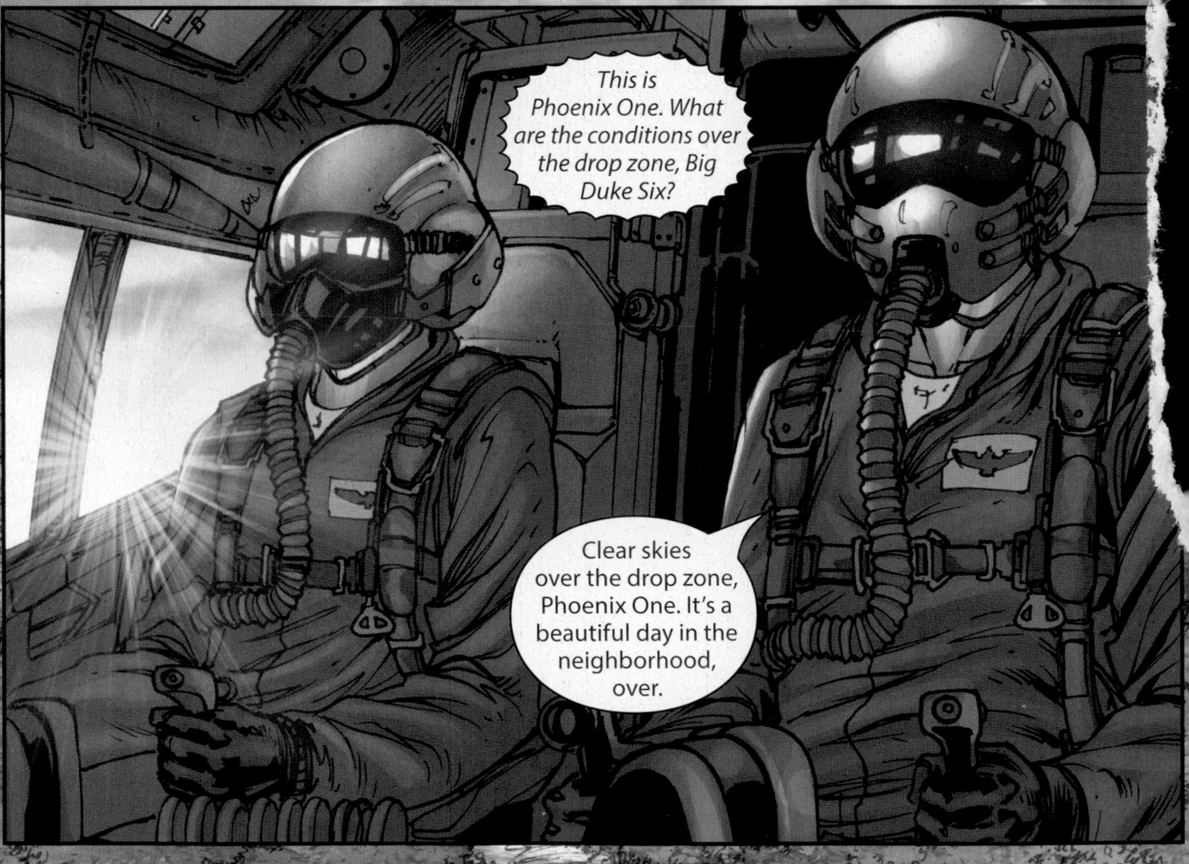

This is Phoenix One. What are the conditions over the drop zone, Big Duke Six?
Clear skies over the drop zone, Phoenix One. It's a beautiful day in the neighborhood, over.

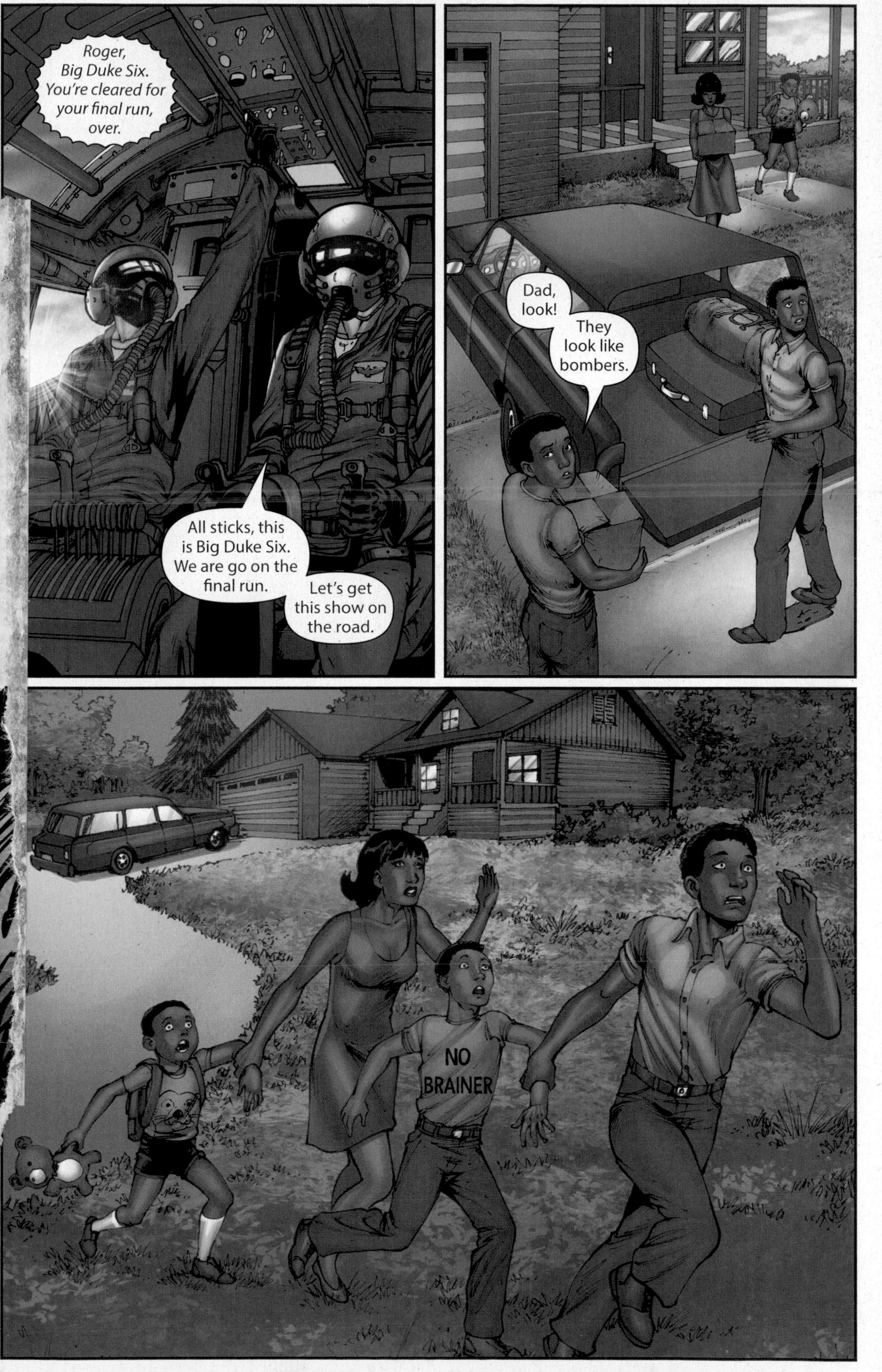
Roger, Big Duke Six. You're cleared for your final run, over.
All sticks, this is Big Duke Six. We are go on the final run.
Let's get this show on the road.
Dad, look!
They look like bombers.
NO BRAINER

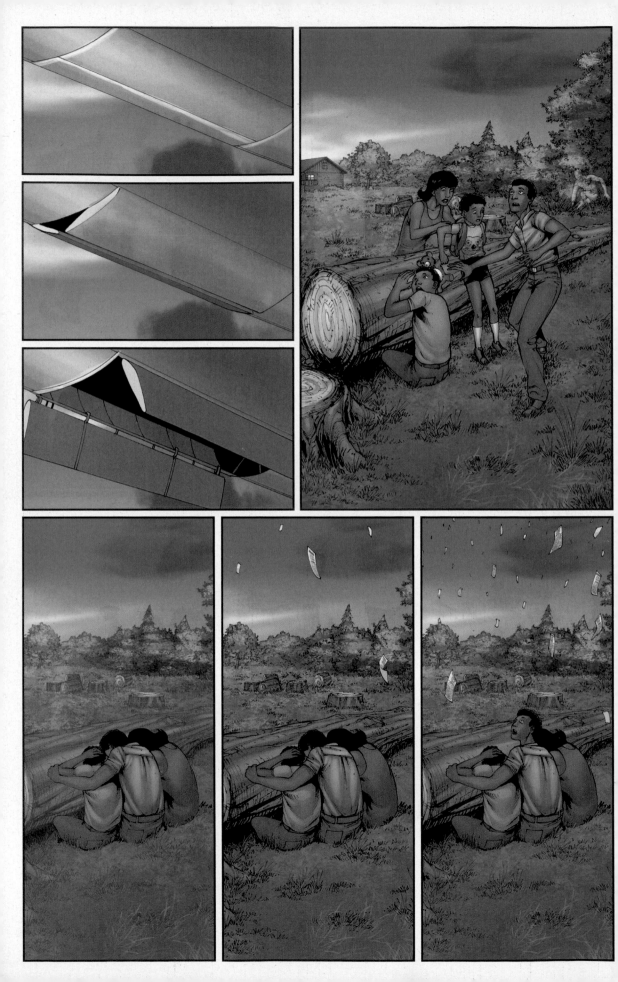

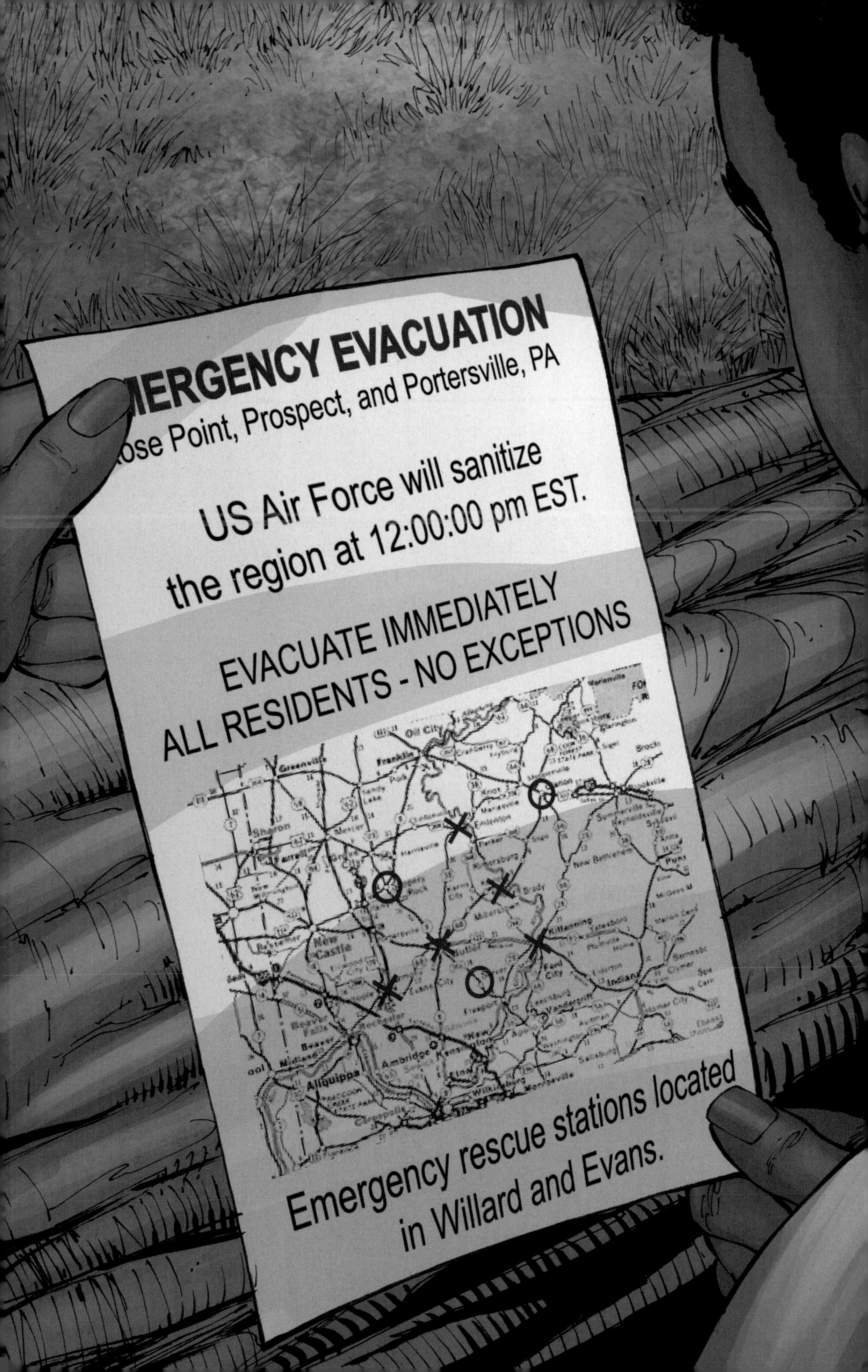

EMERGENCY EVACUATION
Rose Point, Prospect, and Portersville, PA
US Air Force will sanitize the region at 12:00:00 pm EST.
EVACUATE IMMEDIATELY
ALL RESIDENTS - NO EXCEPTIONS
Oil City
Franklin
Greenville
Sharon
New Castle
Butler
Kittanning
Indiana
Beaver Falls
Beaver
Ambridge
Aliquippa
Emergency rescue stations located in Willard and Evans.

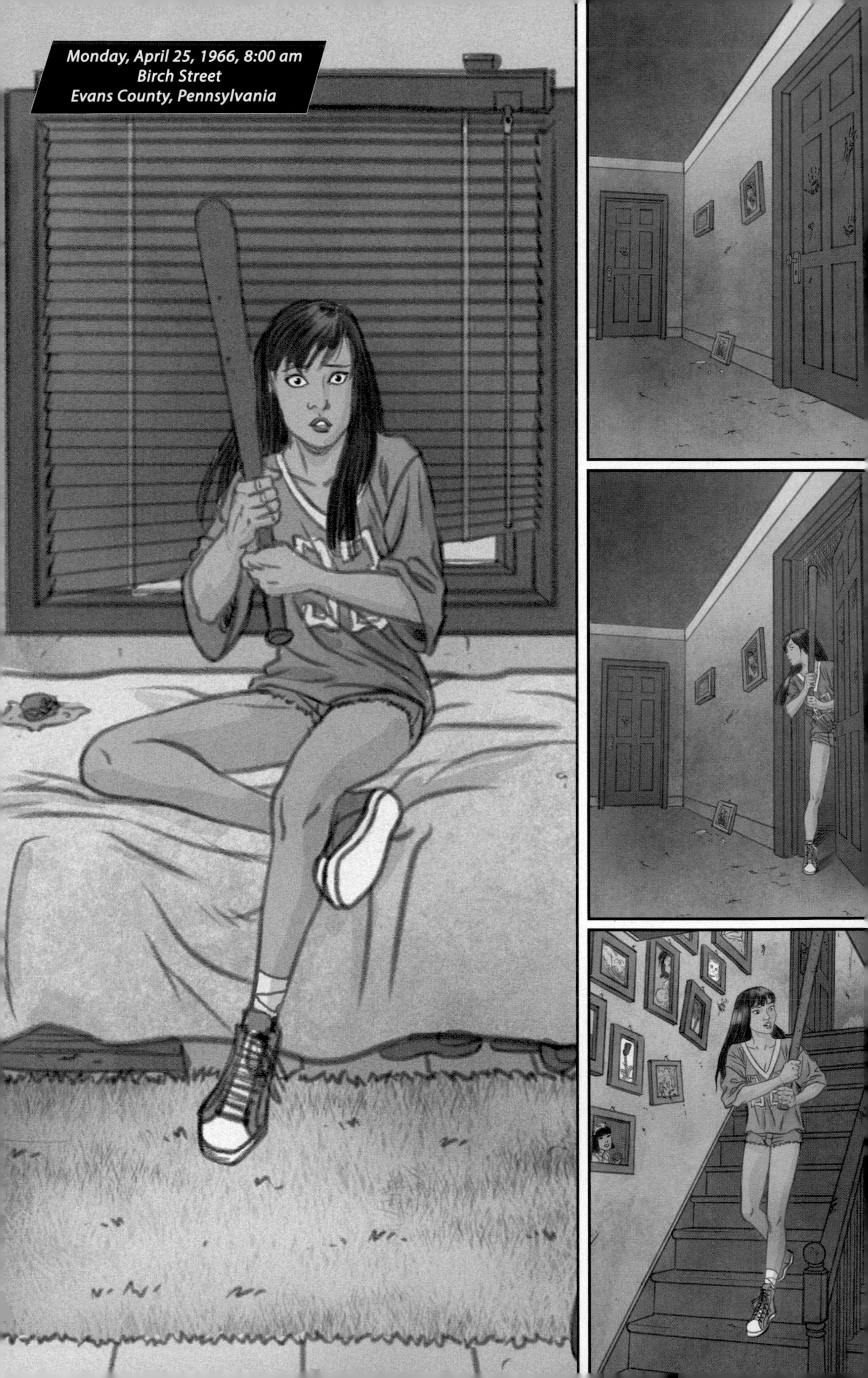
Monday, April 25, 1966, 8:00 am
Birch Street
Evans County, Pennsylvania

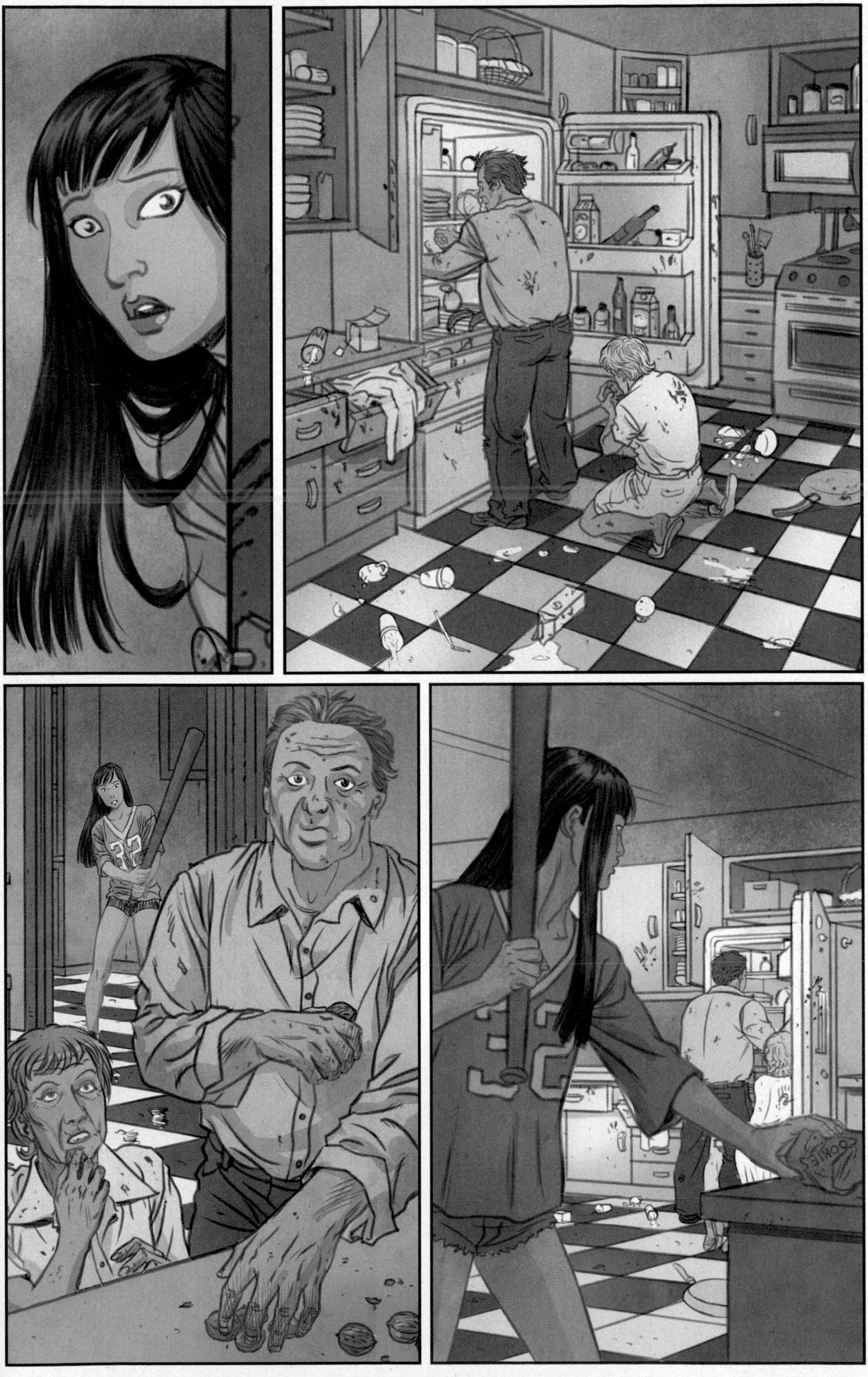

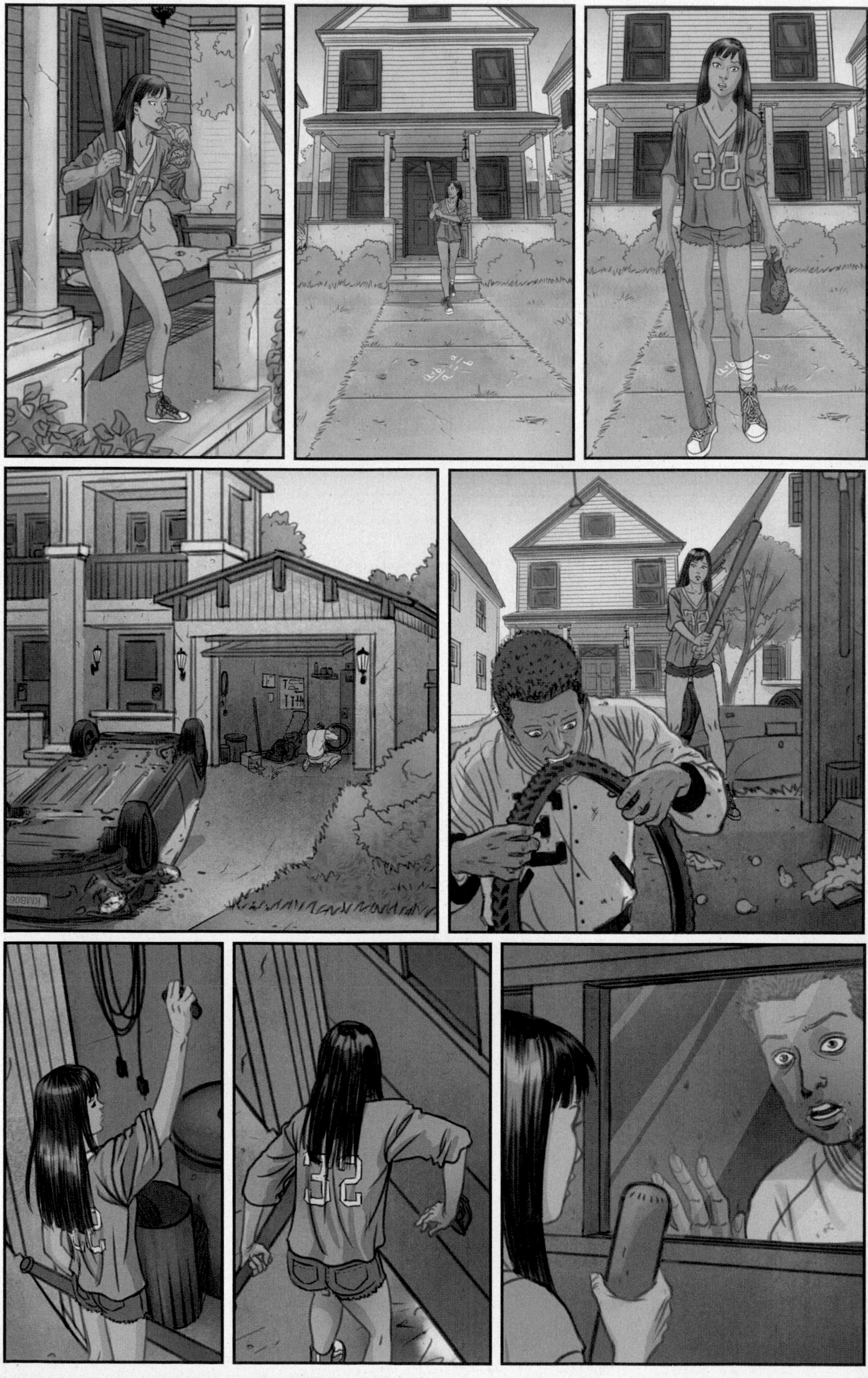

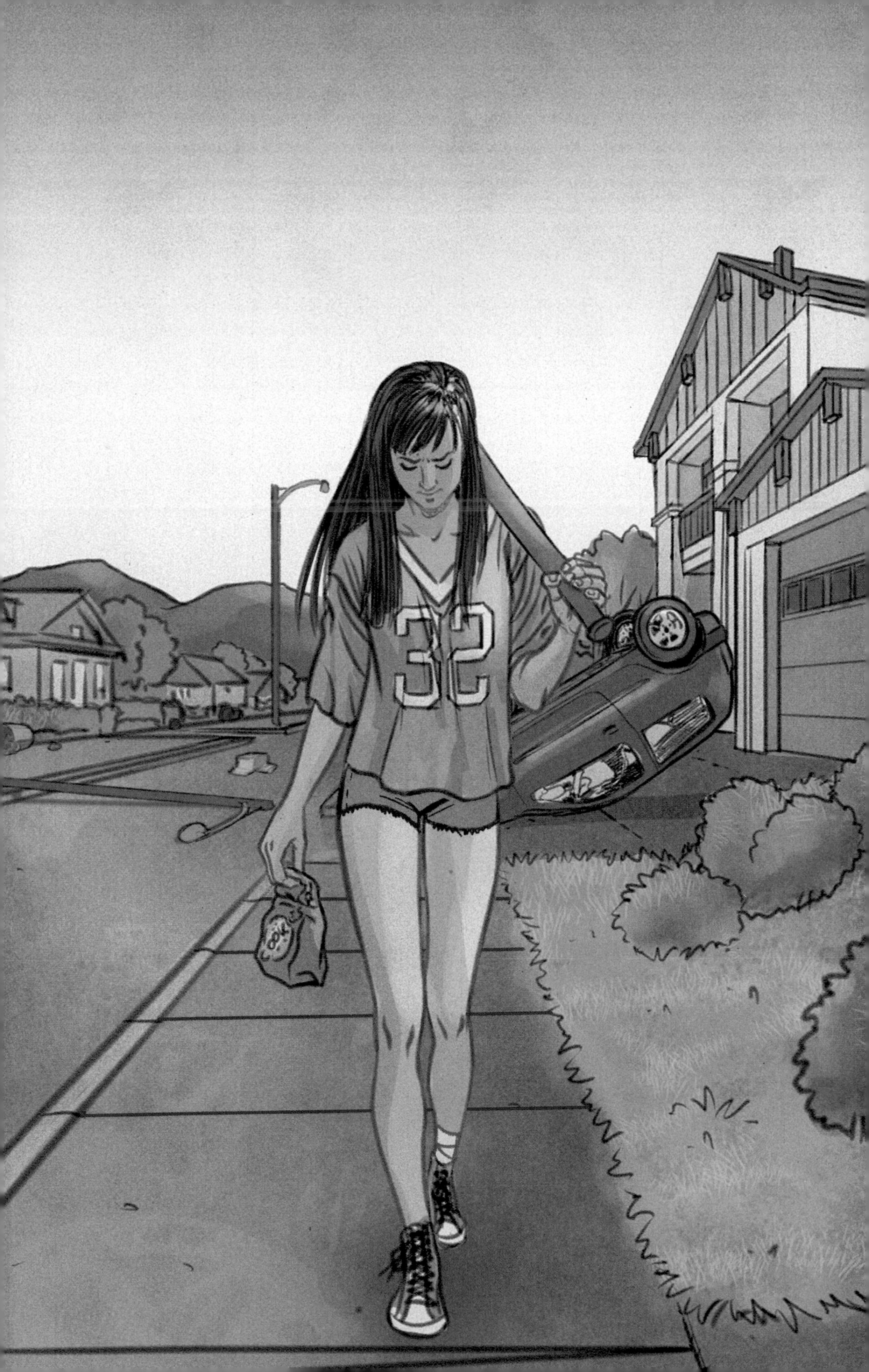

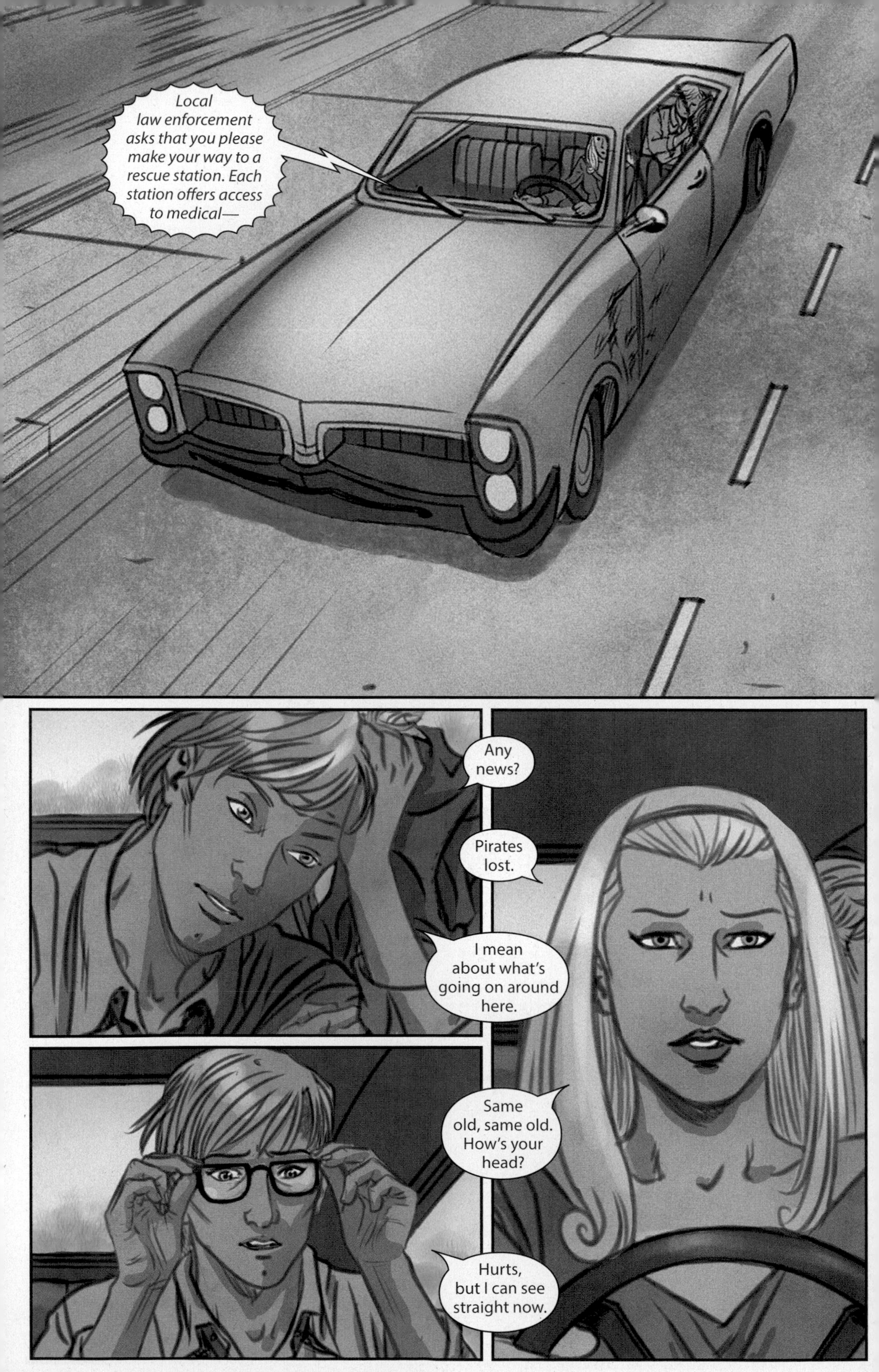
Local law enforcement asks that you please make your way to a rescue station. Each station offers access to medical—
Any news?
Pirates lost.
I mean about what's going on around here.
Same old, same old. How's your head?
Hurts, but I can see straight now.

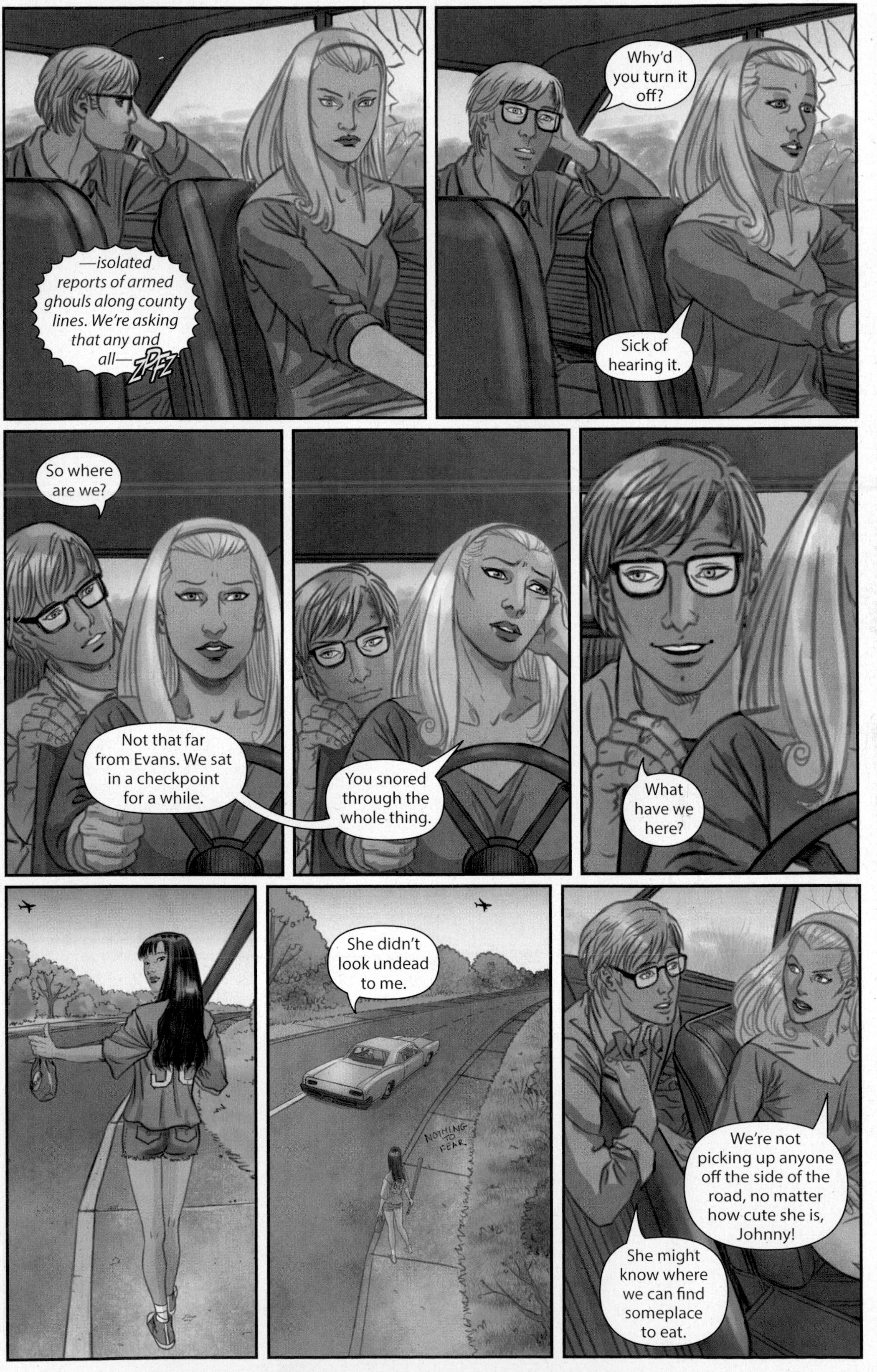
—isolated reports of armed ghouls along county lines. We're asking that any and all—
ZPFZ
Why'd you turn it off?
Sick of hearing it.
So where are we?
Not that far from Evans. We sat in a checkpoint for a while.
You snored through the whole thing.
What have we here?
She didn't look undead to me.
NOTHING TO FEAR
We're not picking up anyone off the side of the road, no matter how cute she is, Johnny!
She might know where we can find someplace to eat.

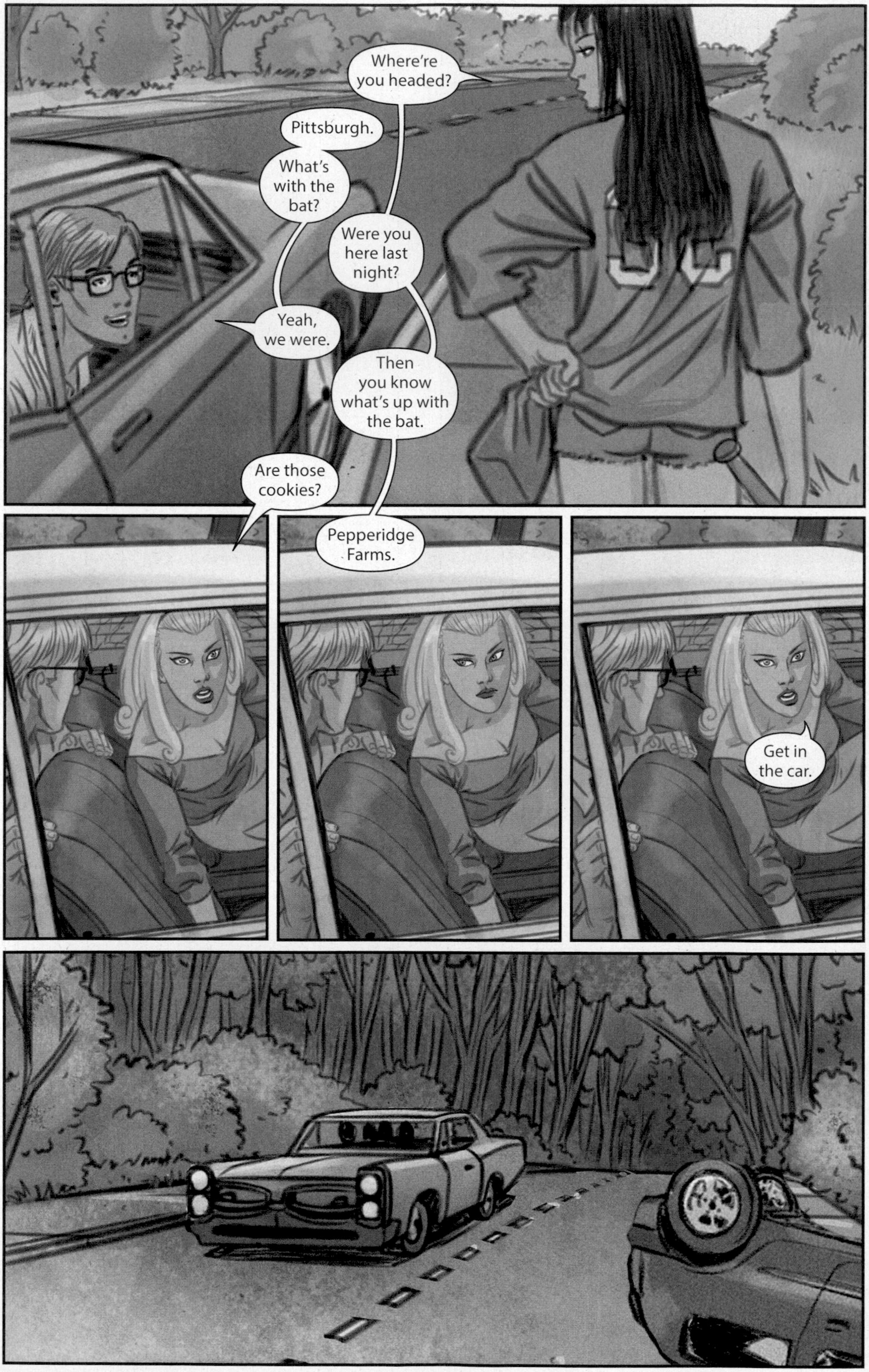
Where're you headed?
Pittsburgh.
What's with the bat?
Were you here last night?
Yeah, we were.
Then you know what's up with the bat.
Are those cookies?
Pepperidge Farms.
Get in the car.

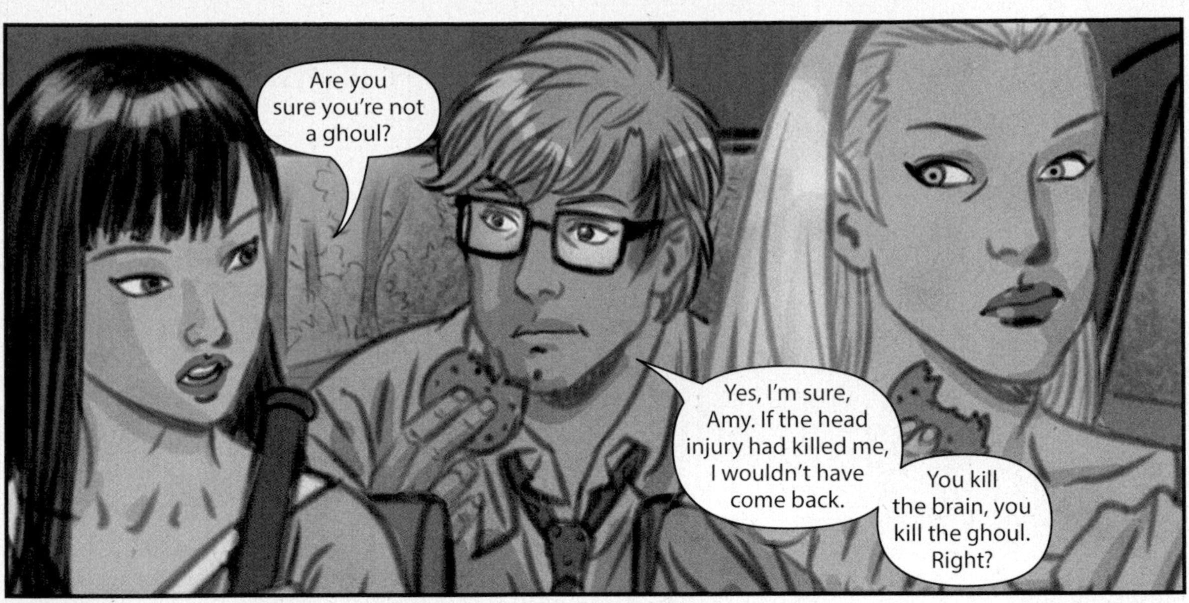
Are you sure you're not a ghoul?
Yes, I'm sure, Amy. If the head injury had killed me, I wouldn't have come back.
You kill the brain, you kill the ghoul. Right?

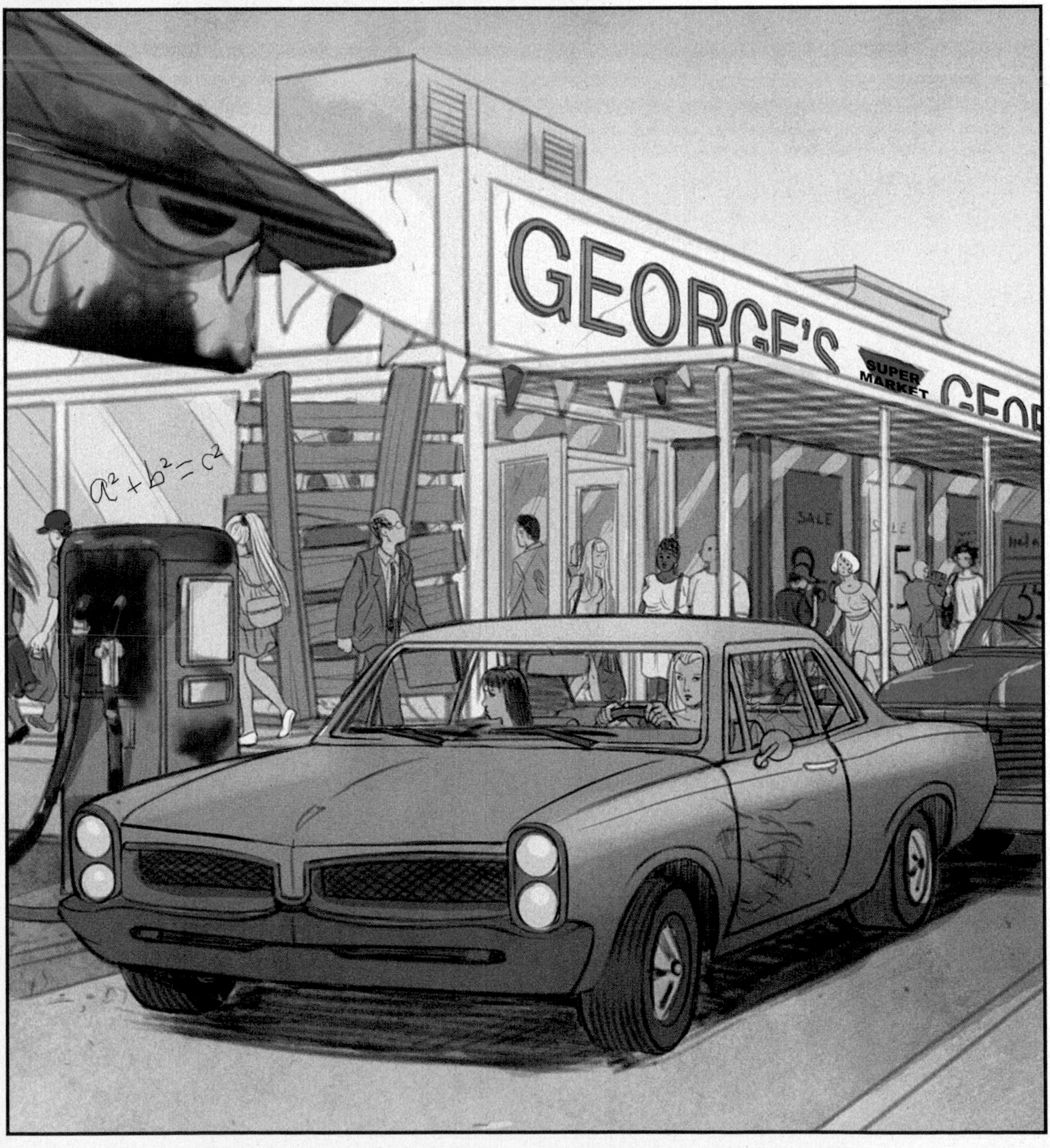
GEORGE'S
SUPER MARKET
$a^2+b^2=c^2$

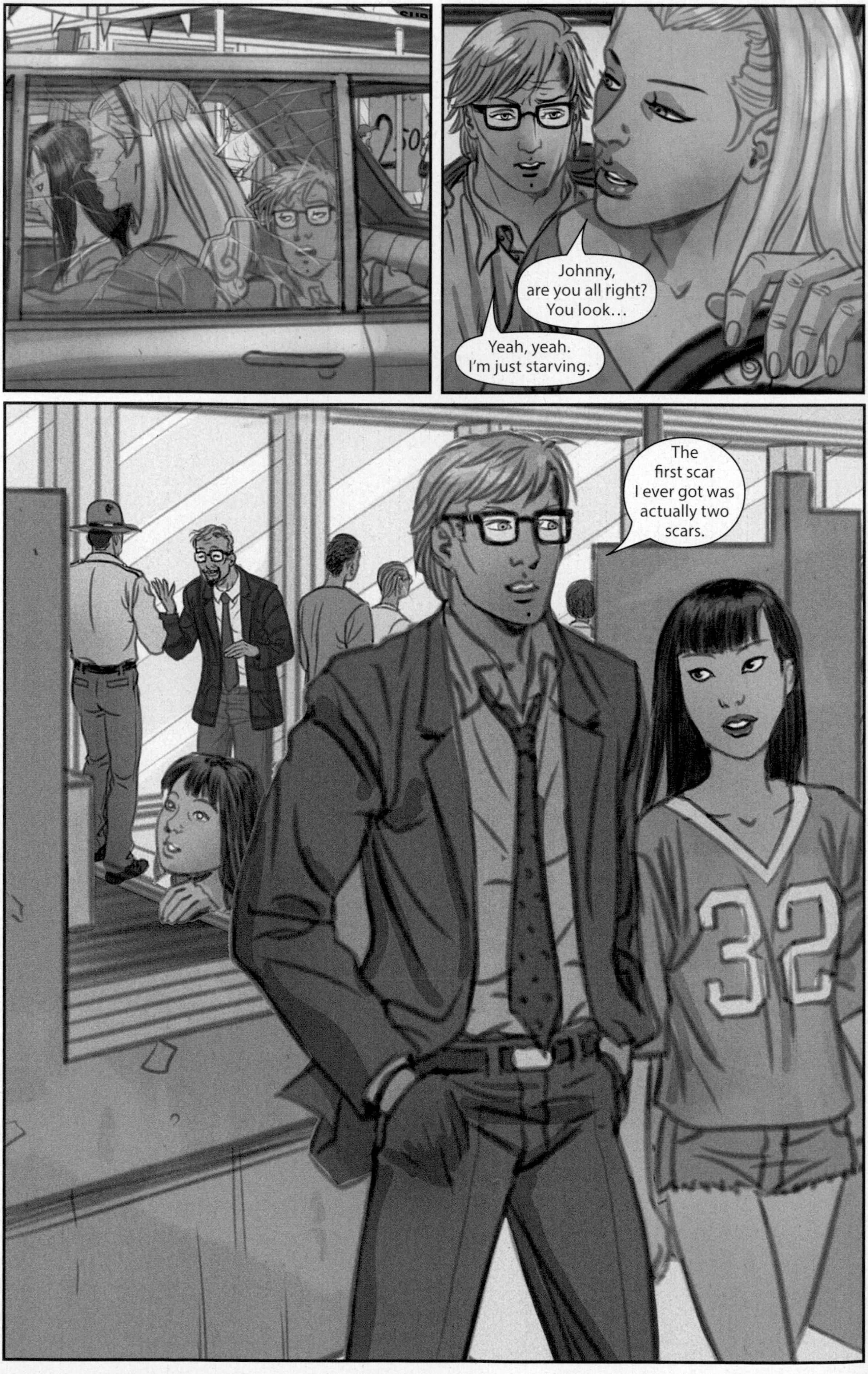
Johnny,
are you all right?
You look…
Yeah, yeah.
I'm just starving.
The first scar I ever got was actually two scars.

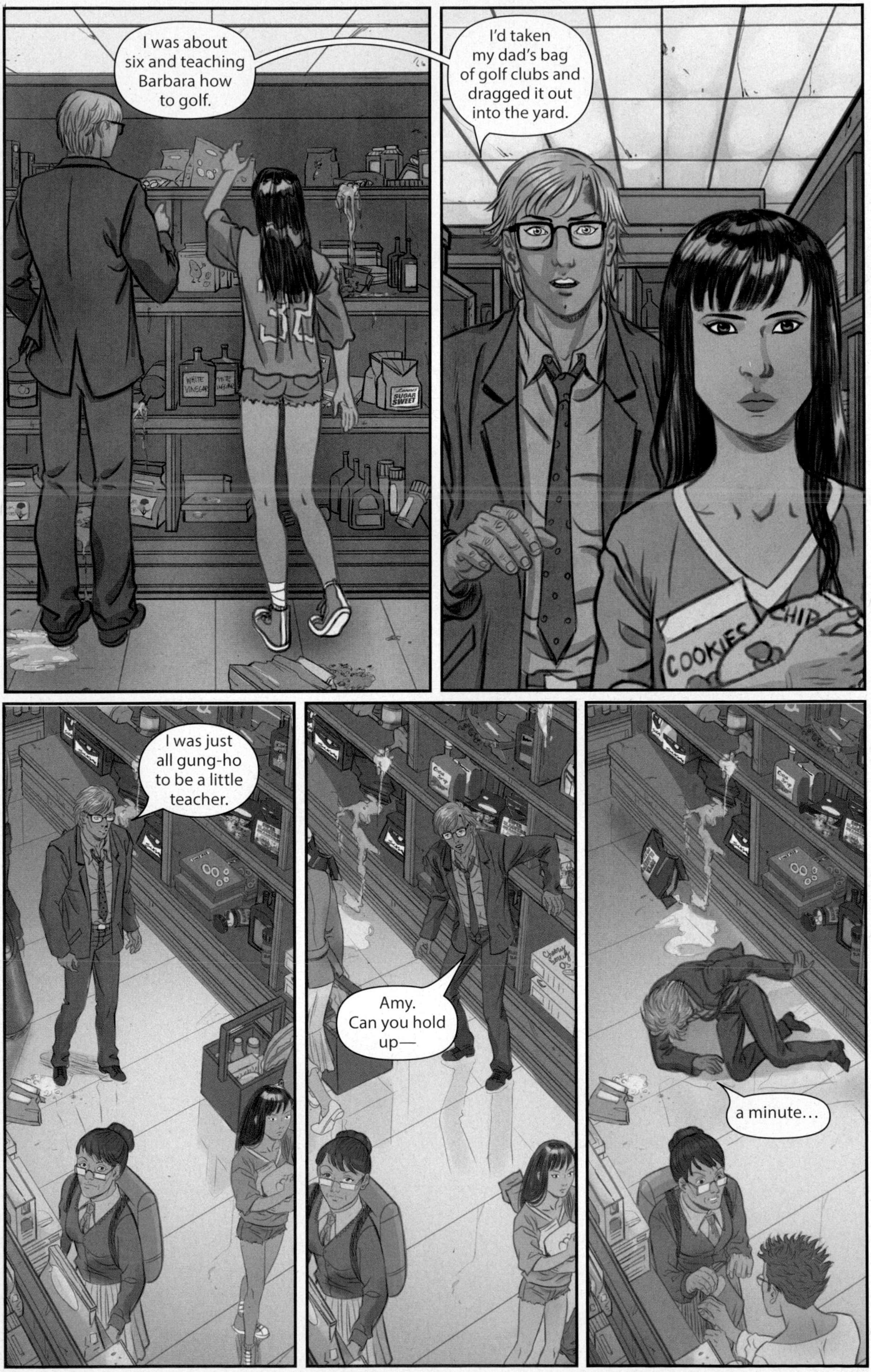
I was about six and teaching Barbara how to golf.
I'd taken my dad's bag of golf clubs and dragged it out into the yard.
WHITE VINEGAR
SUGAR SWEET
COOKIES
I was just all gung-ho to be a little teacher.
Amy. Can you hold up—
a minute…

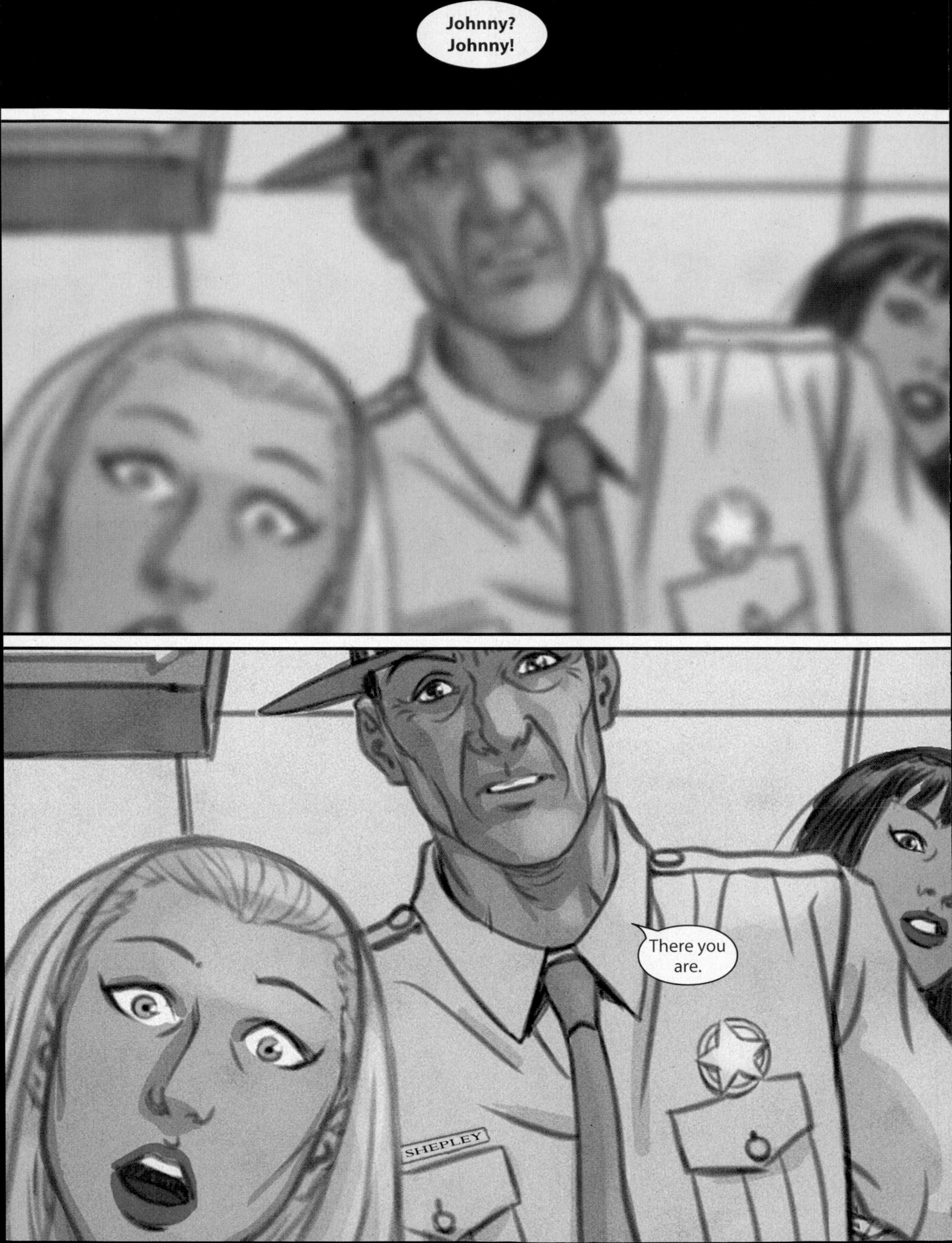
Johnny?
Johnny!
There you are.
SHEPLEY

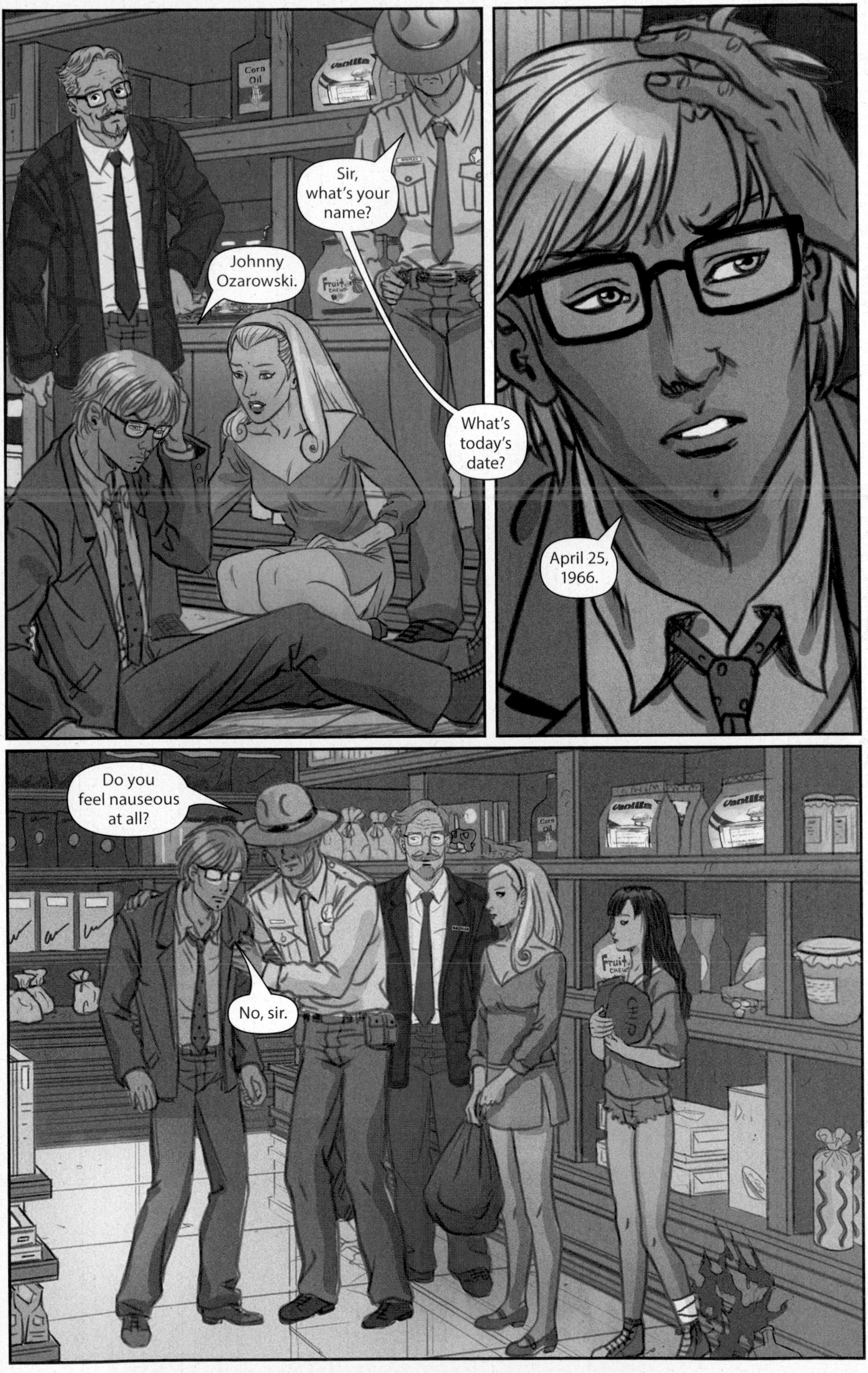
Corn Oil
Vanilla
Sir, what's your name?
Johnny Ozarowski.
Fruit Chews
What's today's date?
April 25, 1966.
Do you feel nauseous at all?
Vanilla
Corn Oil
Vanilla
No, sir.
Fruit Chews

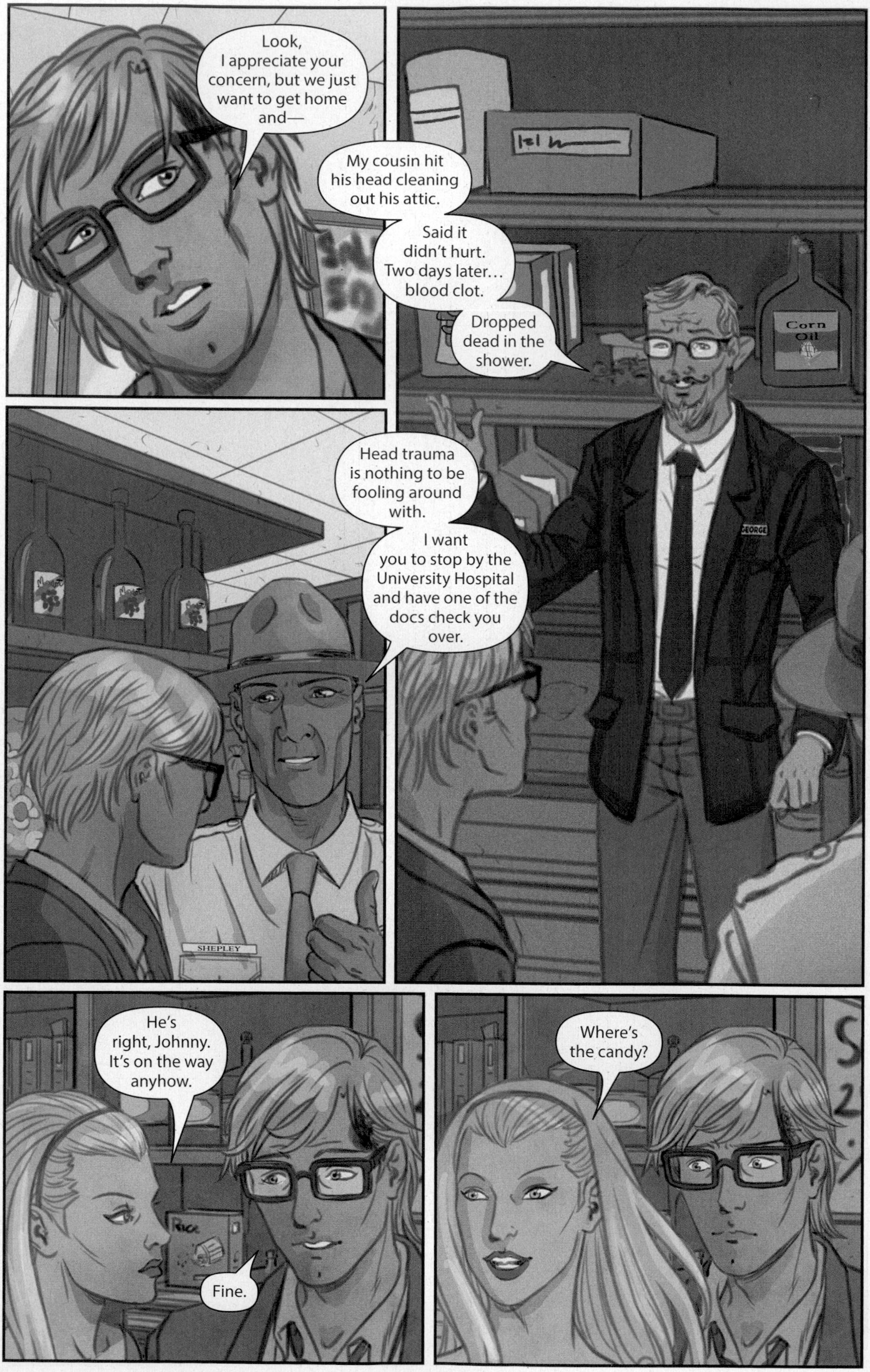
Look, I appreciate your concern, but we just want to get home and—
My cousin hit his head cleaning out his attic.
Said it didn't hurt. Two days later… blood clot.
Dropped dead in the shower.
Corn Oil
GEORGE
Head trauma is nothing to be fooling around with.
I want you to stop by the University Hospital and have one of the docs check you over.
SHEPLEY
He's right, Johnny. It's on the way anyhow.
Fine.
Where's the candy?

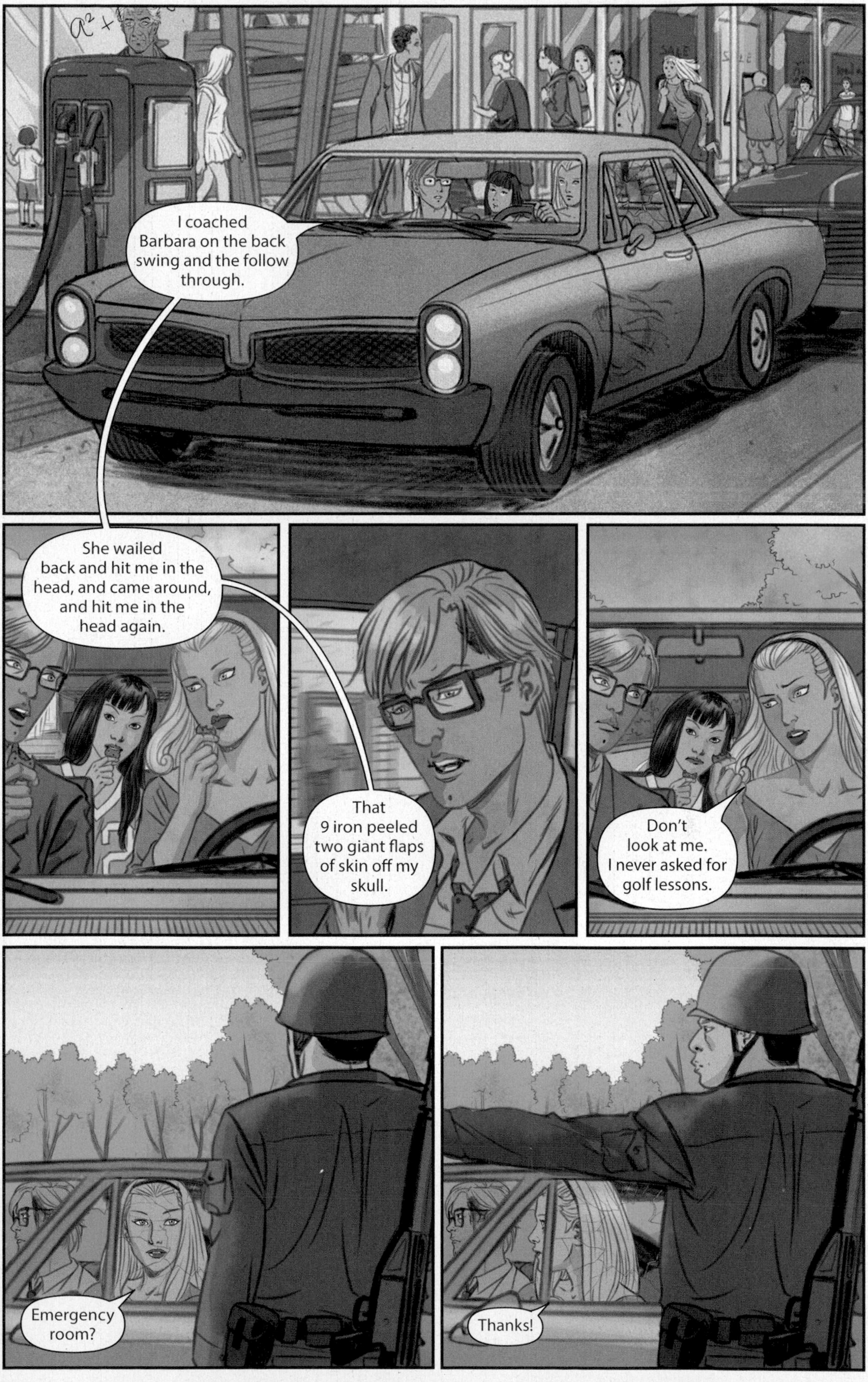
I coached Barbara on the back swing and the follow through.
She wailed back and hit me in the head, and came around, and hit me in the head again.
That 9 iron peeled two giant flaps of skin off my skull.
Don't look at me. I never asked for golf lessons.
Emergency room?
Thanks!

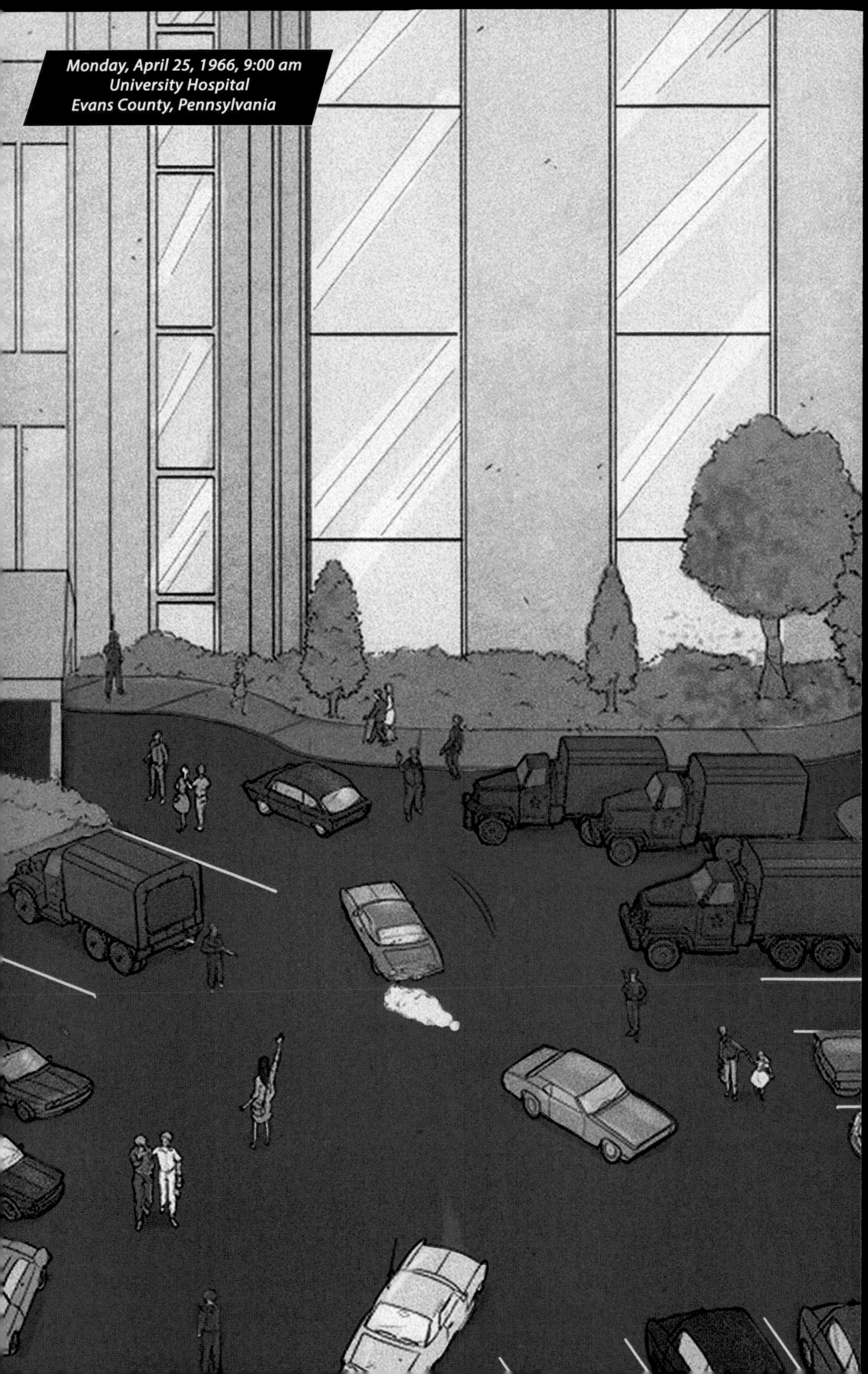
Monday, April 25, 1966, 9:00 am
University Hospital
Evans County, Pennsylvania

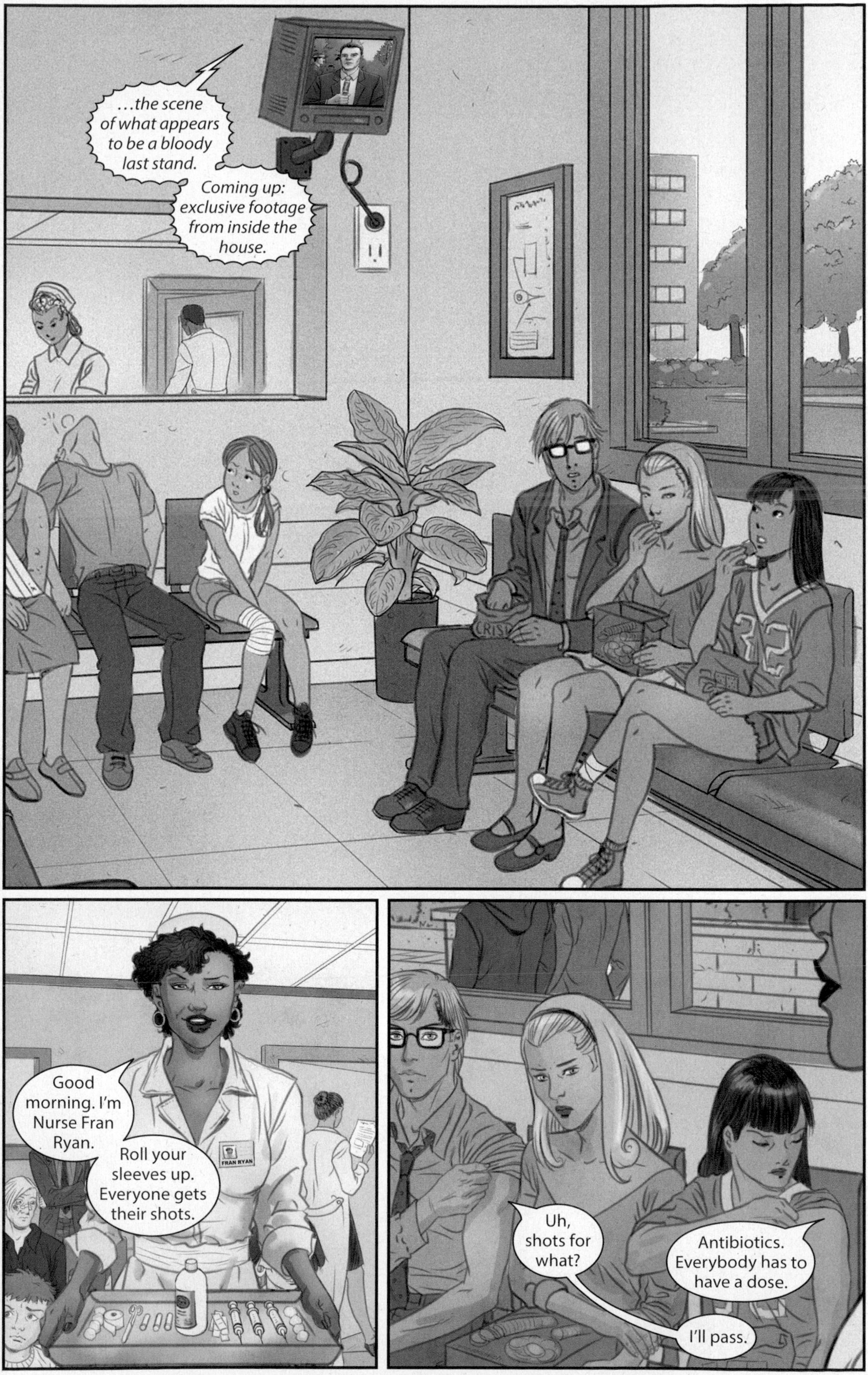

...the scene of what appears to be a bloody last stand.
Coming up: exclusive footage from inside the house.
Good morning. I'm Nurse Fran Ryan.
Roll your sleeves up. Everyone gets their shots.
FRAN RYAN
Uh, shots for what?
Antibiotics. Everybody has to have a dose.
I'll pass.

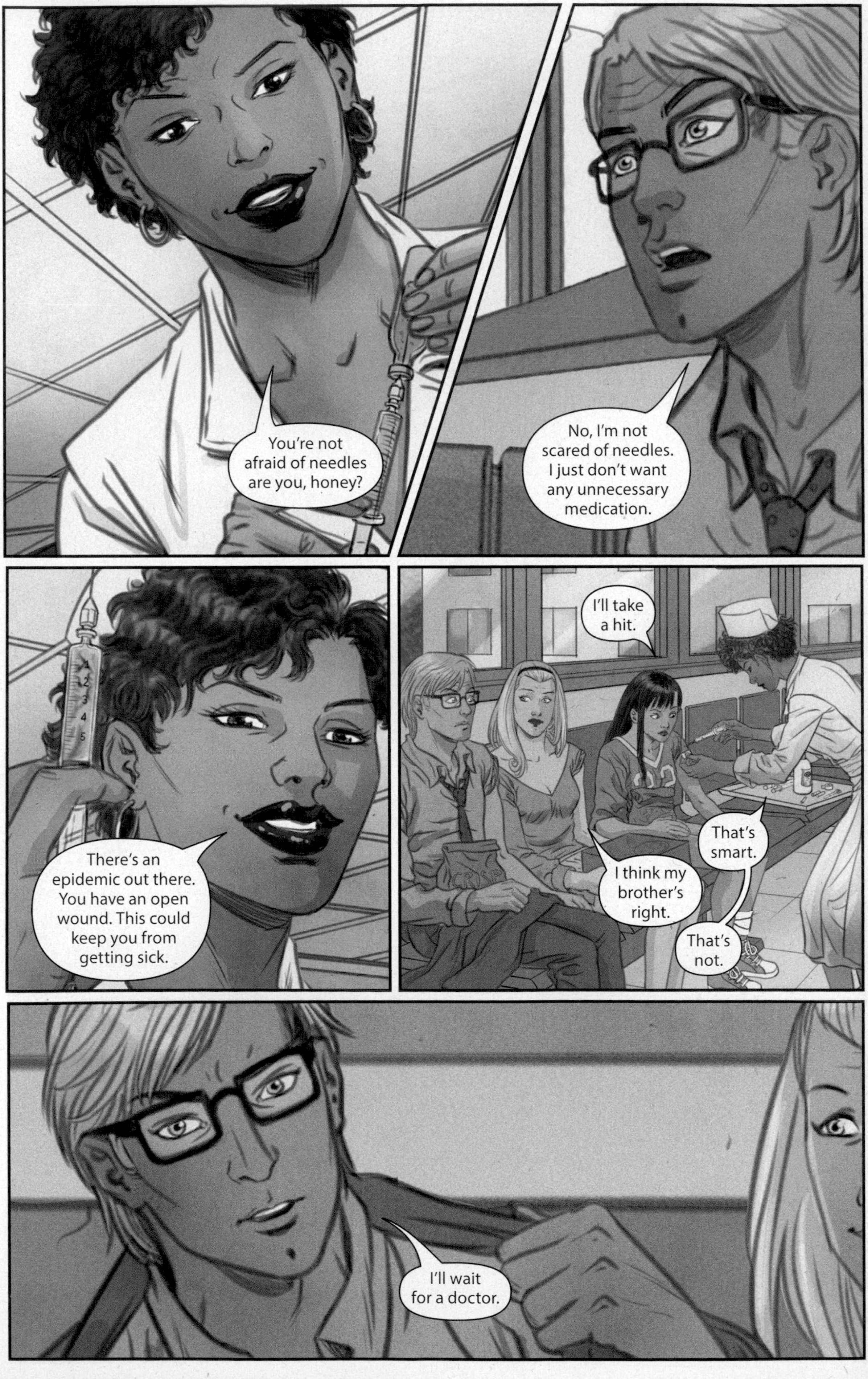
You're not afraid of needles are you, honey?
No, I'm not scared of needles. I just don't want any unnecessary medication.
There's an epidemic out there. You have an open wound. This could keep you from getting sick.
I'll take a hit.
That's smart.
I think my brother's right.
That's not.
I'll wait for a doctor.

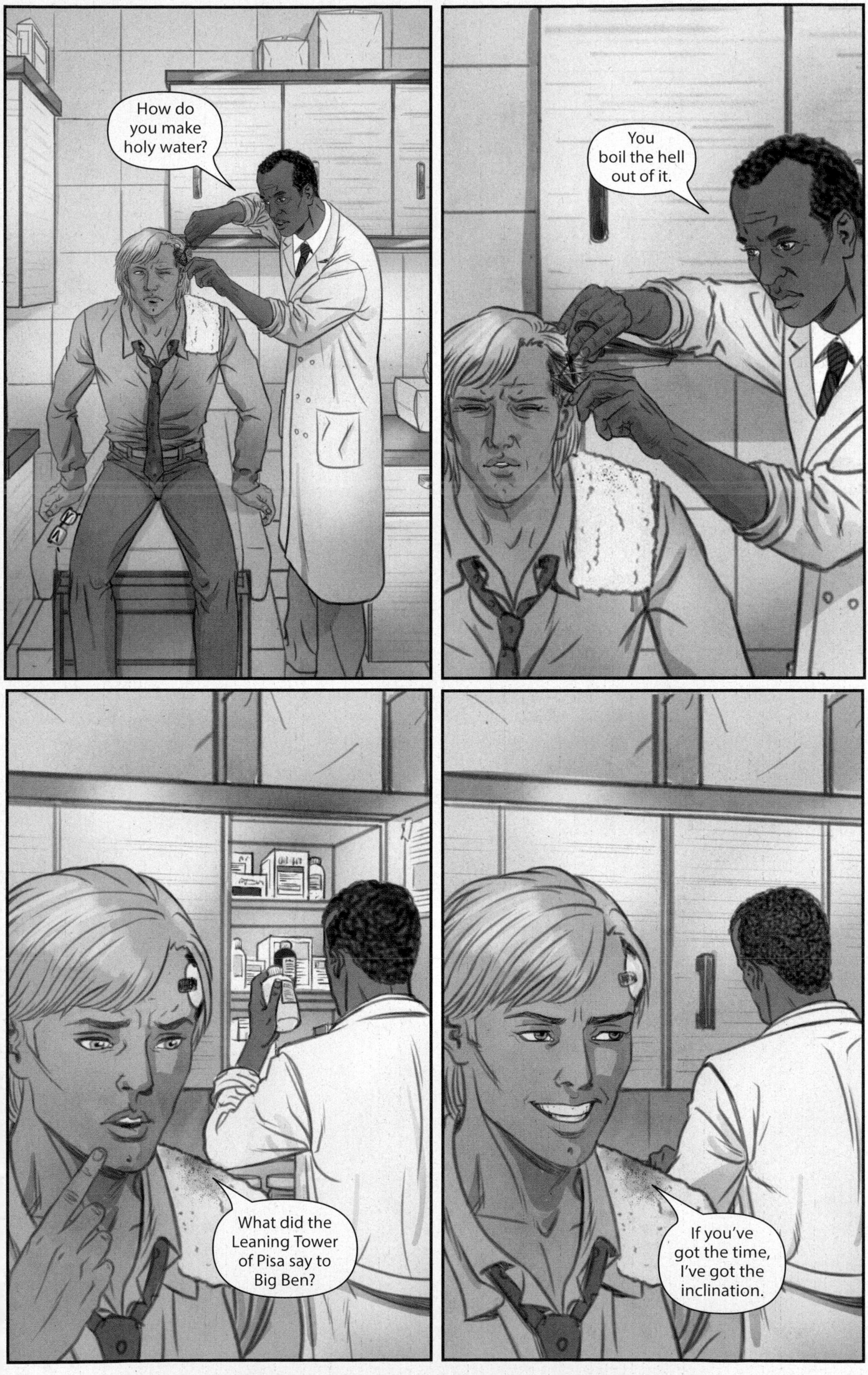
How do you make holy water?
You boil the hell out of it.
What did the Leaning Tower of Pisa say to Big Ben?
If you've got the time, I've got the inclination.

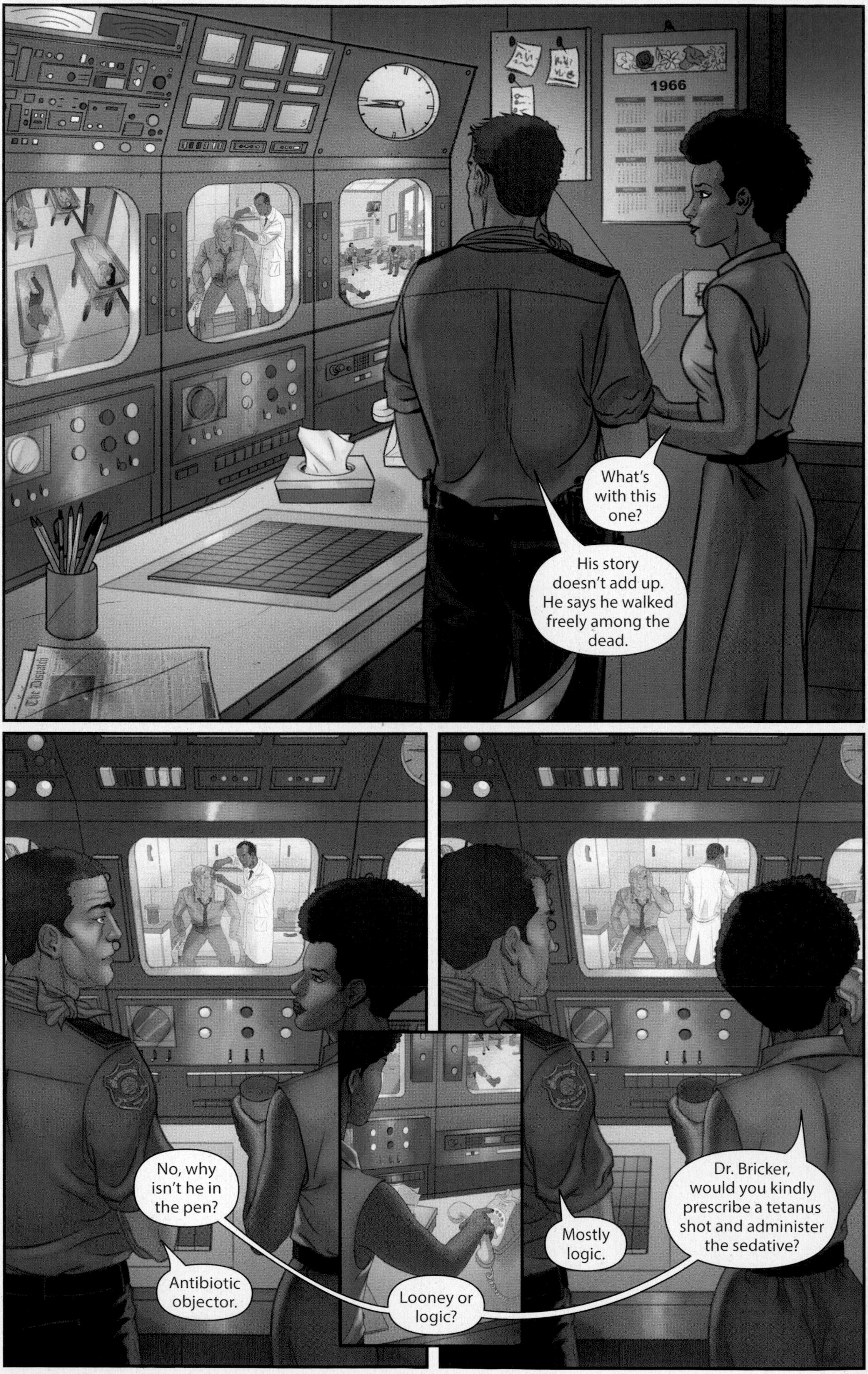
1966
The Dispatch
What's with this one?
His story doesn't add up. He says he walked freely among the dead.
No, why isn't he in the pen?
Antibiotic objector.
Looney or logic?
Mostly logic.
Dr. Bricker, would you kindly prescribe a tetanus shot and administer the sedative?

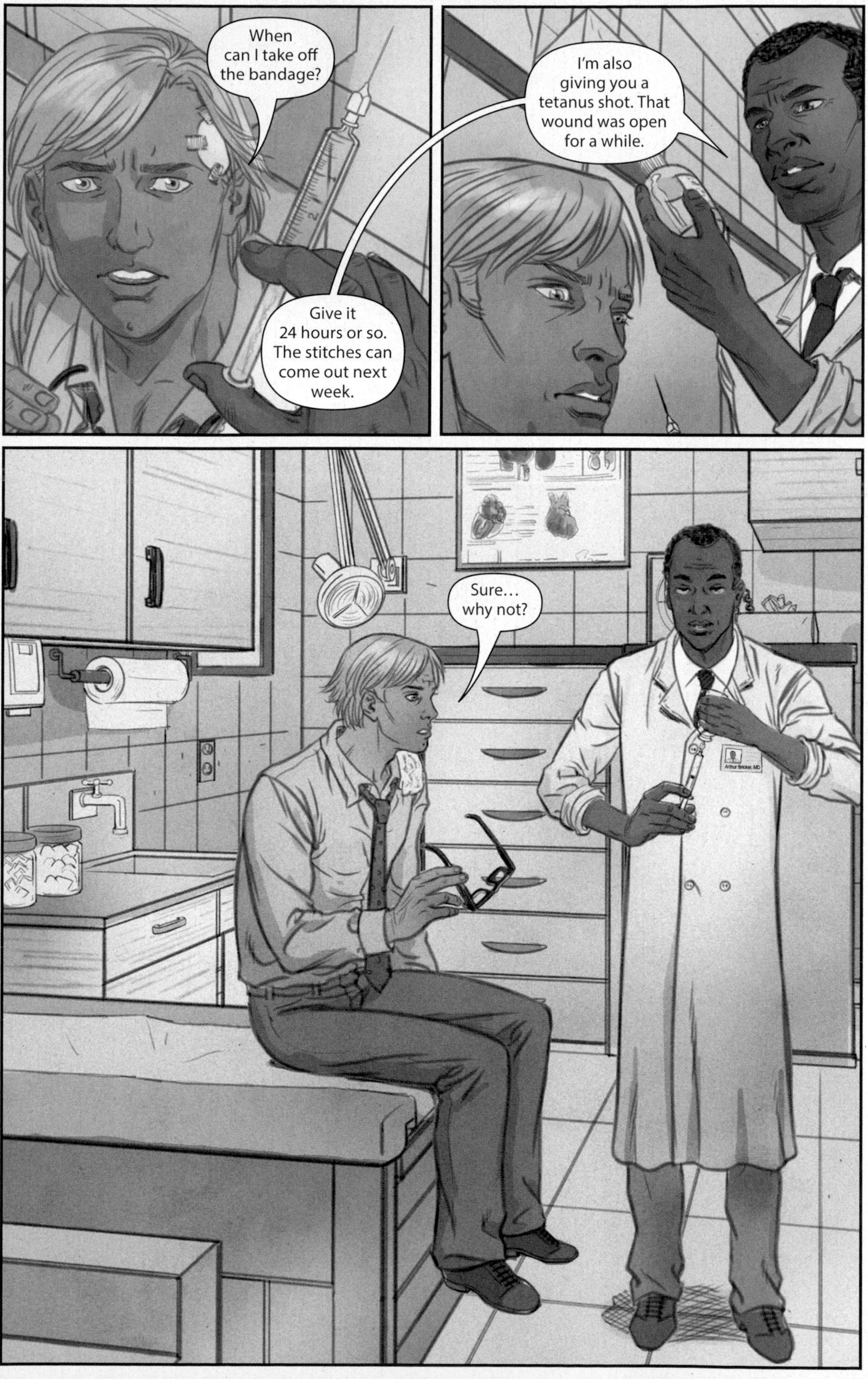
When can I take off the bandage?
Give it 24 hours or so. The stitches can come out next week.
I'm also giving you a tetanus shot. That wound was open for a while.
Sure… why not?

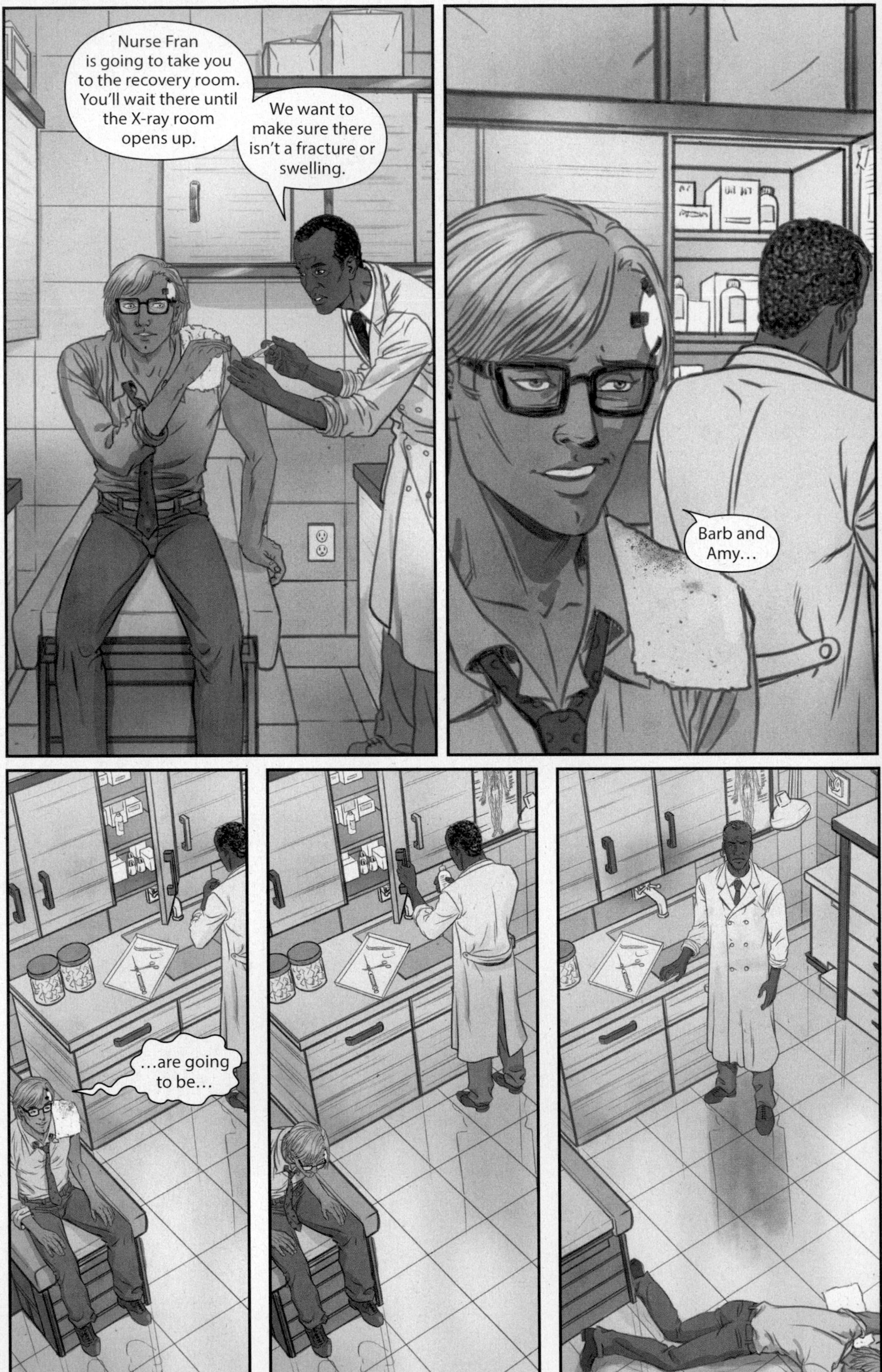
Nurse Fran is going to take you to the recovery room. You'll wait there until the X-ray room opens up.
We want to make sure there isn't a fracture or swelling.
Barb and Amy…
…are going to be…

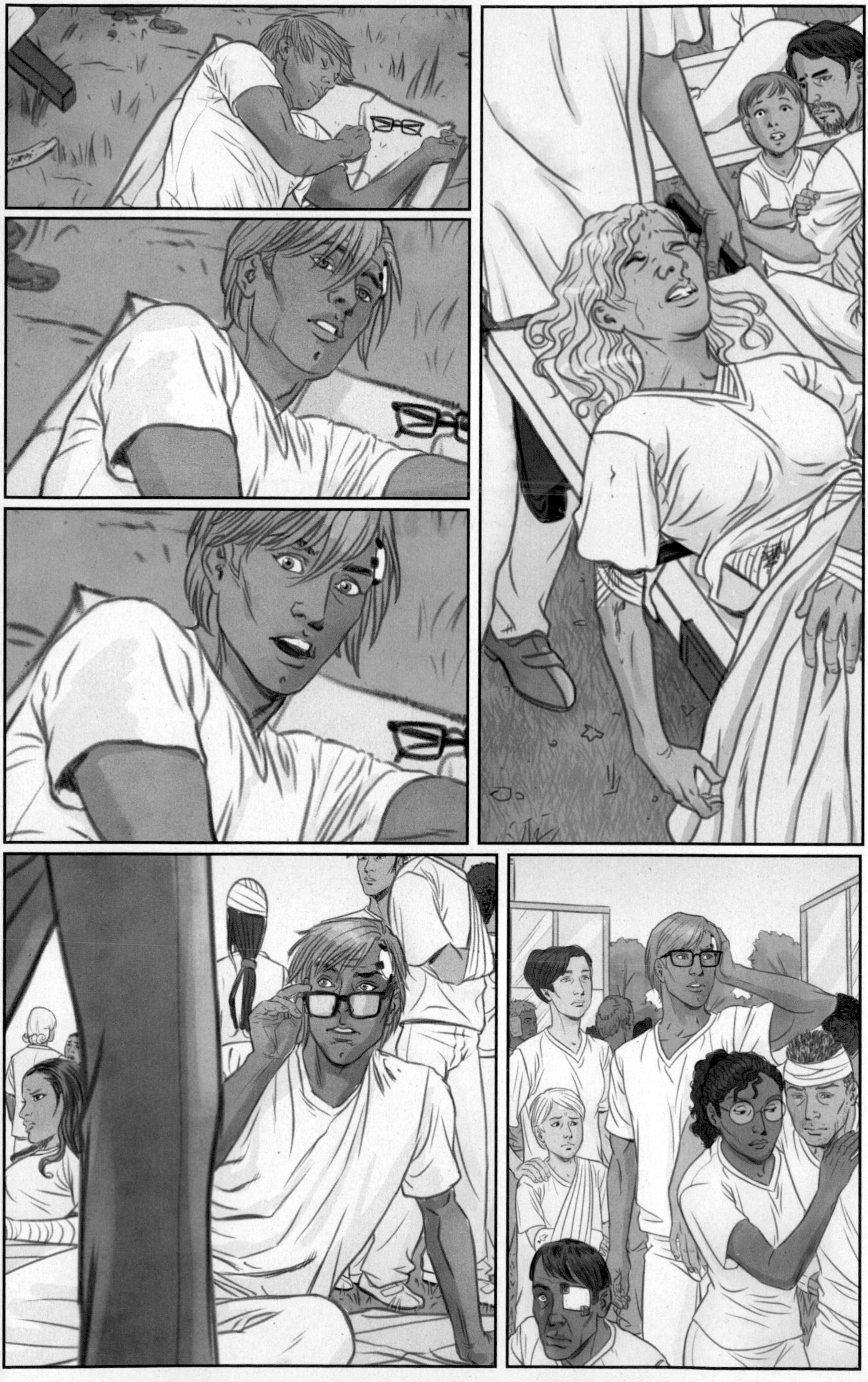

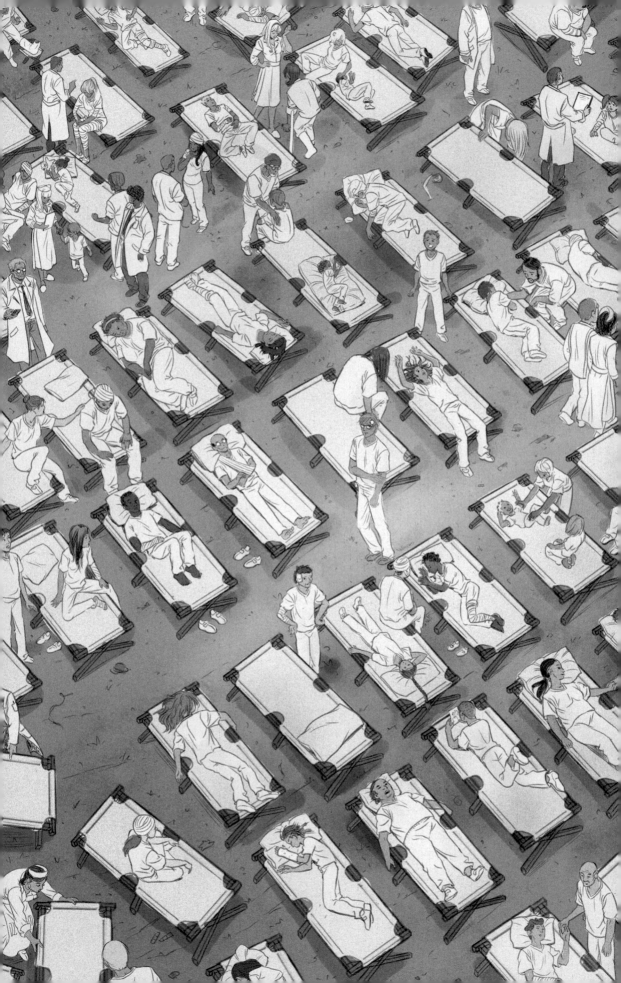

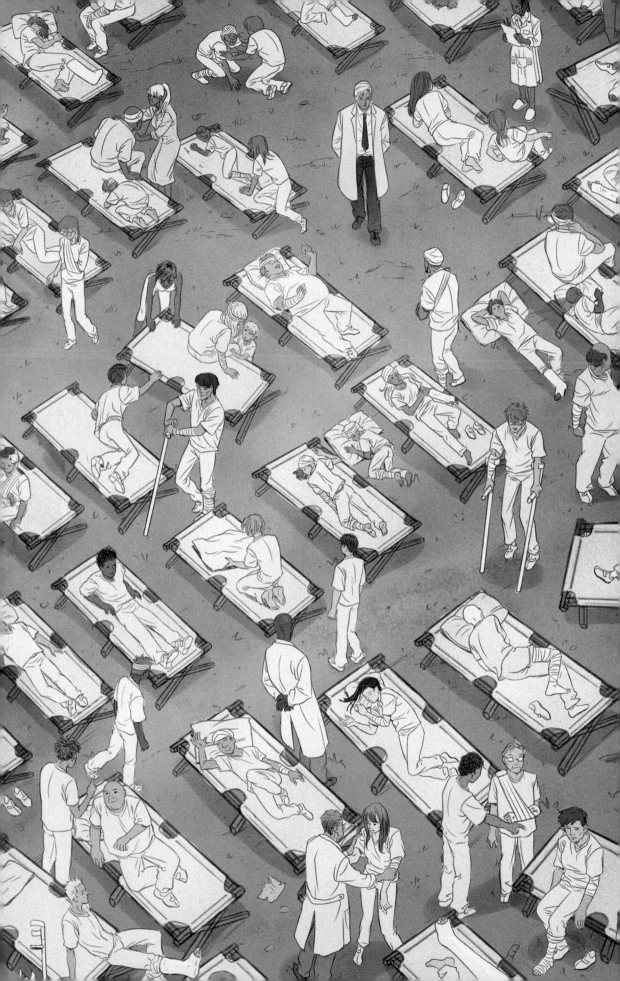

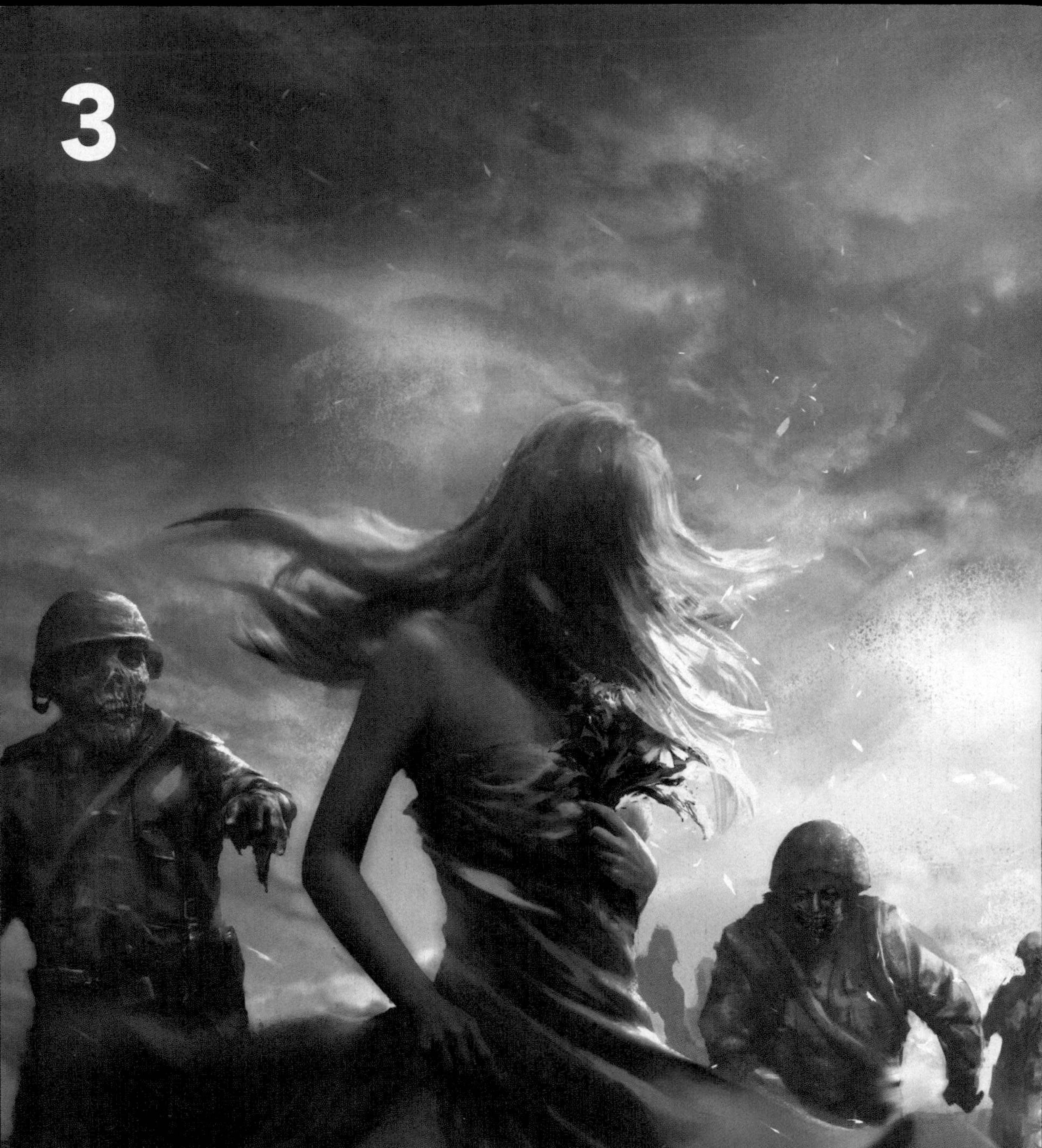
3

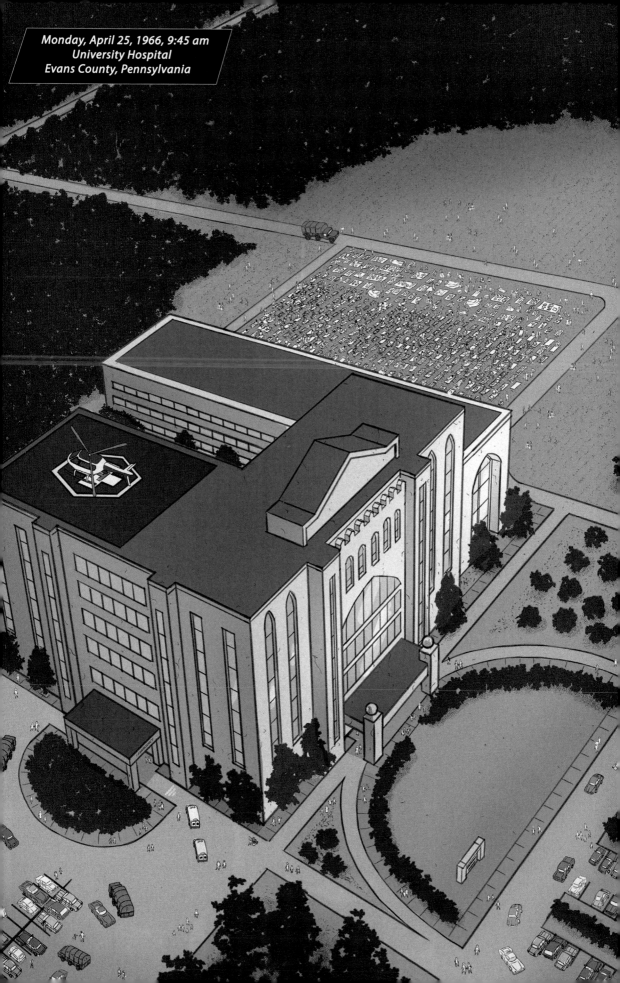

Monday, April 25, 1966, 9:45 am
University Hospital
Evans County, Pennsylvania

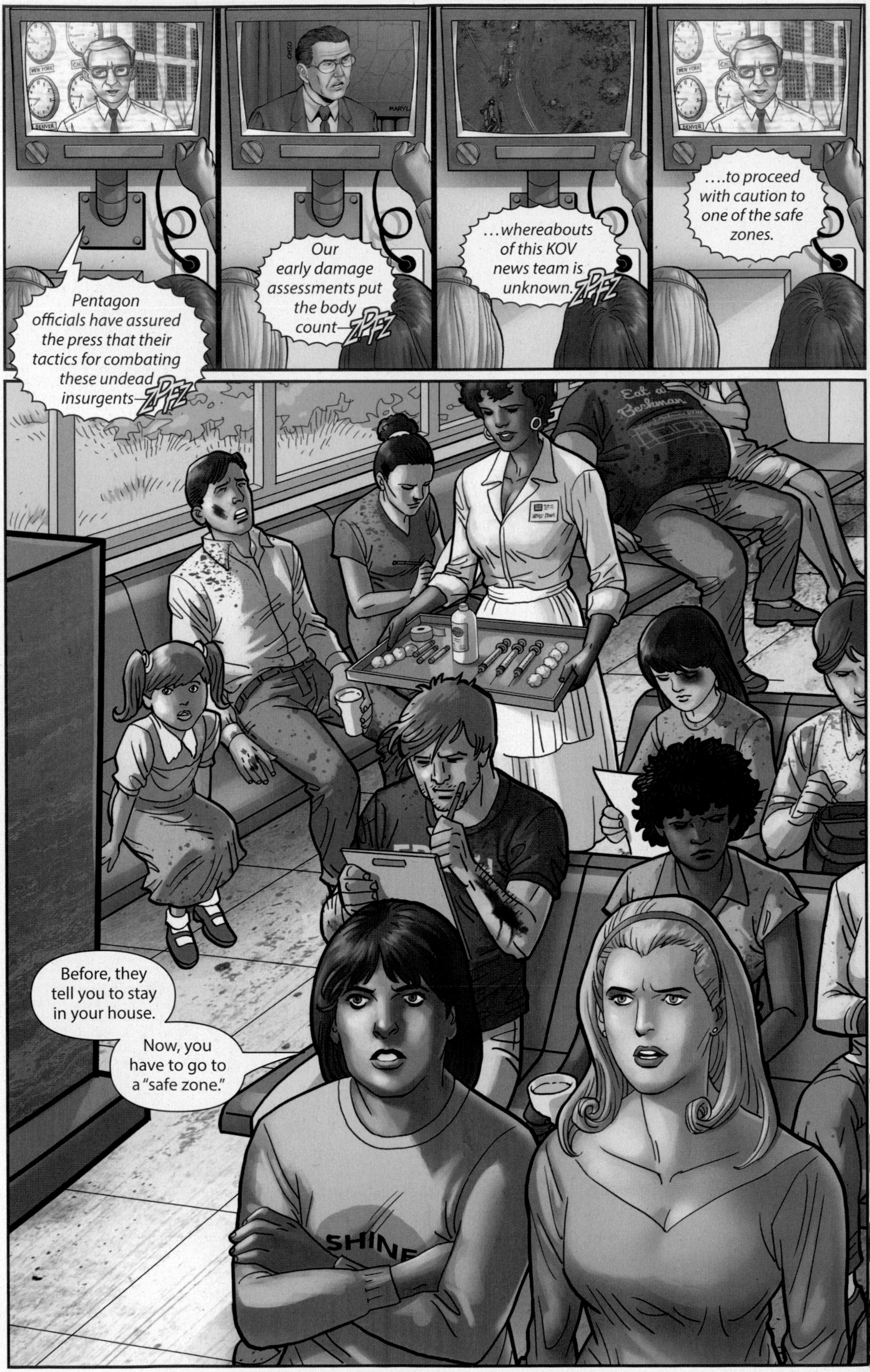
Pentagon officials have assured the press that their tactics for combating these undead insurgents—ZPFZ
Our early damage assessments put the body count—ZPFZ
...whereabouts of this KOV news team is unknown. ZPFZ
....to proceed with caution to one of the safe zones.
Before, they tell you to stay in your house.
Now, you have to go to a "safe zone."

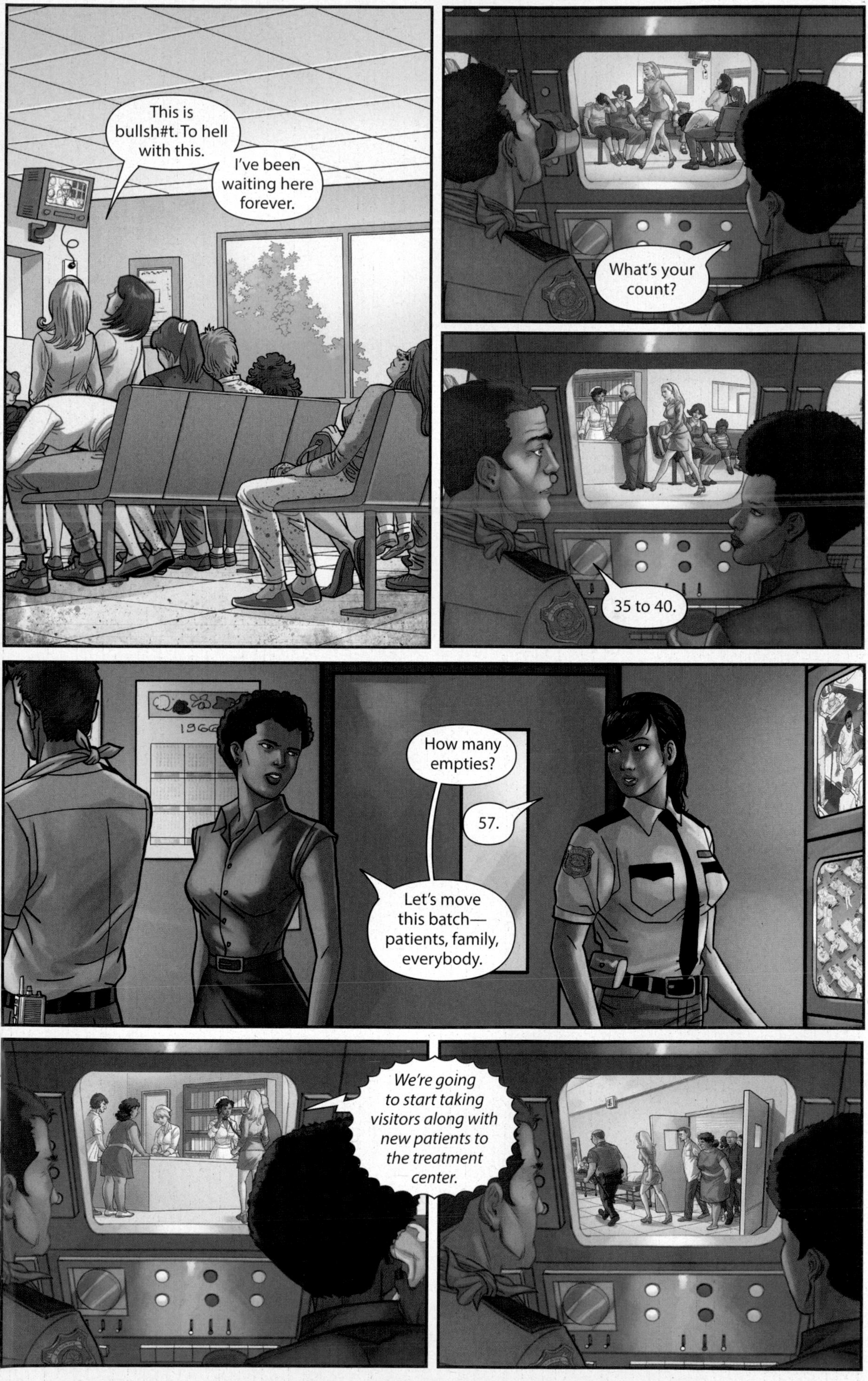
This is bullsh#t. To hell with this.
I've been waiting here forever.
What's your count?
35 to 40.
How many empties?
57.
Let's move this batch— patients, family, everybody.
We're going to start taking visitors along with new patients to the treatment center.

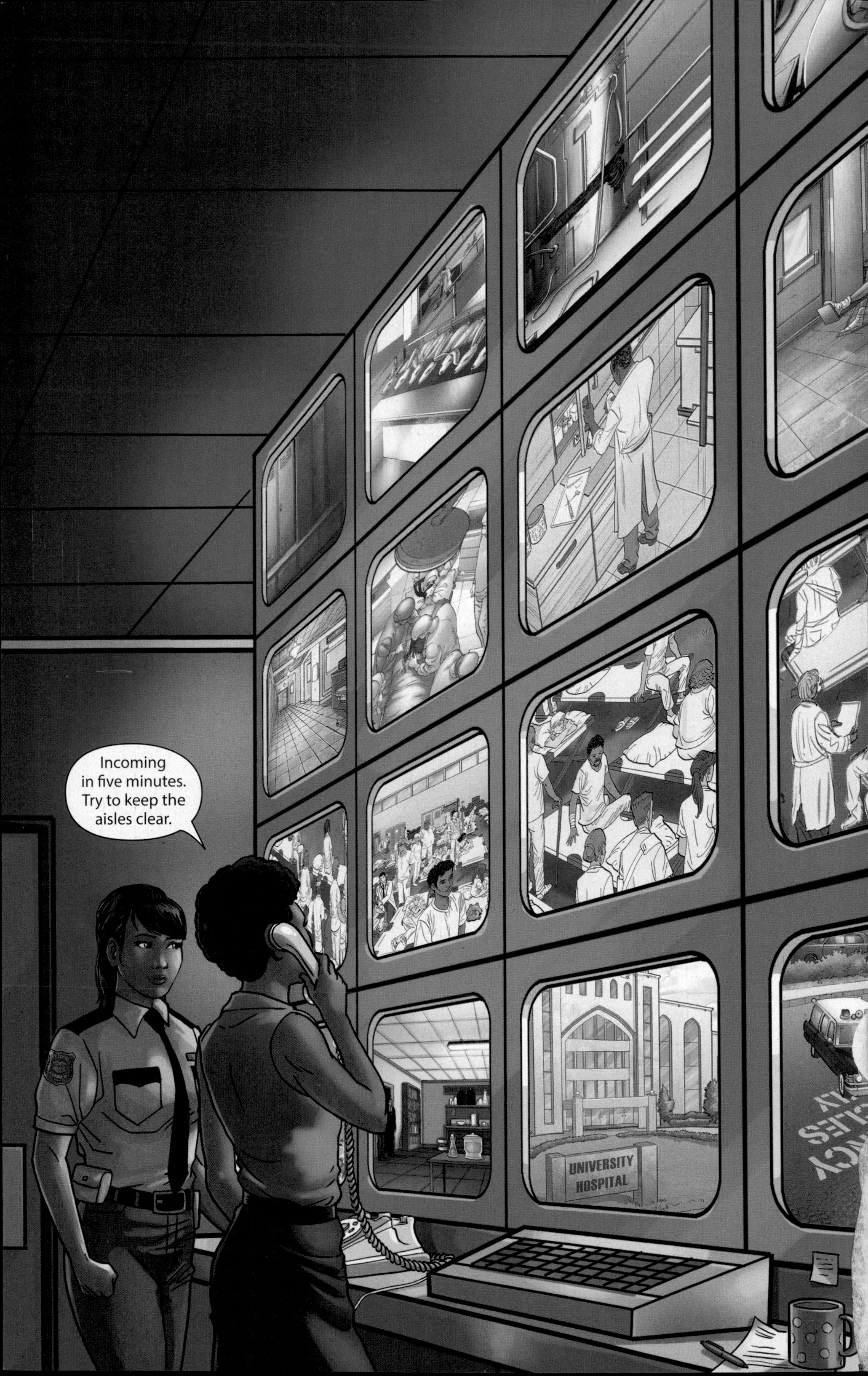
Incoming in five minutes. Try to keep the aisles clear.
UNIVERSITY HOSPITAL

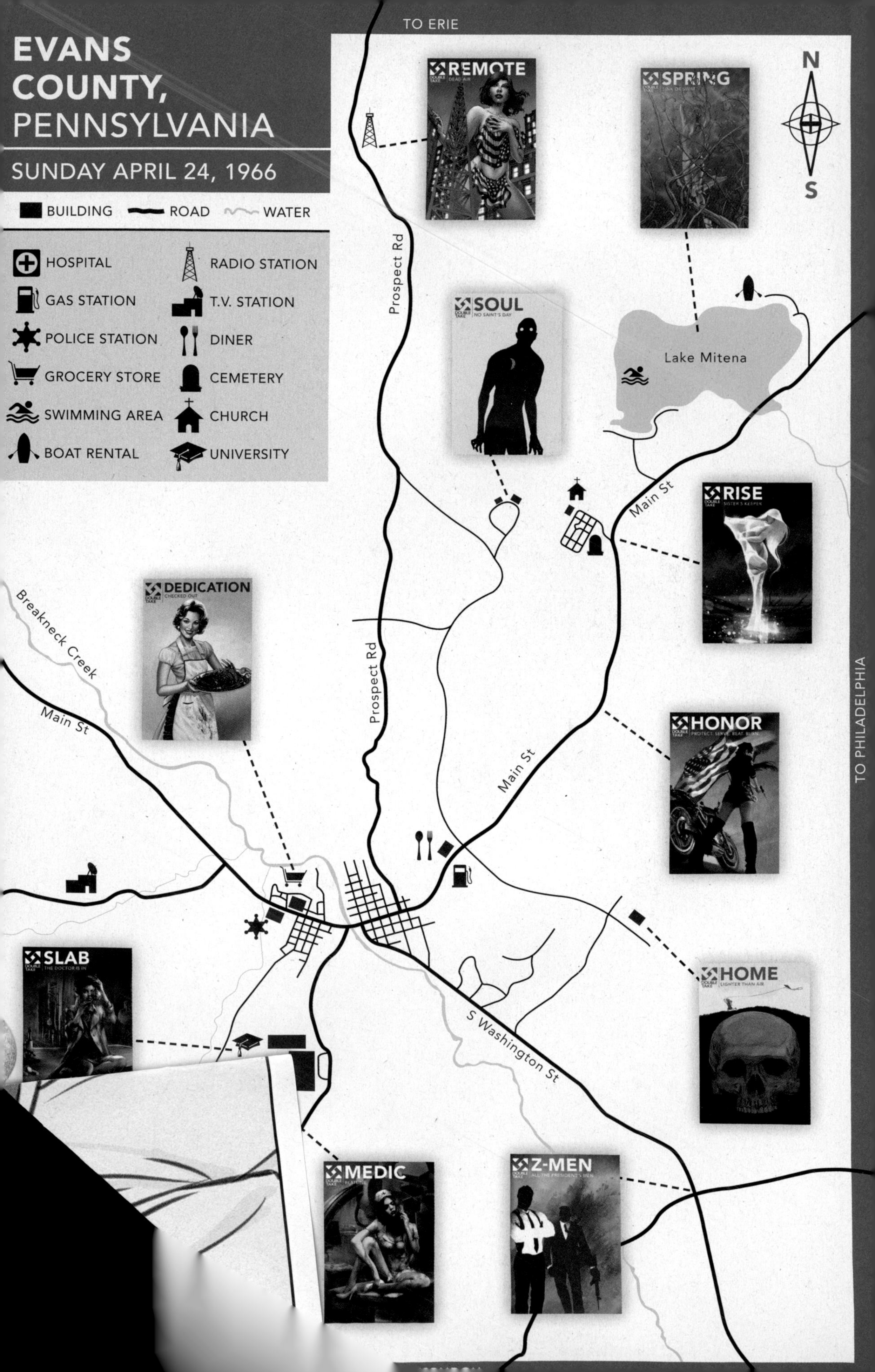

EVANS COUNTY, PENNSYLVANIA
SUNDAY APRIL 24, 1966
BUILDING
ROAD
WATER
HOSPITAL
RADIO STATION
GAS STATION
T.V. STATION
POLICE STATION
DINER
GROCERY STORE
CEMETERY
SWIMMING AREA
CHURCH
BOAT RENTAL
UNIVERSITY
TO ERIE
TO PHILADELPHIA
N
S
REMOTE
SPRING
SOUL
RISE
DEDICATION
HONOR
HOME
SLAB
MEDIC
Z-MEN
Prospect Rd
Prospect Rd
Lake Mitena
Main St
Main St
Main St
Breakneck Creek
S Washington St

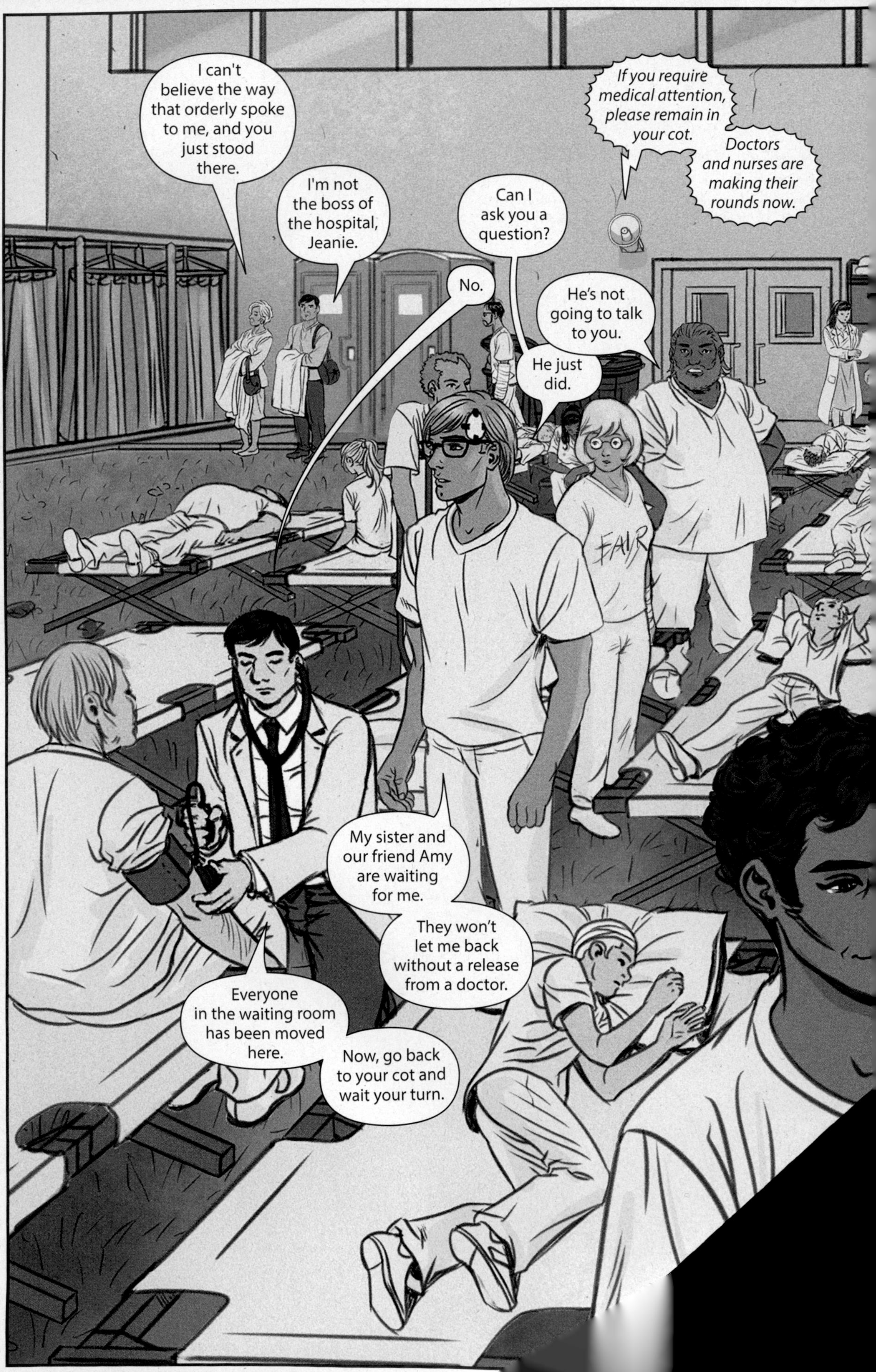
I can't believe the way that orderly spoke to me, and you just stood there.
I'm not the boss of the hospital, Jeanie.
Can I ask you a question?
No.
He's not going to talk to you.
He just did.
If you require medical attention, please remain in your cot.
Doctors and nurses are making their rounds now.
My sister and our friend Amy are waiting for me.
They won't let me back without a release from a doctor.
Everyone in the waiting room has been moved here.
Now, go back to your cot and wait your turn.

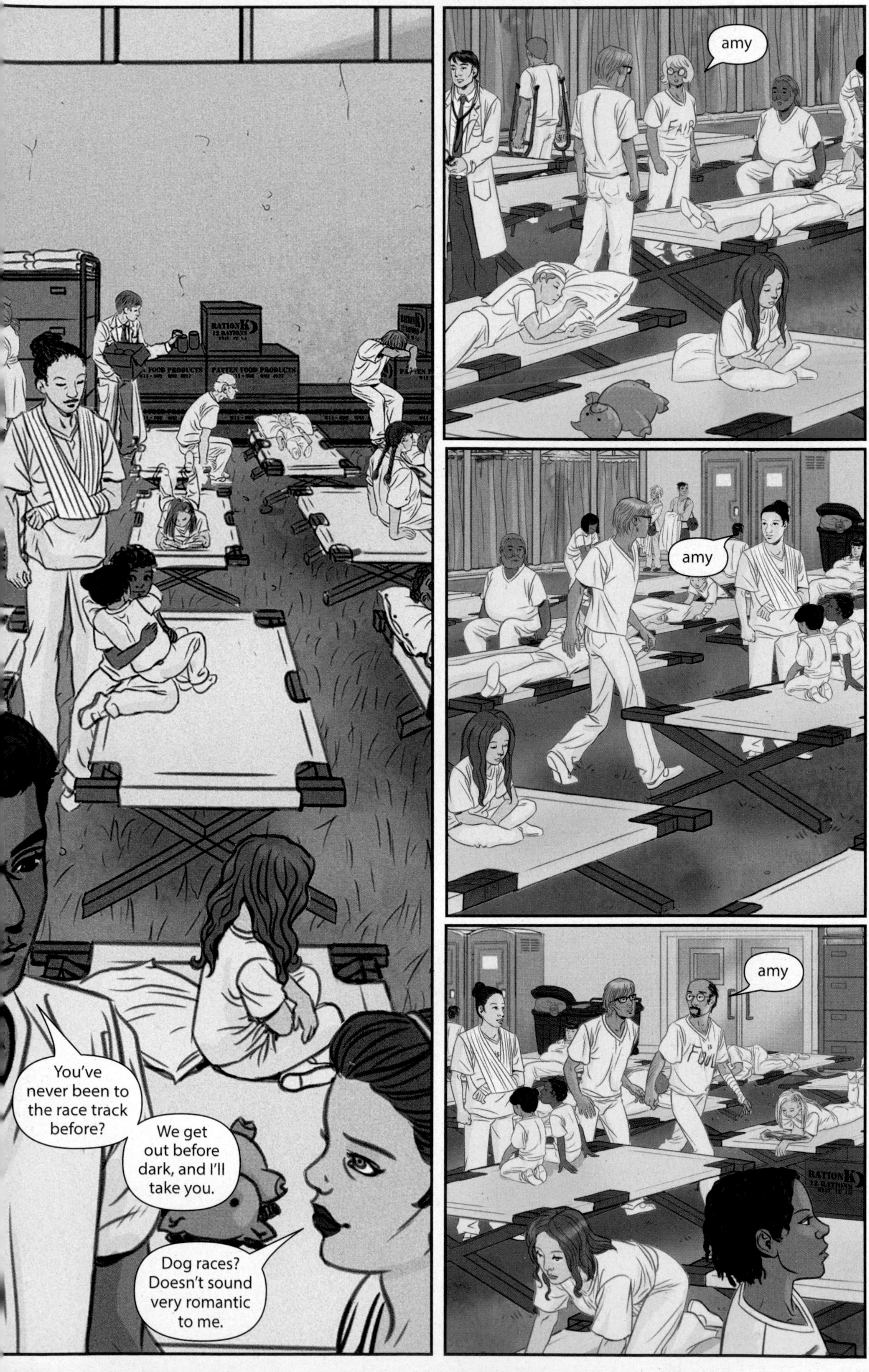
RATION K
12 RATIONS
PATTEN FOOD PRODUCTS
You've never been to the race track before?
We get out before dark, and I'll take you.
Dog races? Doesn't sound very romantic to me.
FAIR
amy
amy
amy
FOUL
RATION K
12 RATIONS

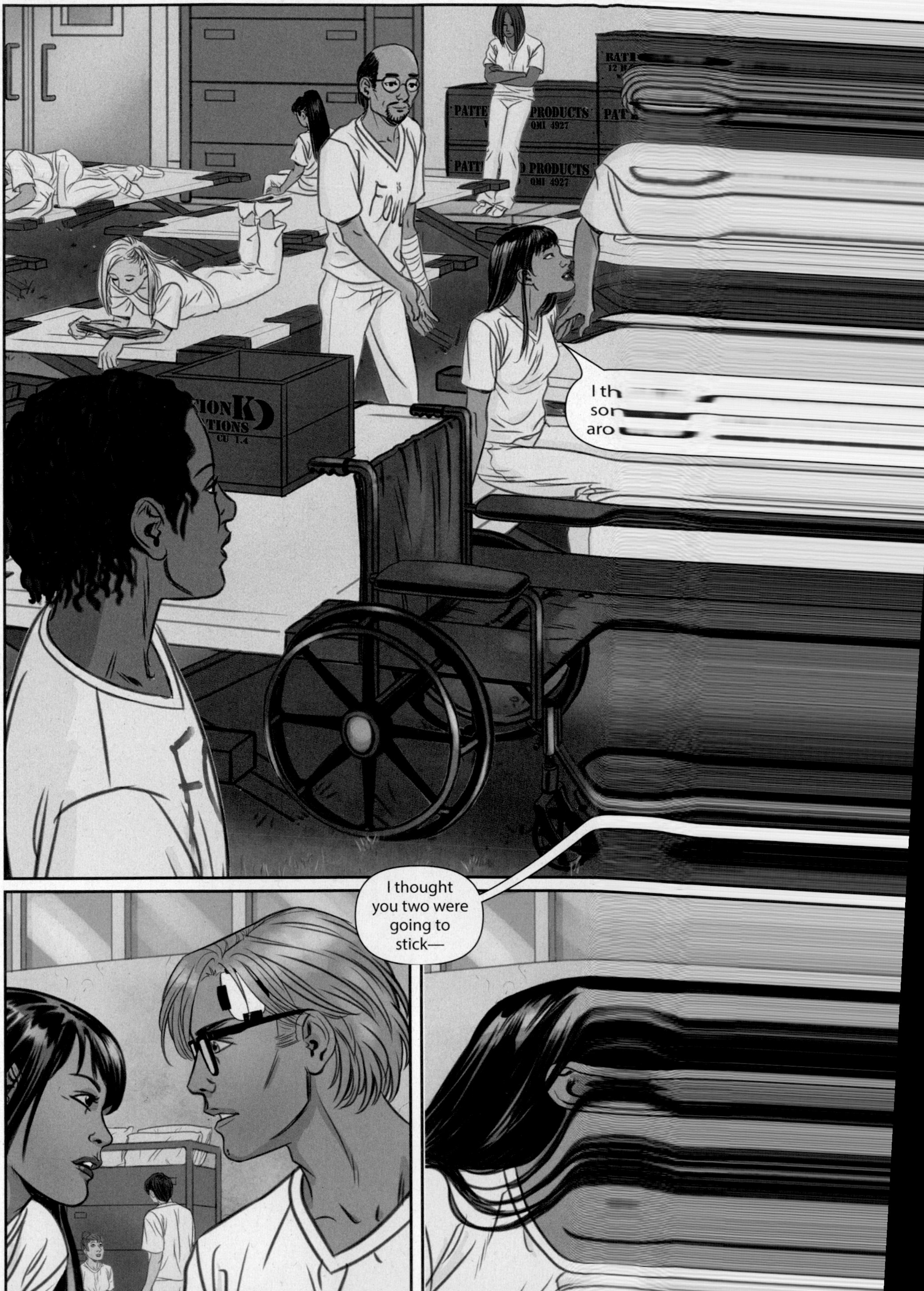
I thought you two were going to stick—

You've never been to the race track before?

We get out before dark, and I'll take you.

Dog races? Doesn't sound very romantic to me.

amy

amy

amy

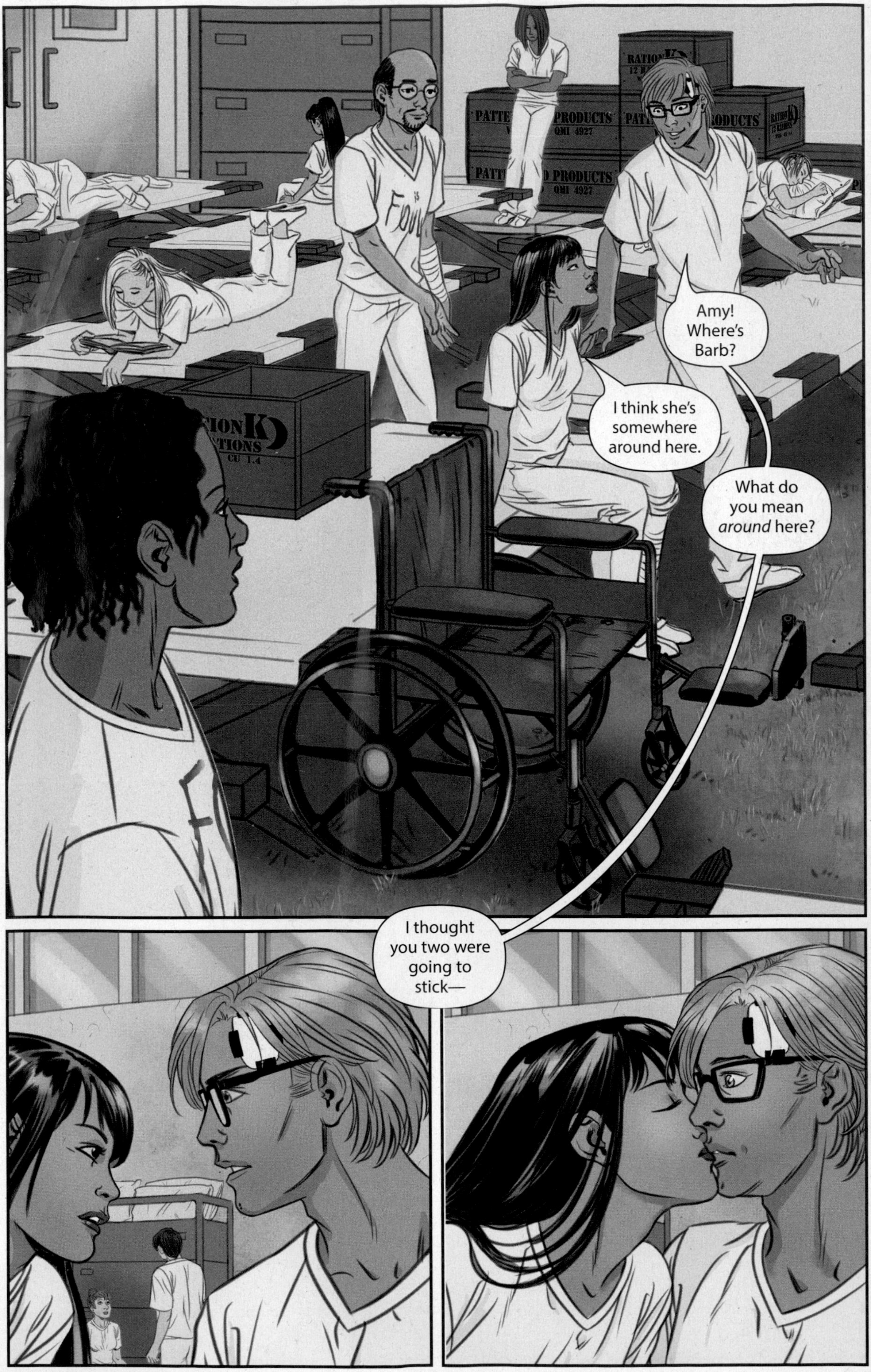
Amy! Where's Barb?
I think she's somewhere around here.
What do you mean *around* here?
I thought you two were going to stick—

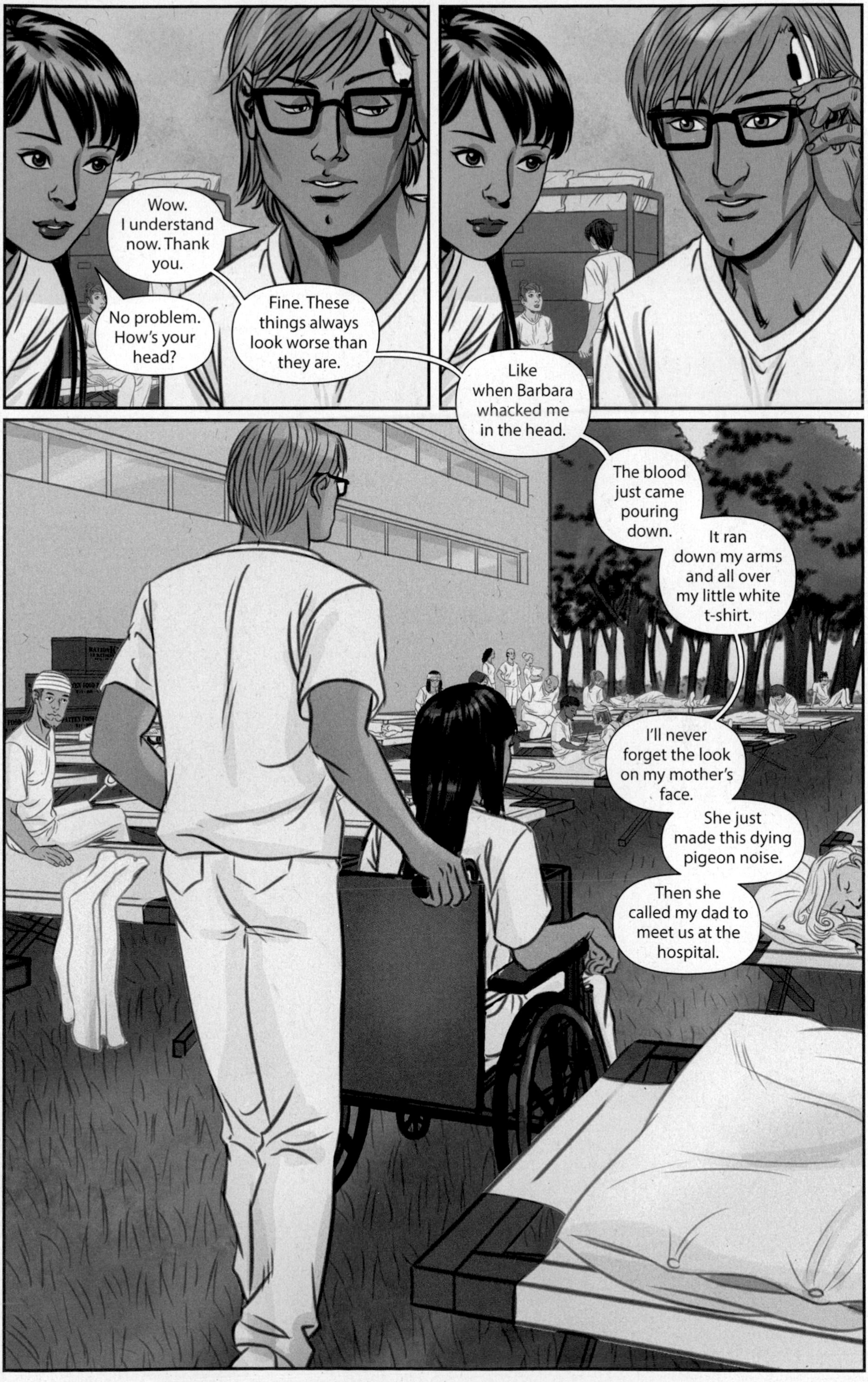
Wow. I understand now. Thank you.
No problem. How's your head?
Fine. These things always look worse than they are.
Like when Barbara whacked me in the head.
The blood just came pouring down.
It ran down my arms and all over my little white t-shirt.
I'll never forget the look on my mother's face.
She just made this dying pigeon noise.
Then she called my dad to meet us at the hospital.

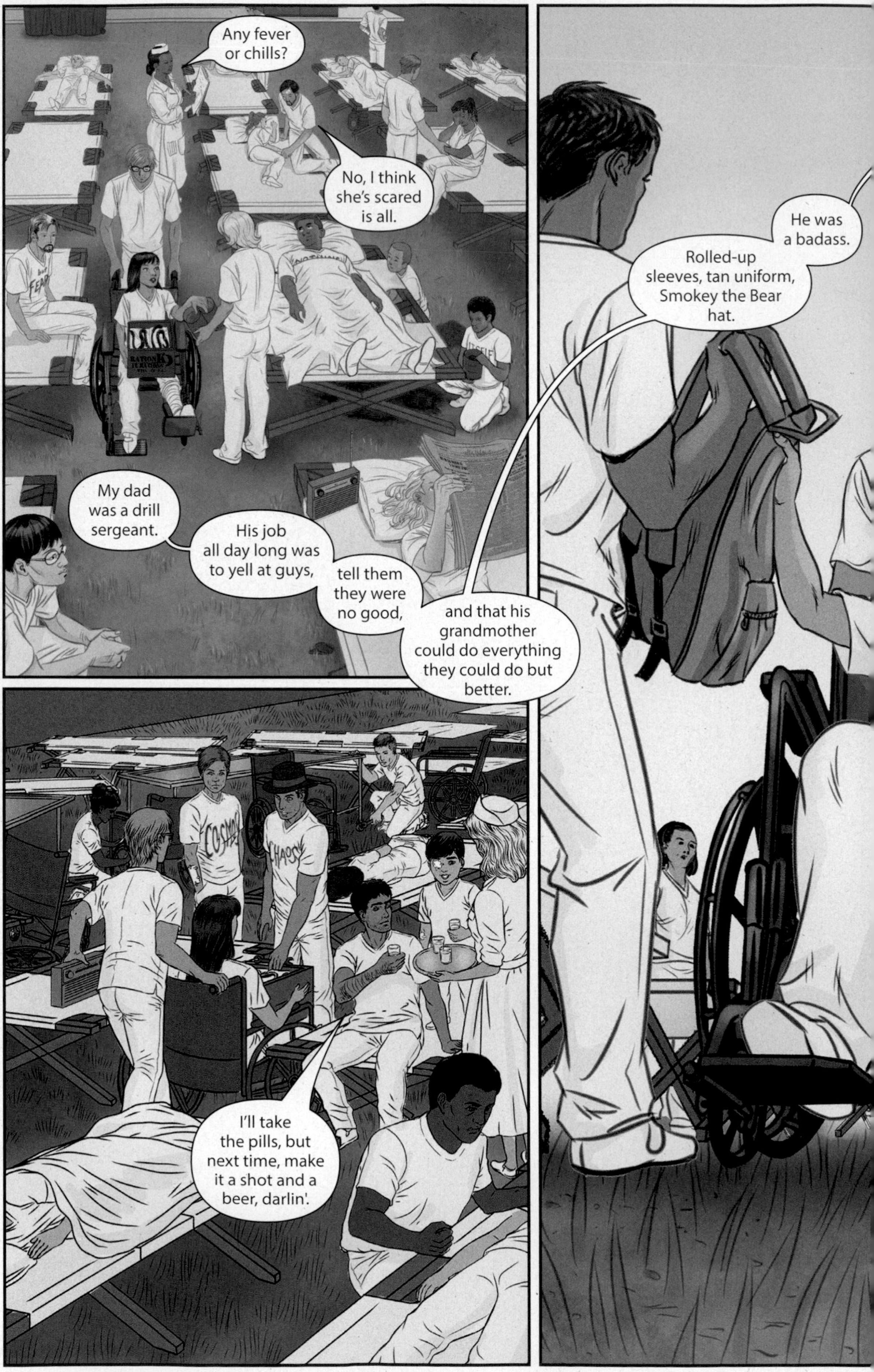
Any fever or chills?
No, I think she's scared is all.
My dad was a drill sergeant.
His job all day long was to yell at guys,
tell them they were no good,
and that his grandmother could do everything they could do but better.
He was a badass.
Rolled-up sleeves, tan uniform, Smokey the Bear hat.
I'll take the pills, but next time, make it a shot and a beer, darlin'.

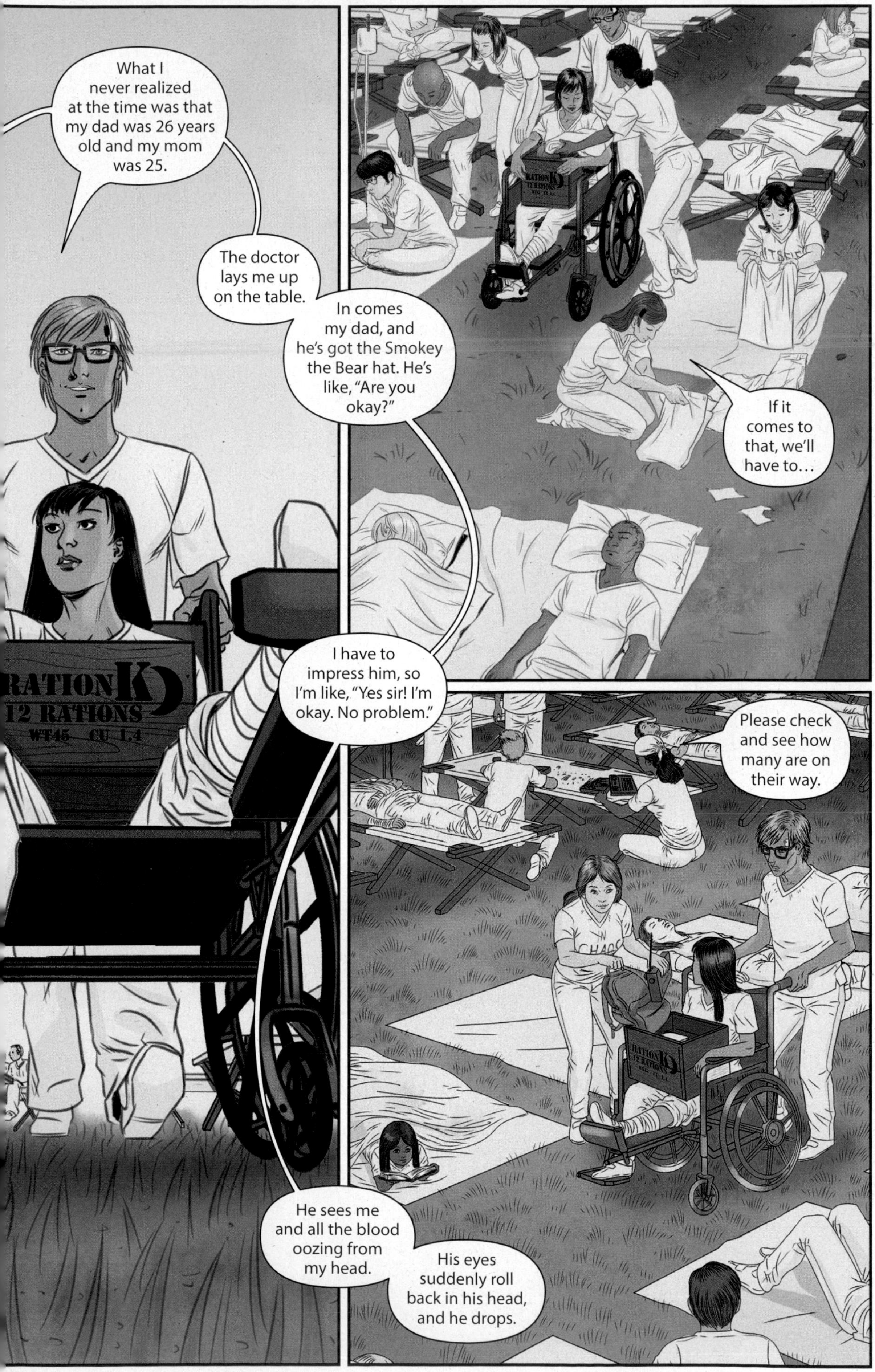
What I never realized at the time was that my dad was 26 years old and my mom was 25.
The doctor lays me up on the table.
In comes my dad, and he's got the Smokey the Bear hat. He's like, "Are you okay?"
I have to impress him, so I'm like, "Yes sir! I'm okay. No problem."
He sees me and all the blood oozing from my head.
His eyes suddenly roll back in his head, and he drops.
RATION K
12 RATIONS
WT45 CU 1.4
If it comes to that, we'll have to…
Please check and see how many are on their way.

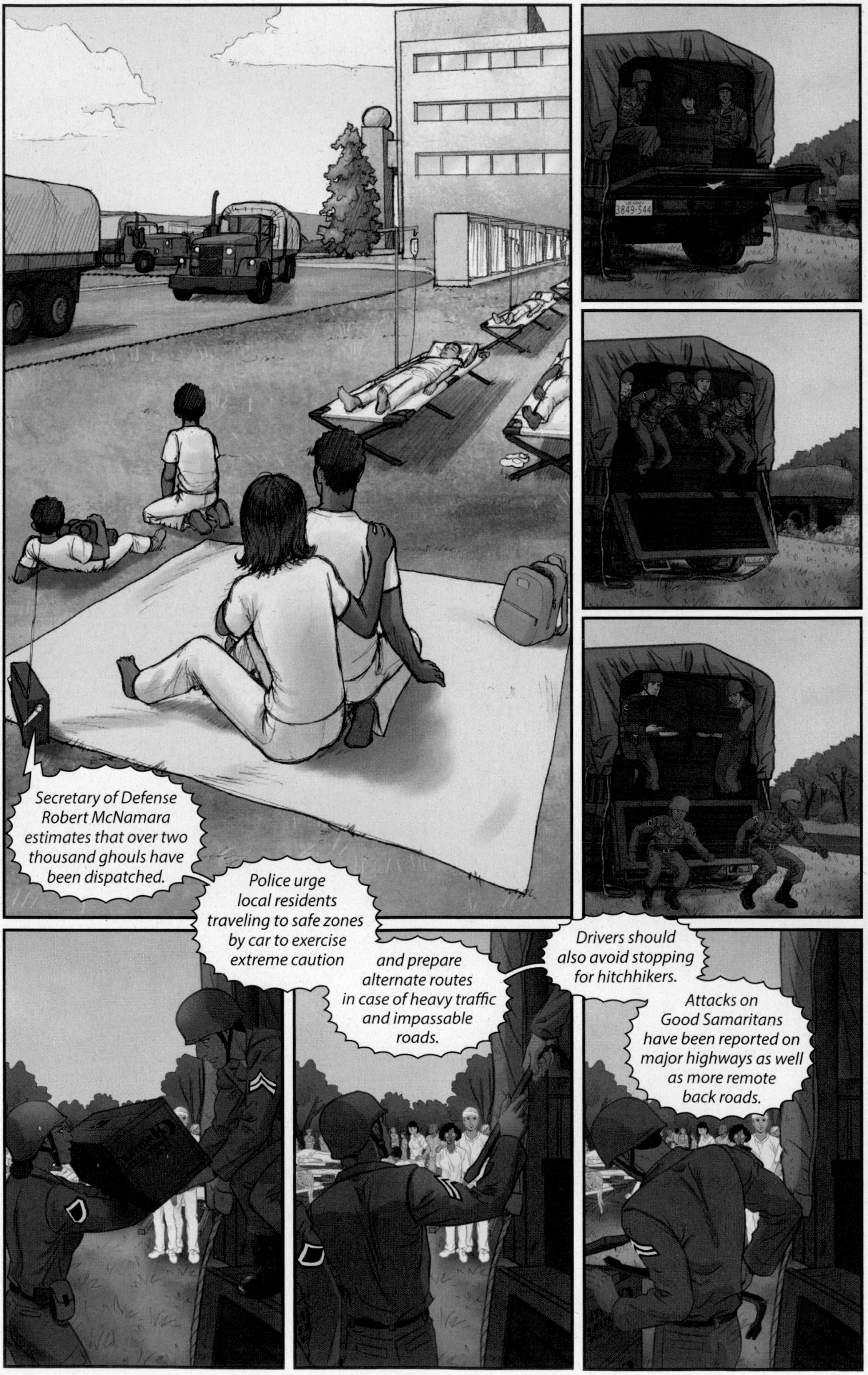

US ARMY
3849-544
Secretary of Defense Robert McNamara estimates that over two thousand ghouls have been dispatched.
Police urge local residents traveling to safe zones by car to exercise extreme caution
and prepare alternate routes in case of heavy traffic and impassable roads.
Drivers should also avoid stopping for hitchhikers.
Attacks on Good Samaritans have been reported on major highways as well as more remote back roads.

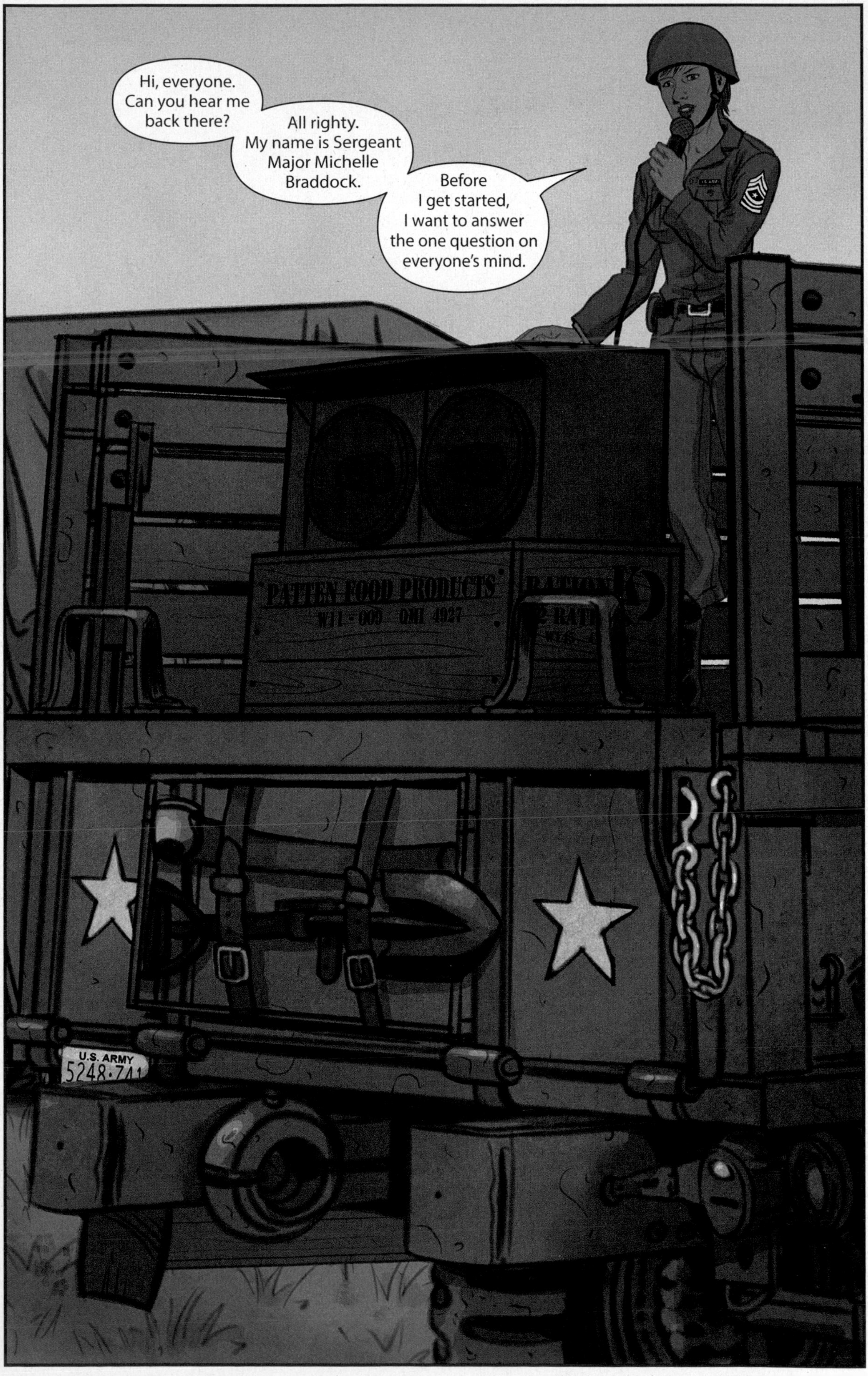
Hi, everyone. Can you hear me back there?
All righty. My name is Sergeant Major Michelle Braddock.
Before I get started, I want to answer the one question on everyone's mind.
PATTEN FOOD PRODUCTS
U.S. ARMY
5248·741

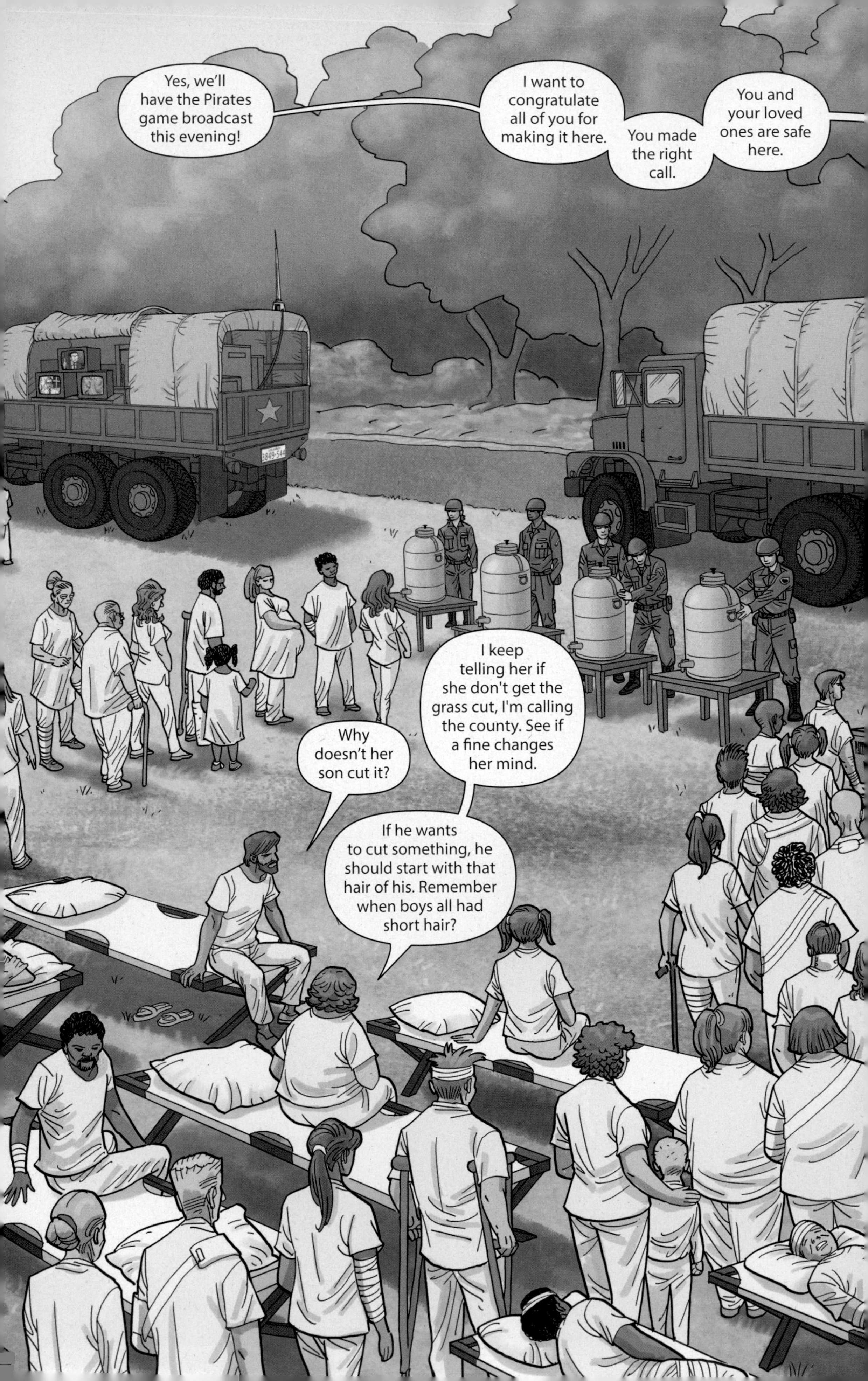

Yes, we'll have the Pirates game broadcast this evening!
I want to congratulate all of you for making it here.
You made the right call.
You and your loved ones are safe here.
Why doesn't her son cut it?
I keep telling her if she don't get the grass cut, I'm calling the county. See if a fine changes her mind.
If he wants to cut something, he should start with that hair of his. Remember when boys all had short hair?

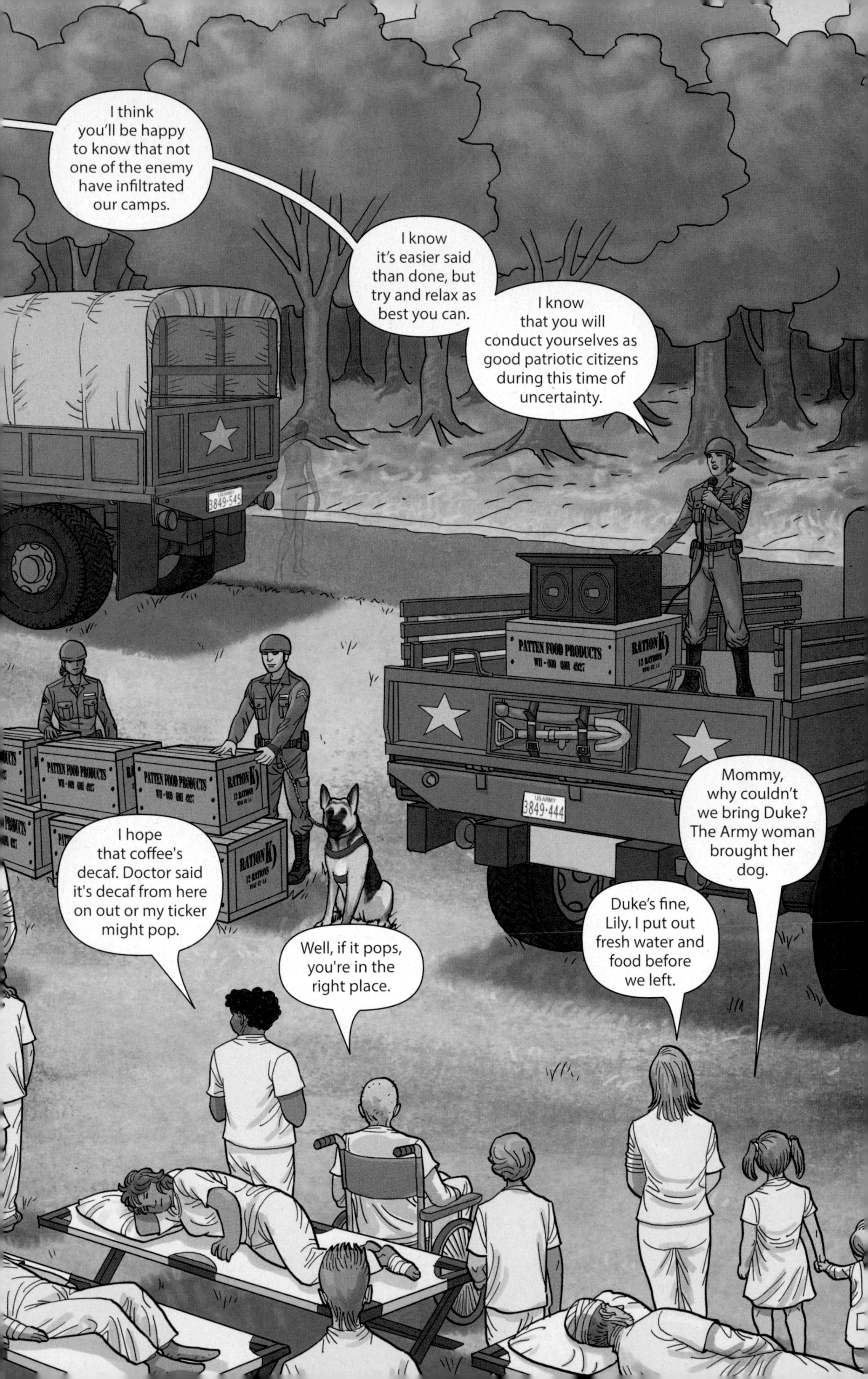
I think you'll be happy to know that not one of the enemy have infiltrated our camps.
I know it's easier said than done, but try and relax as best you can.
I know that you will conduct yourselves as good patriotic citizens during this time of uncertainty.
US ARMY 3849·545
PATTEN FOOD PRODUCTS WII · 009 QMI 4927
RATION K 12 RATIONS
US ARMY 3849·444
Mommy, why couldn't we bring Duke? The Army woman brought her dog.
I hope that coffee's decaf. Doctor said it's decaf from here on out or my ticker might pop.
Well, if it pops, you're in the right place.
Duke's fine, Lily. I put out fresh water and food before we left.

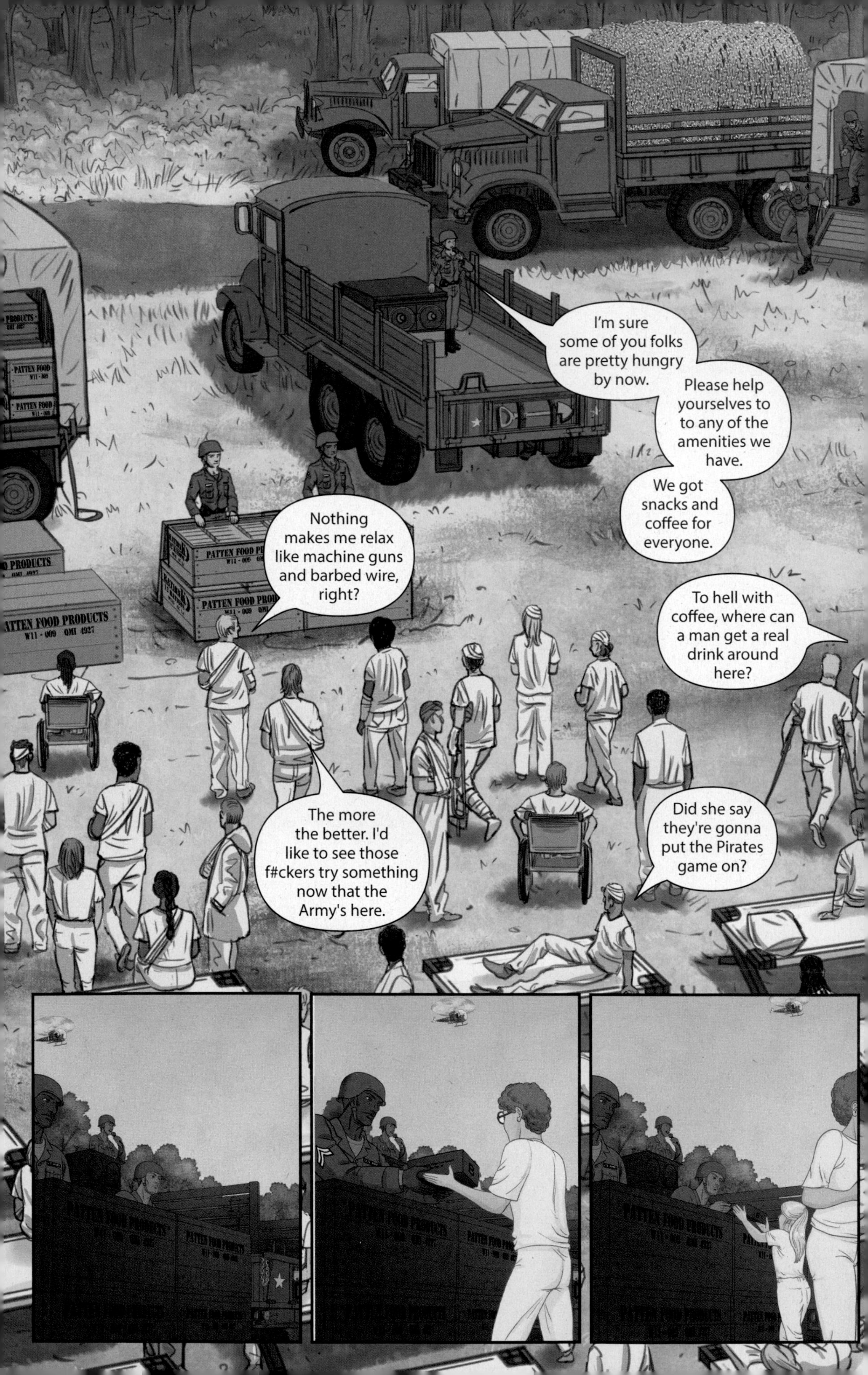
I'm sure some of you folks are pretty hungry by now.
Please help yourselves to to any of the amenities we have.
We got snacks and coffee for everyone.
Nothing makes me relax like machine guns and barbed wire, right?
To hell with coffee, where can a man get a real drink around here?
The more the better. I'd like to see those f#ckers try something now that the Army's here.
Did she say they're gonna put the Pirates game on?
PATTEN FOOD PRODUCTS
W11 - 009 QMI 4927

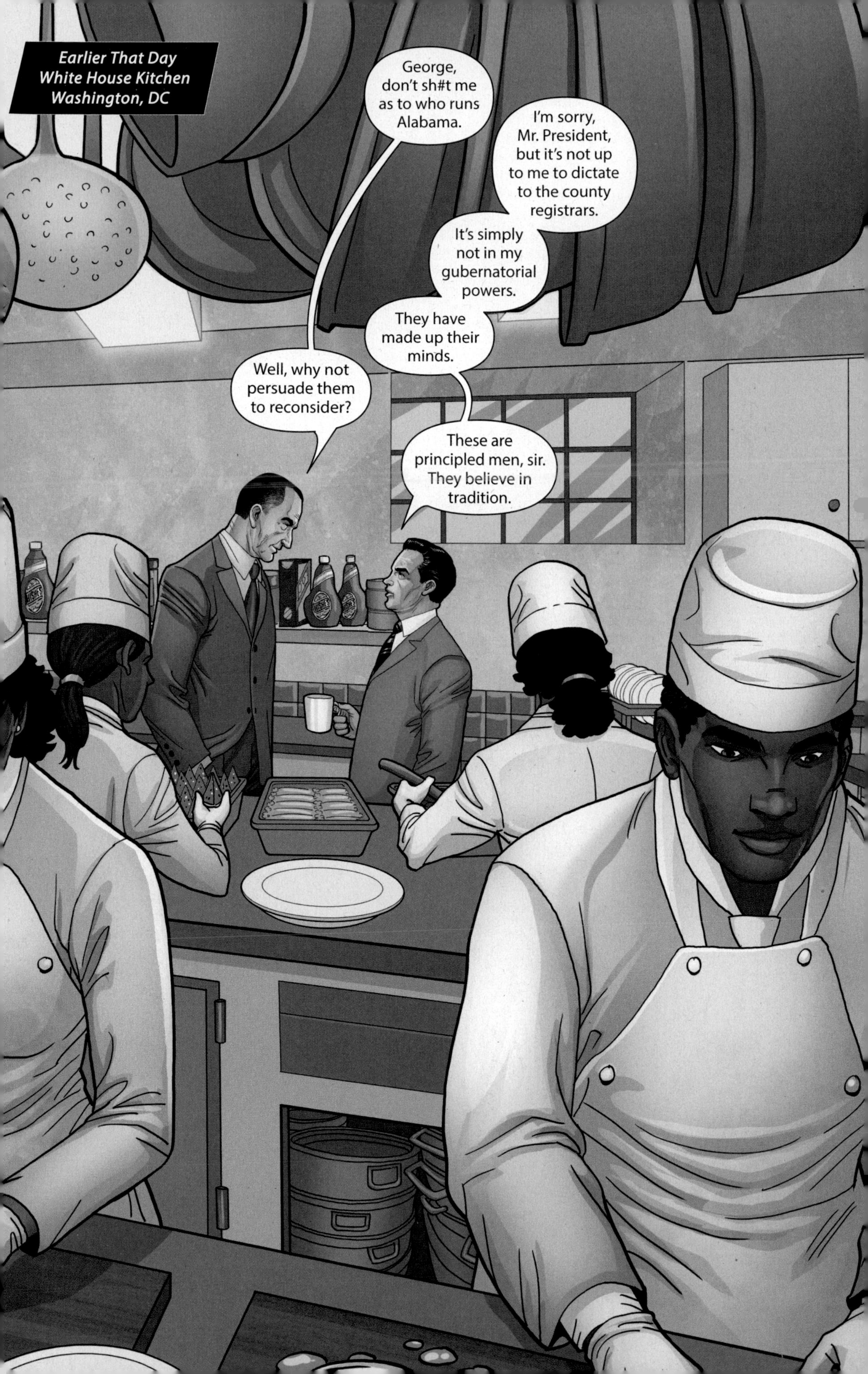
Earlier That Day
White House Kitchen
Washington, DC
George, don't sh#t me as to who runs Alabama.
I'm sorry, Mr. President, but it's not up to me to dictate to the county registrars.
It's simply not in my gubernatorial powers.
They have made up their minds.
Well, why not persuade them to reconsider?
These are principled men, sir. They believe in tradition.

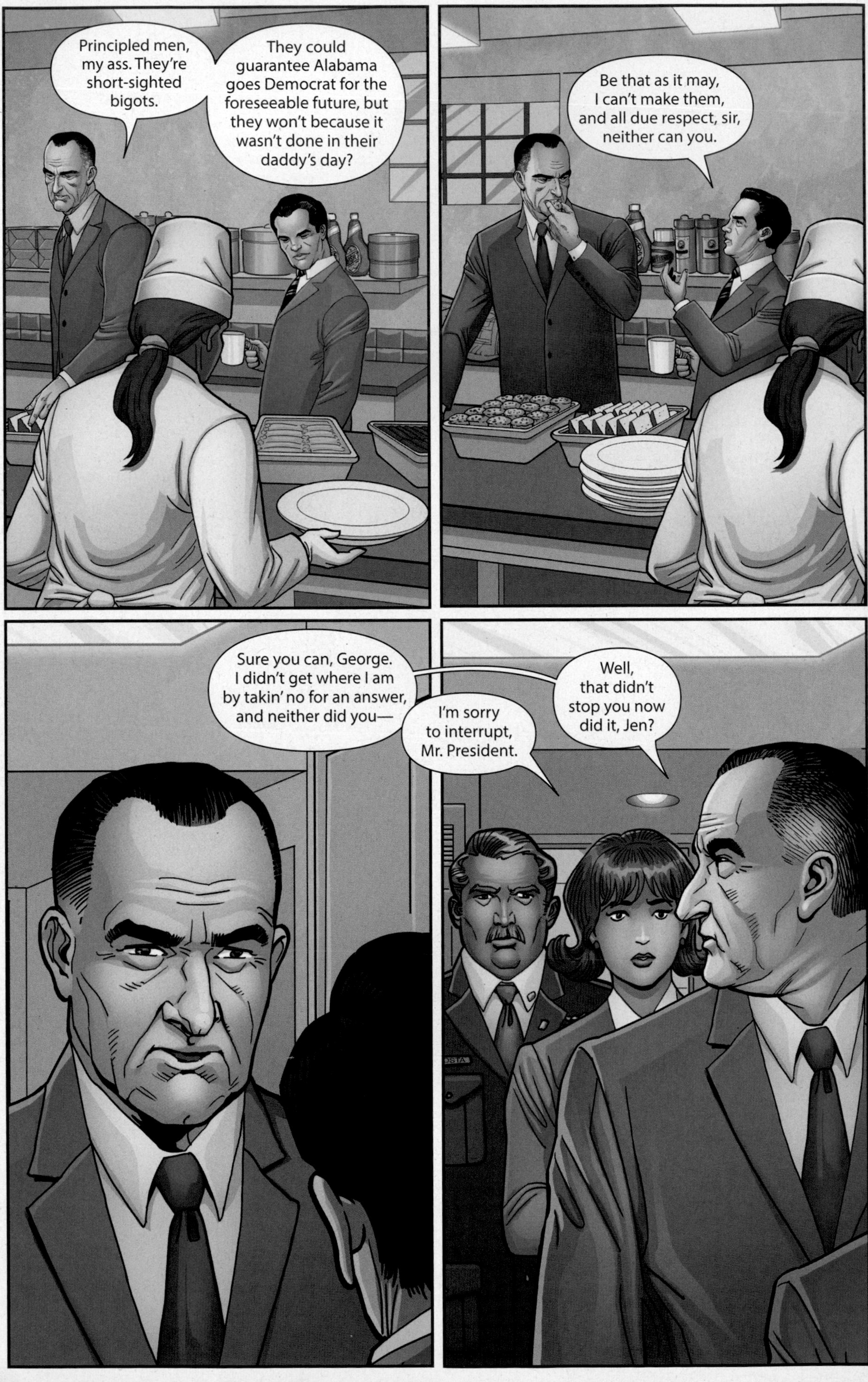
Principled men, my ass. They're short-sighted bigots.
They could guarantee Alabama goes Democrat for the foreseeable future, but they won't because it wasn't done in their daddy's day?
Be that as it may, I can't make them, and all due respect, sir, neither can you.
Sure you can, George. I didn't get where I am by takin' no for an answer, and neither did you—
I'm sorry to interrupt, Mr. President.
Well, that didn't stop you now did it, Jen?

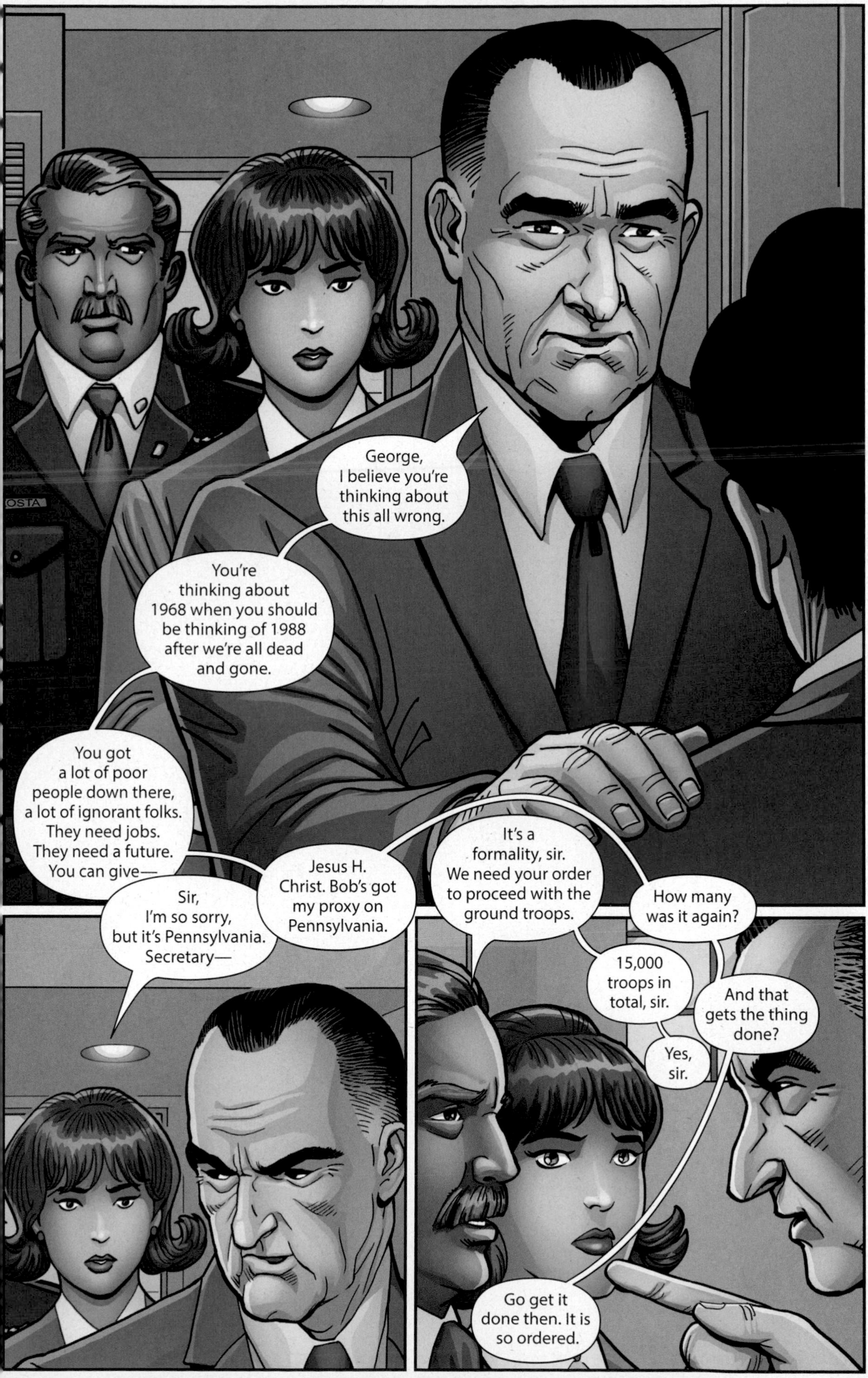
OSTA
George, I believe you're thinking about this all wrong.
You're thinking about 1968 when you should be thinking of 1988 after we're all dead and gone.
You got a lot of poor people down there, a lot of ignorant folks. They need jobs. They need a future. You can give—
Sir, I'm so sorry, but it's Pennsylvania. Secretary—
Jesus H. Christ. Bob's got my proxy on Pennsylvania.
It's a formality, sir. We need your order to proceed with the ground troops.
How many was it again?
15,000 troops in total, sir.
And that gets the thing done?
Yes, sir.
Go get it done then. It is so ordered.

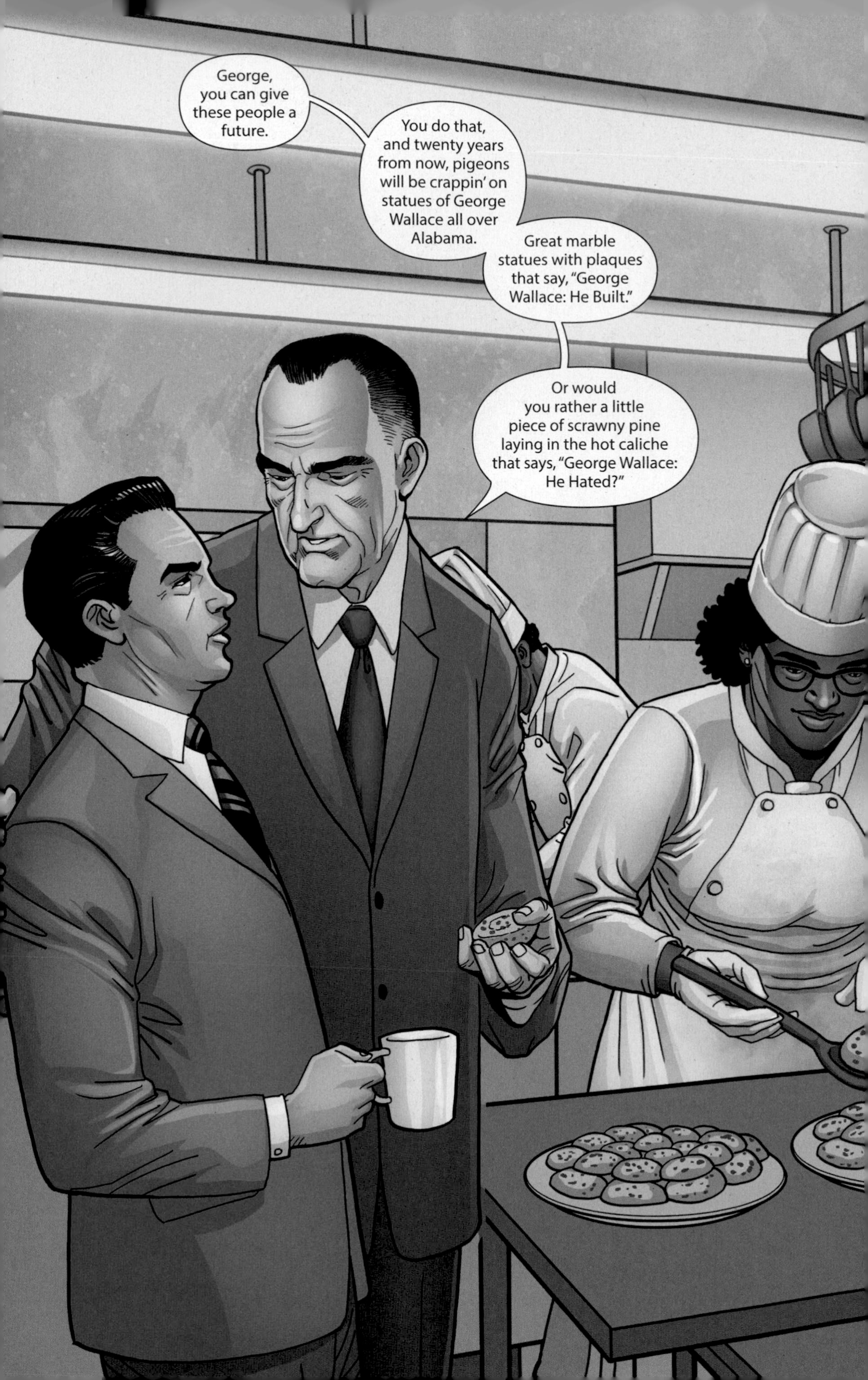
George, you can give these people a future.
You do that, and twenty years from now, pigeons will be crappin' on statues of George Wallace all over Alabama.
Great marble statues with plaques that say, "George Wallace: He Built."
Or would you rather a little piece of scrawny pine laying in the hot caliche that says, "George Wallace: He Hated?"

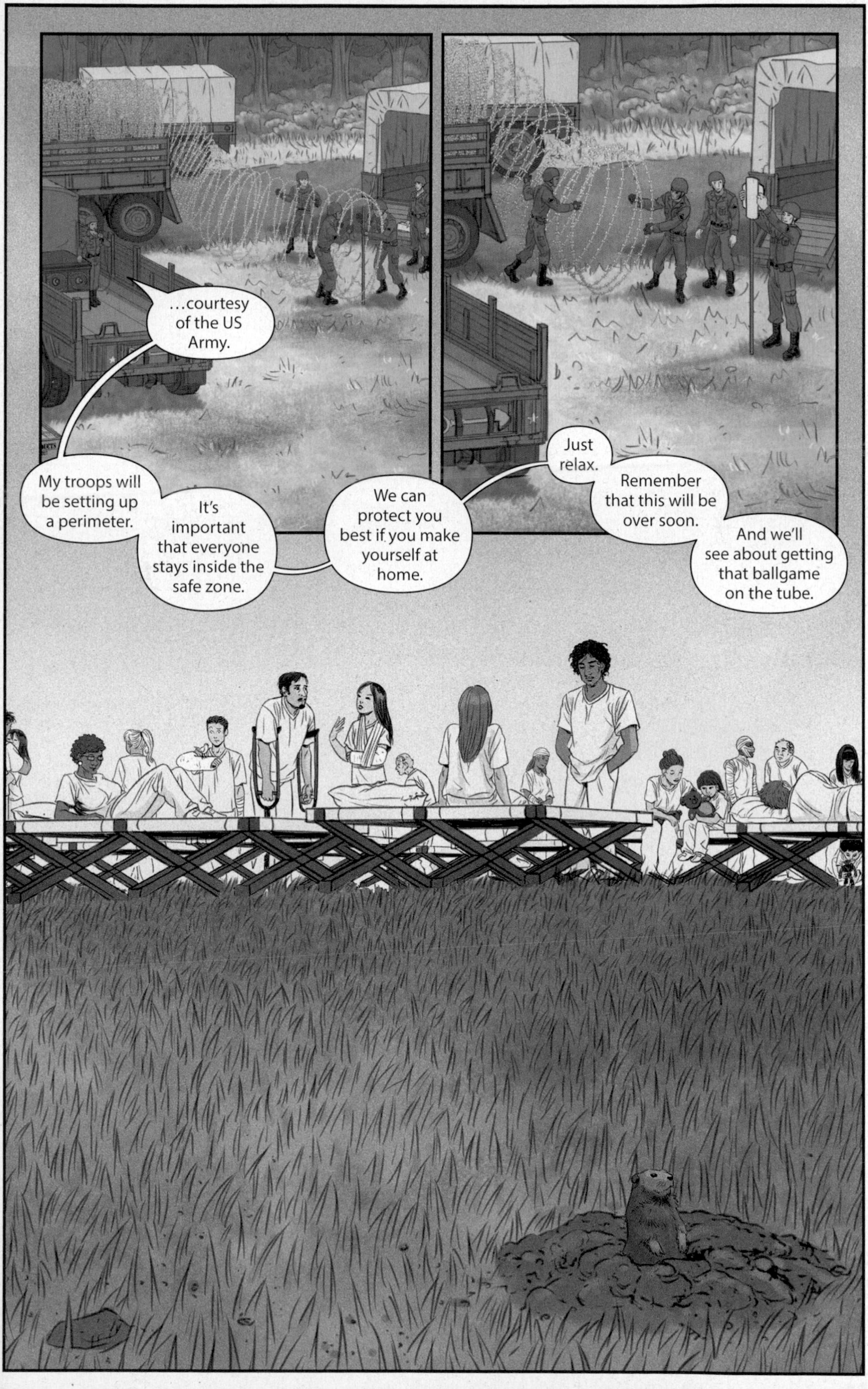
...courtesy of the US Army.
My troops will be setting up a perimeter.
It's important that everyone stays inside the safe zone.
We can protect you best if you make yourself at home.
Just relax.
Remember that this will be over soon.
And we'll see about getting that ballgame on the tube.

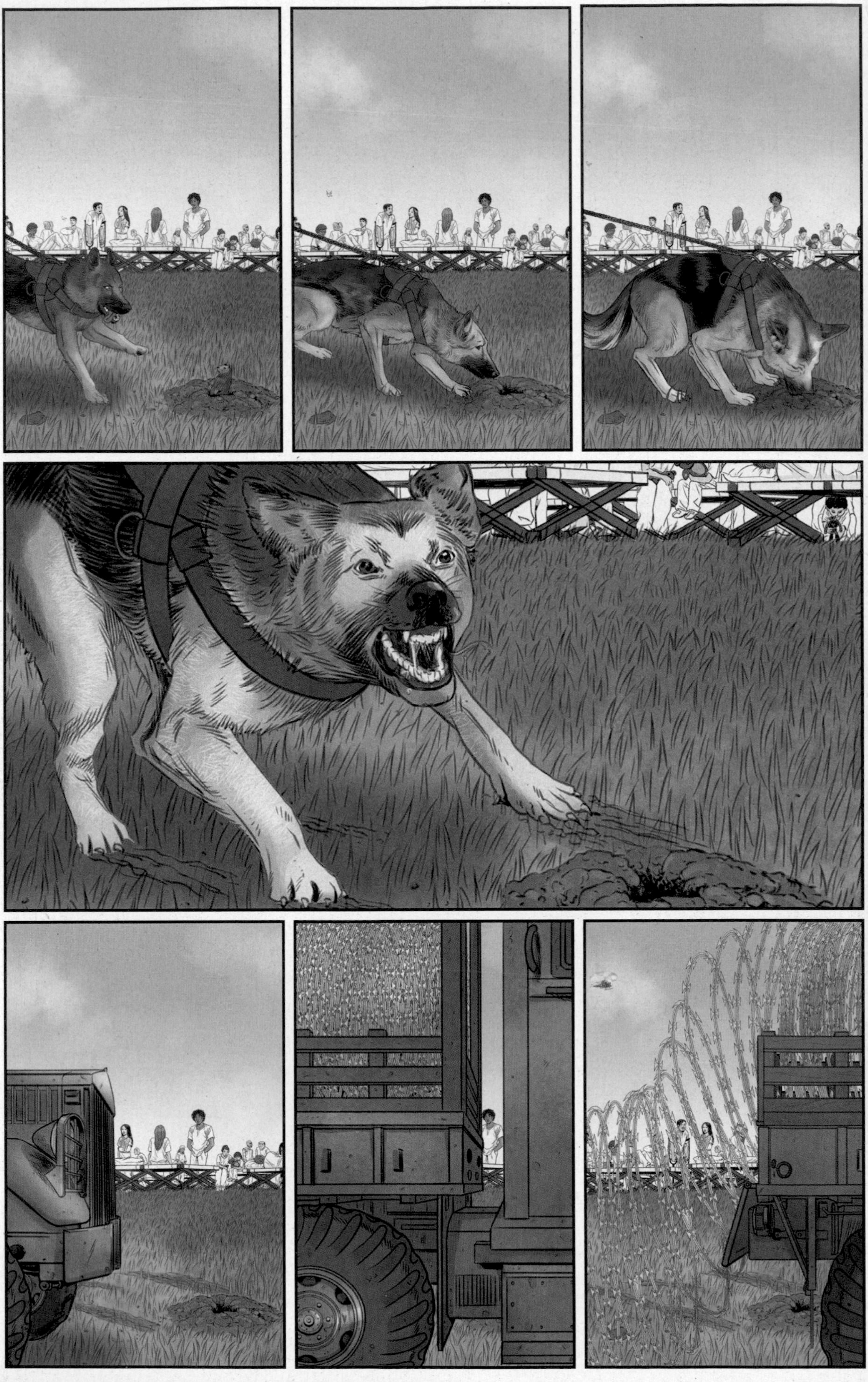

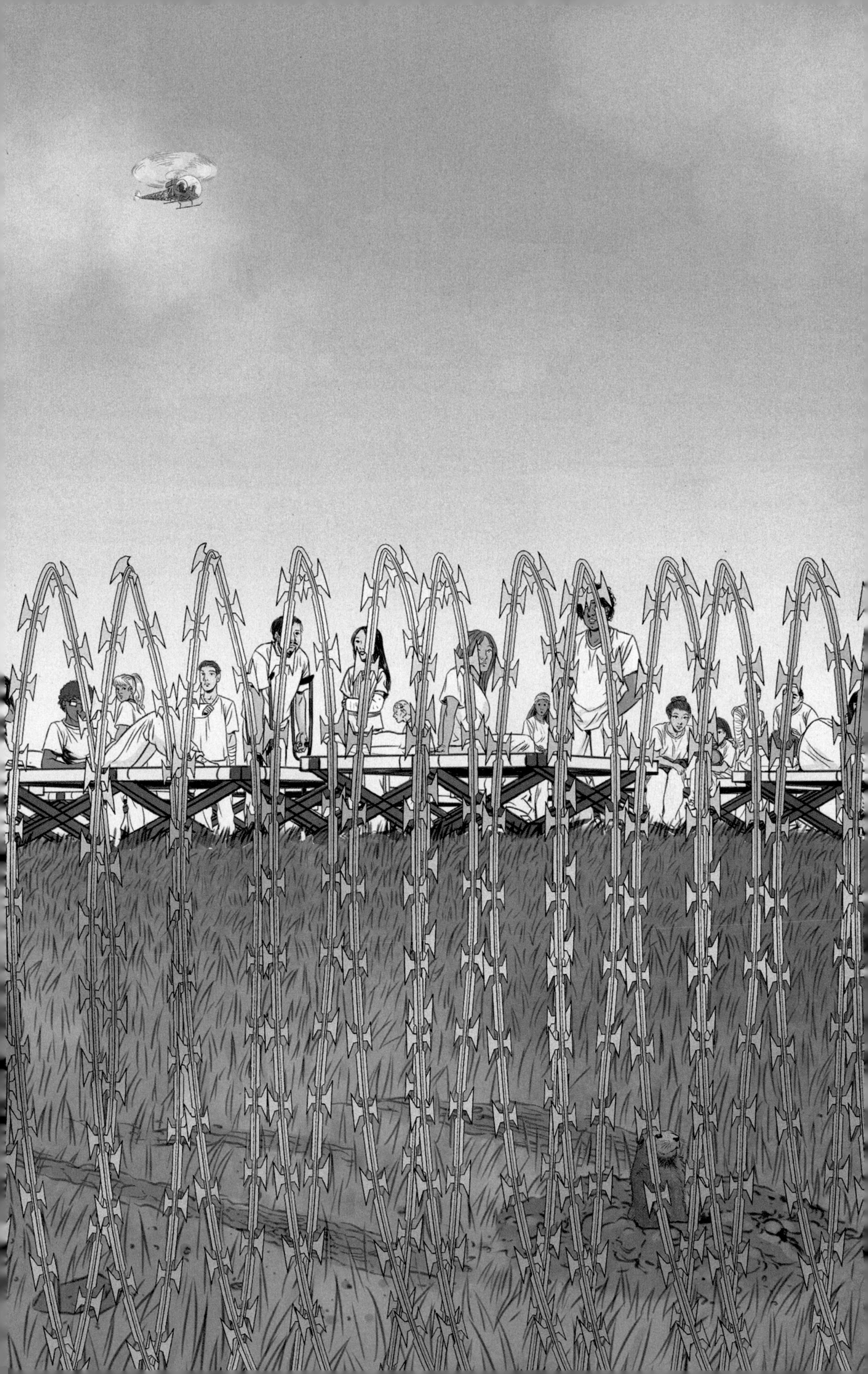

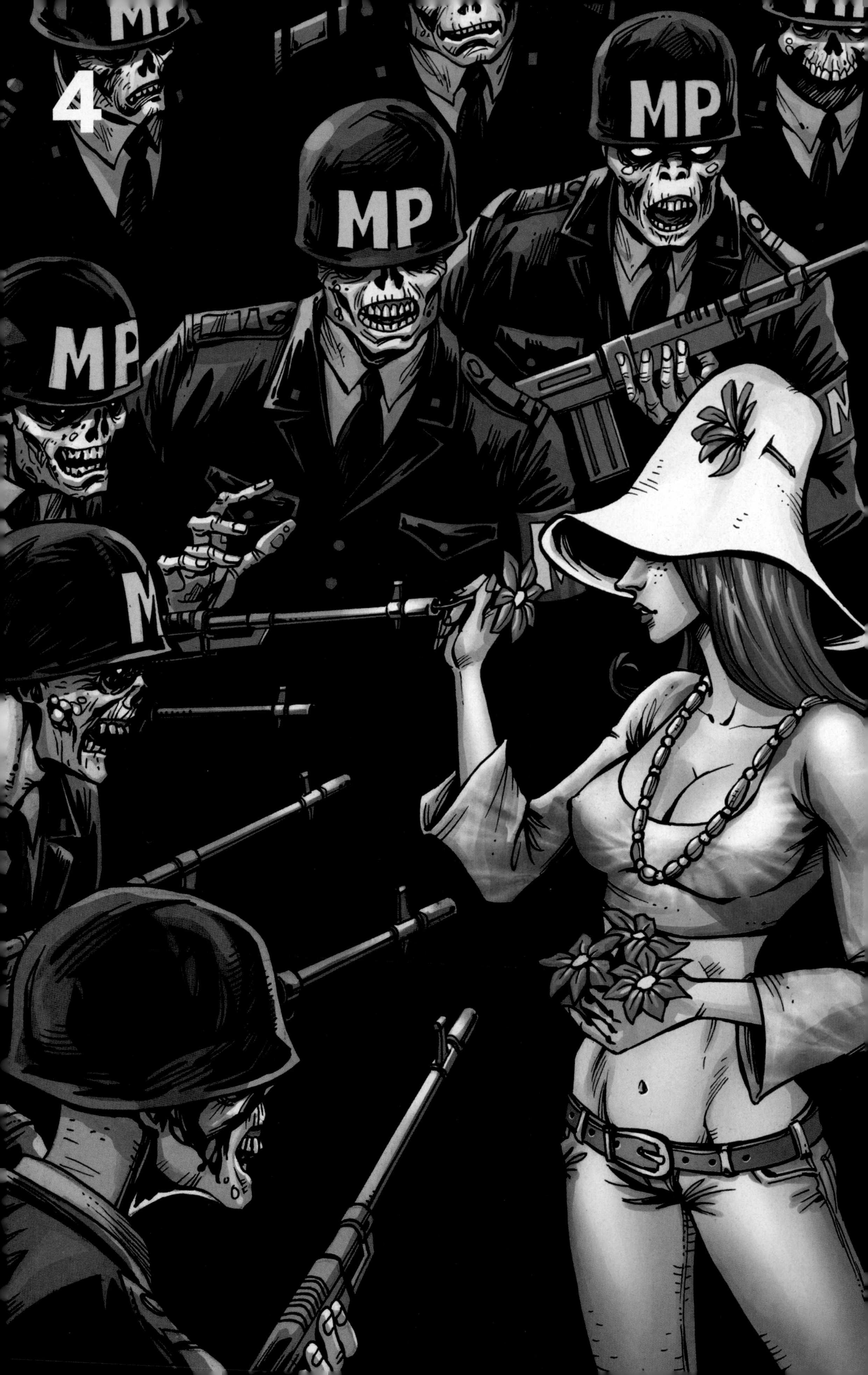
4
MP
MP
MP

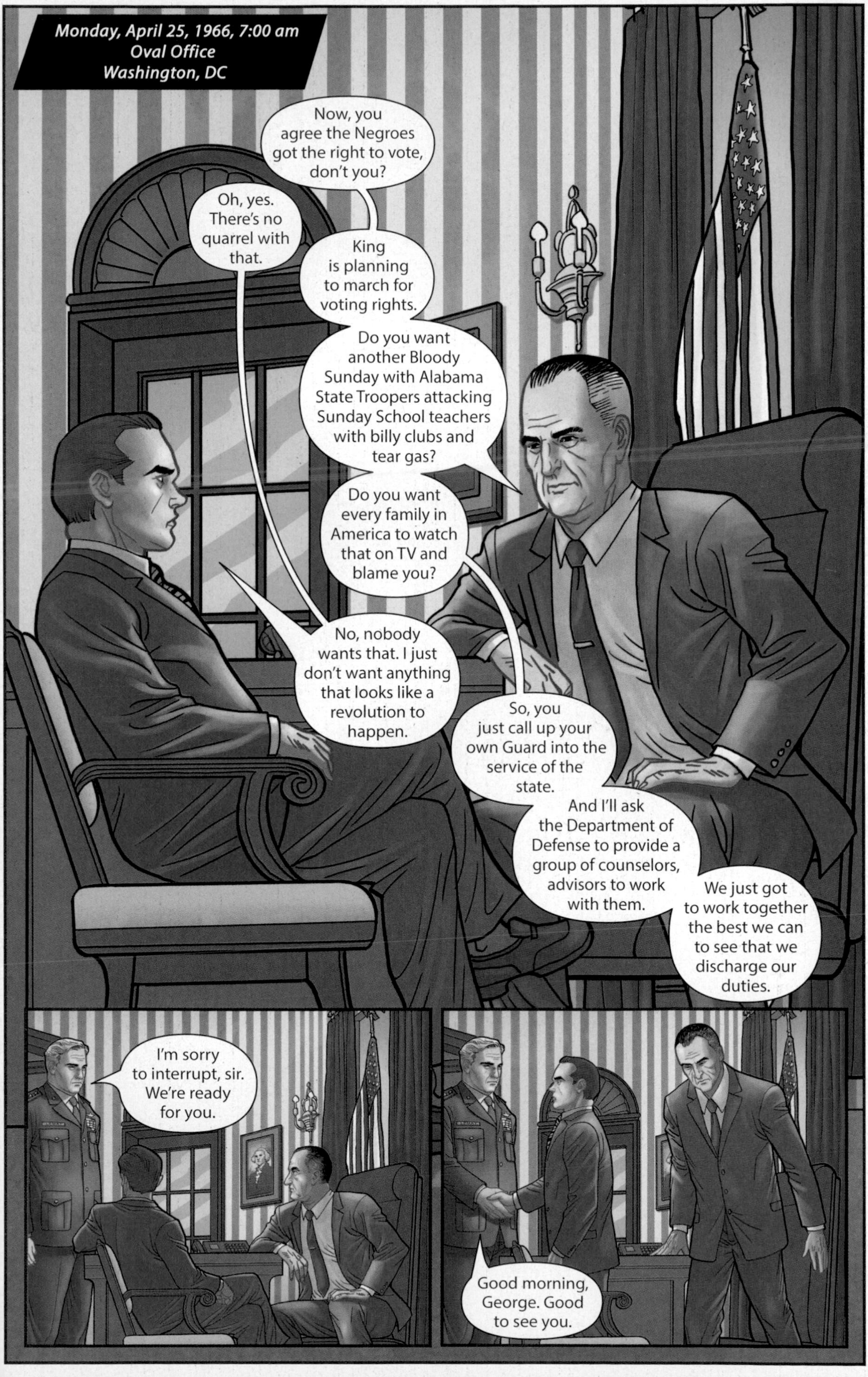

Monday, April 25, 1966, 7:00 am
Oval Office
Washington, DC
Now, you agree the Negroes got the right to vote, don't you?
Oh, yes. There's no quarrel with that.
King is planning to march for voting rights.
Do you want another Bloody Sunday with Alabama State Troopers attacking Sunday School teachers with billy clubs and tear gas?
Do you want every family in America to watch that on TV and blame you?
No, nobody wants that. I just don't want anything that looks like a revolution to happen.
So, you just call up your own Guard into the service of the state.
And I'll ask the Department of Defense to provide a group of counselors, advisors to work with them.
We just got to work together the best we can to see that we discharge our duties.
I'm sorry to interrupt, sir. We're ready for you.
Good morning, George. Good to see you.

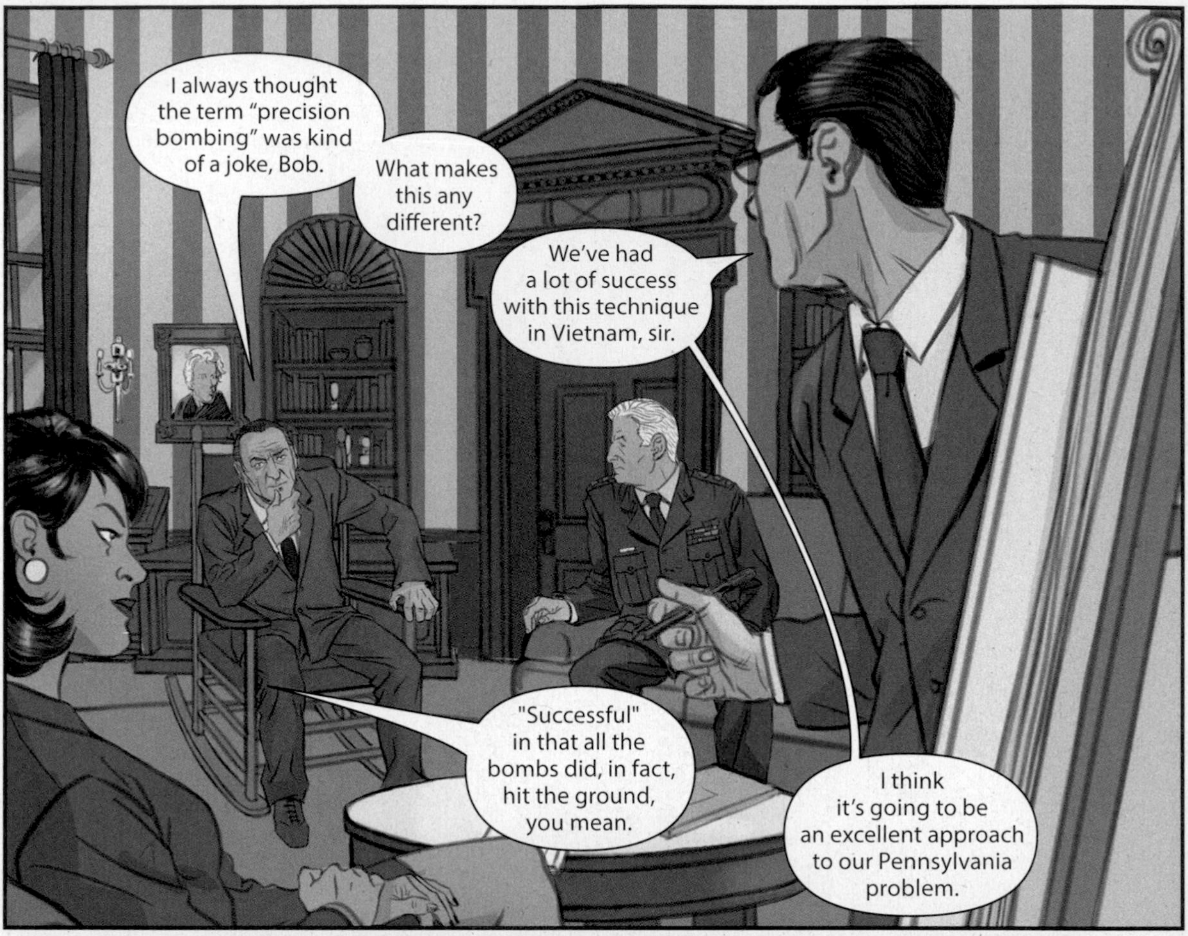
I always thought the term "precision bombing" was kind of a joke, Bob.
What makes this any different?
We've had a lot of success with this technique in Vietnam, sir.
"Successful" in that all the bombs did, in fact, hit the ground, you mean.
I think it's going to be an excellent approach to our Pennsylvania problem.

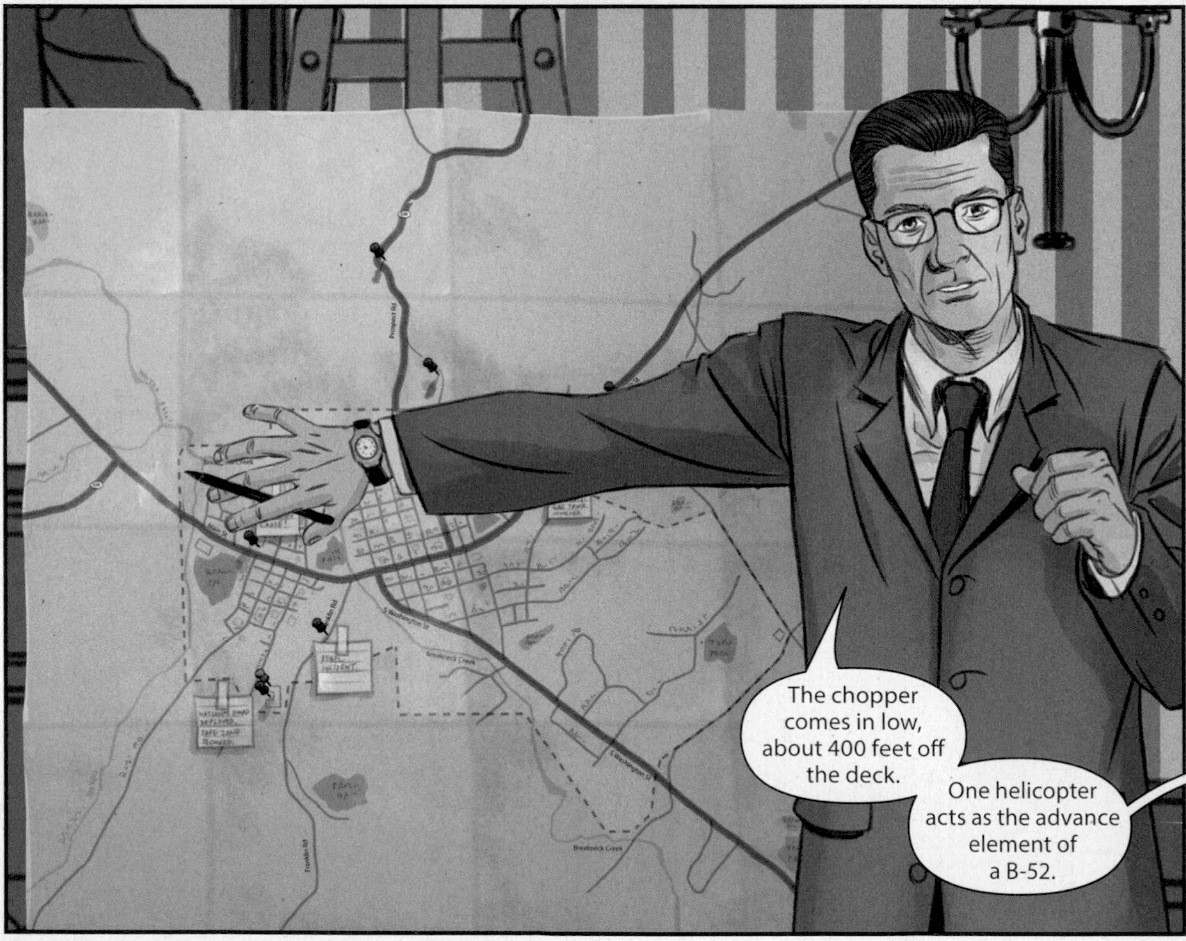
The chopper comes in low, about 400 feet off the deck.
One helicopter acts as the advance element of a B-52.

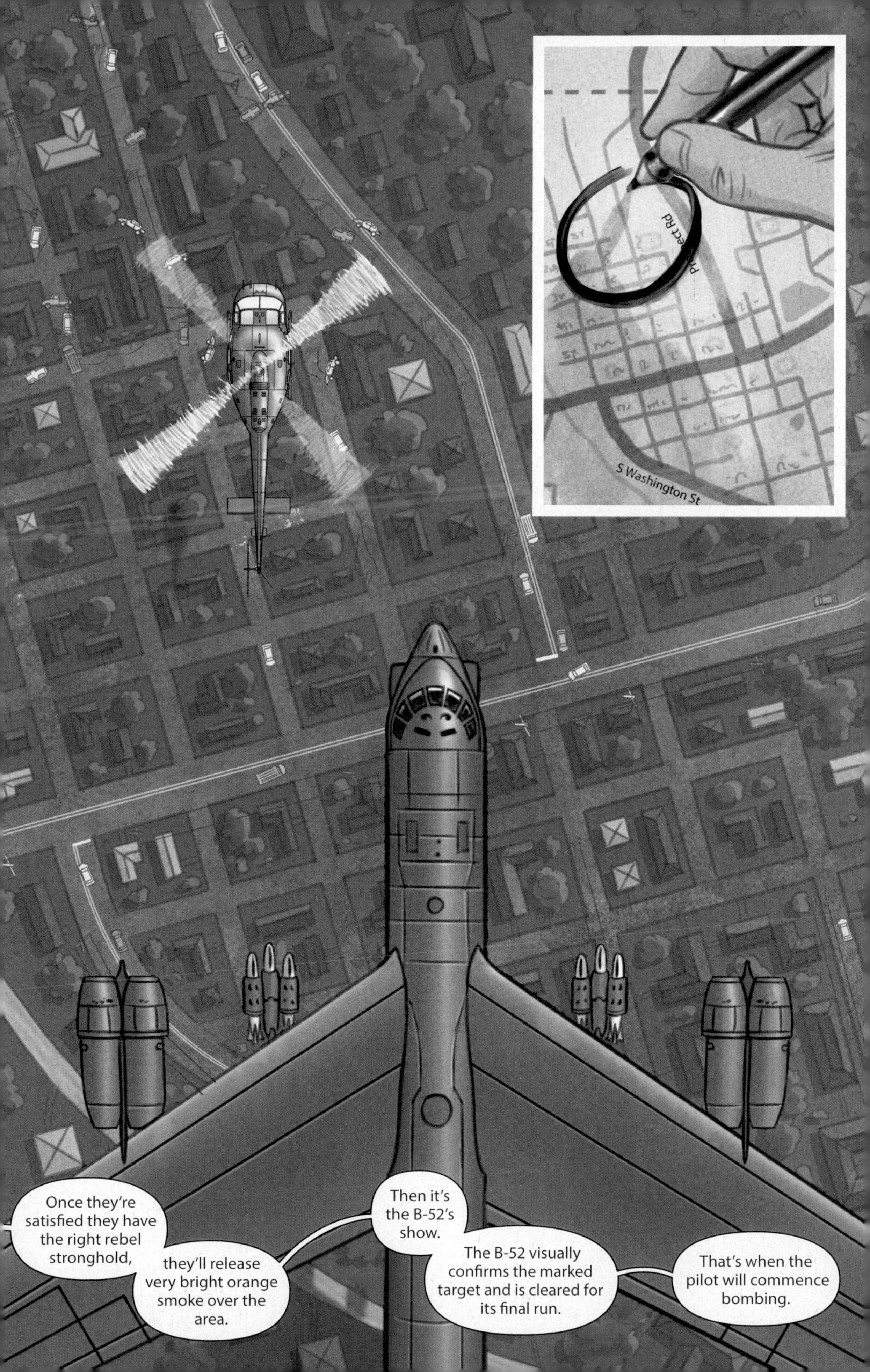
Pro...ect Rd
S Washington St
Once they're satisfied they have the right rebel stronghold,
they'll release very bright orange smoke over the area.
Then it's the B-52's show.
The B-52 visually confirms the marked target and is cleared for its final run.
That's when the pilot will commence bombing.

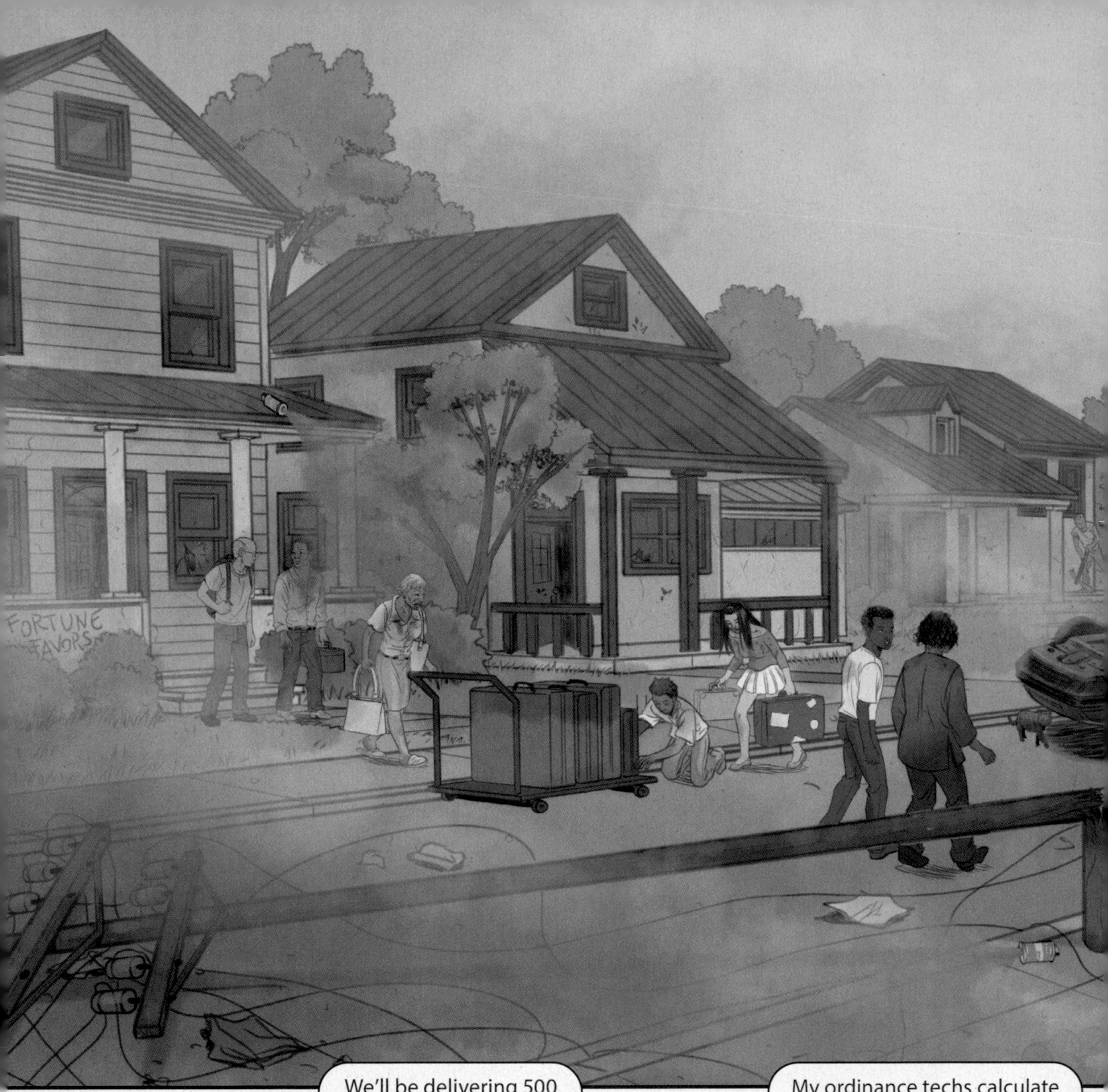
FORTUNE FAVORS

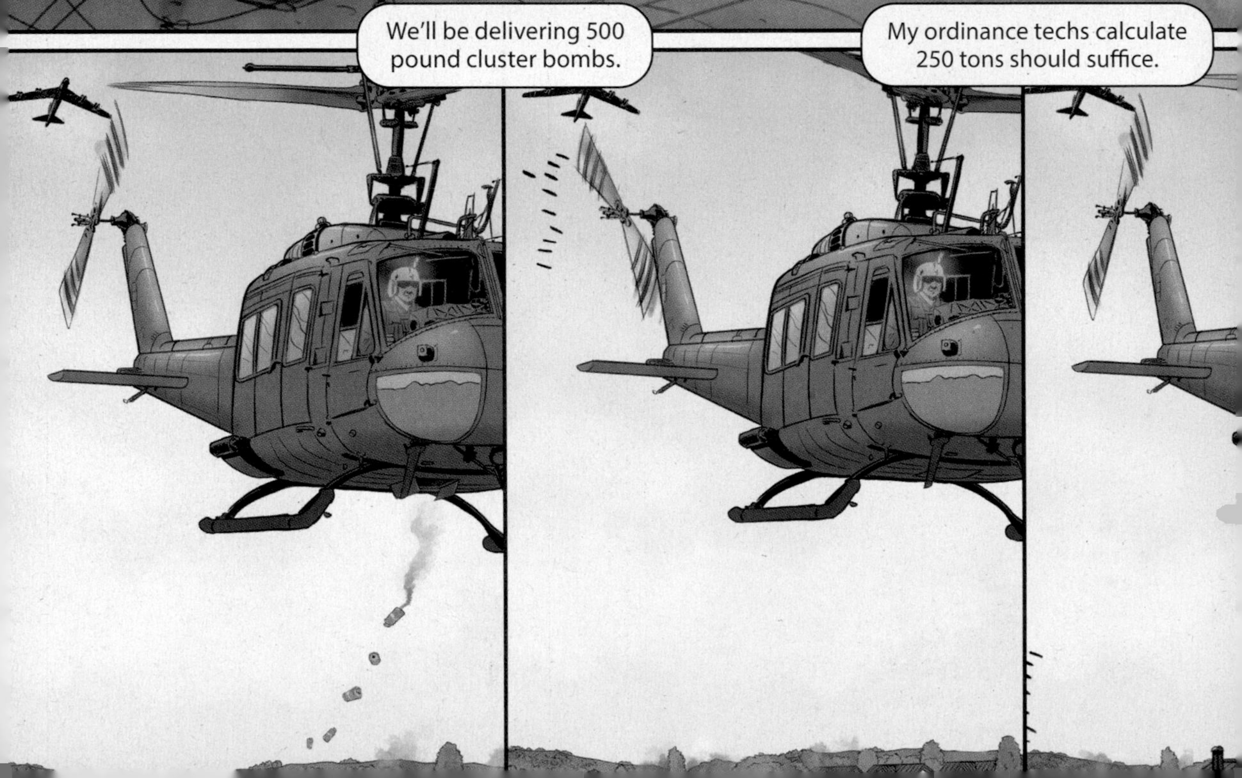
We'll be delivering 500 pound cluster bombs.
My ordinance techs calculate 250 tons should suffice.

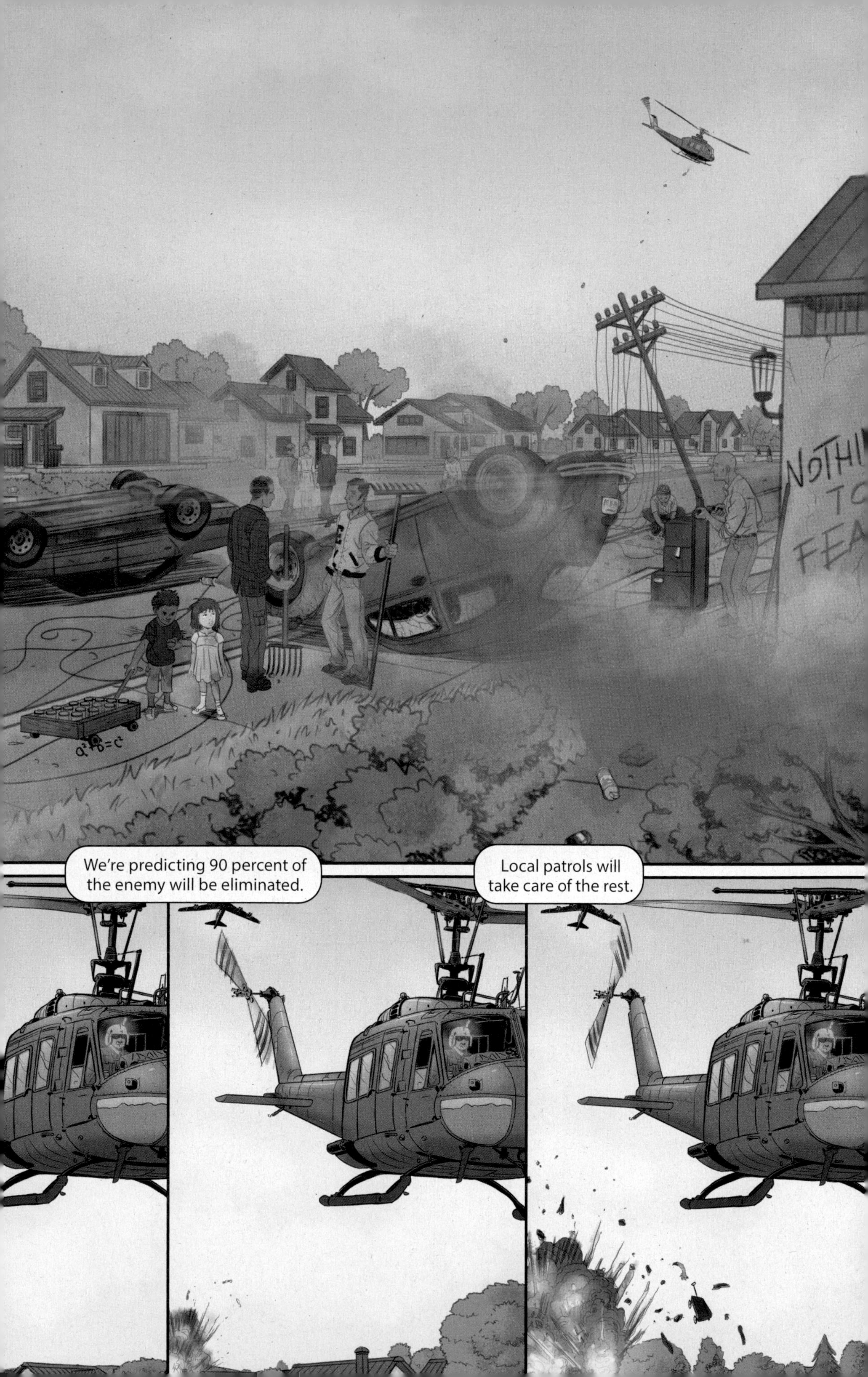
We're predicting 90 percent of the enemy will be eliminated.
Local patrols will take care of the rest.

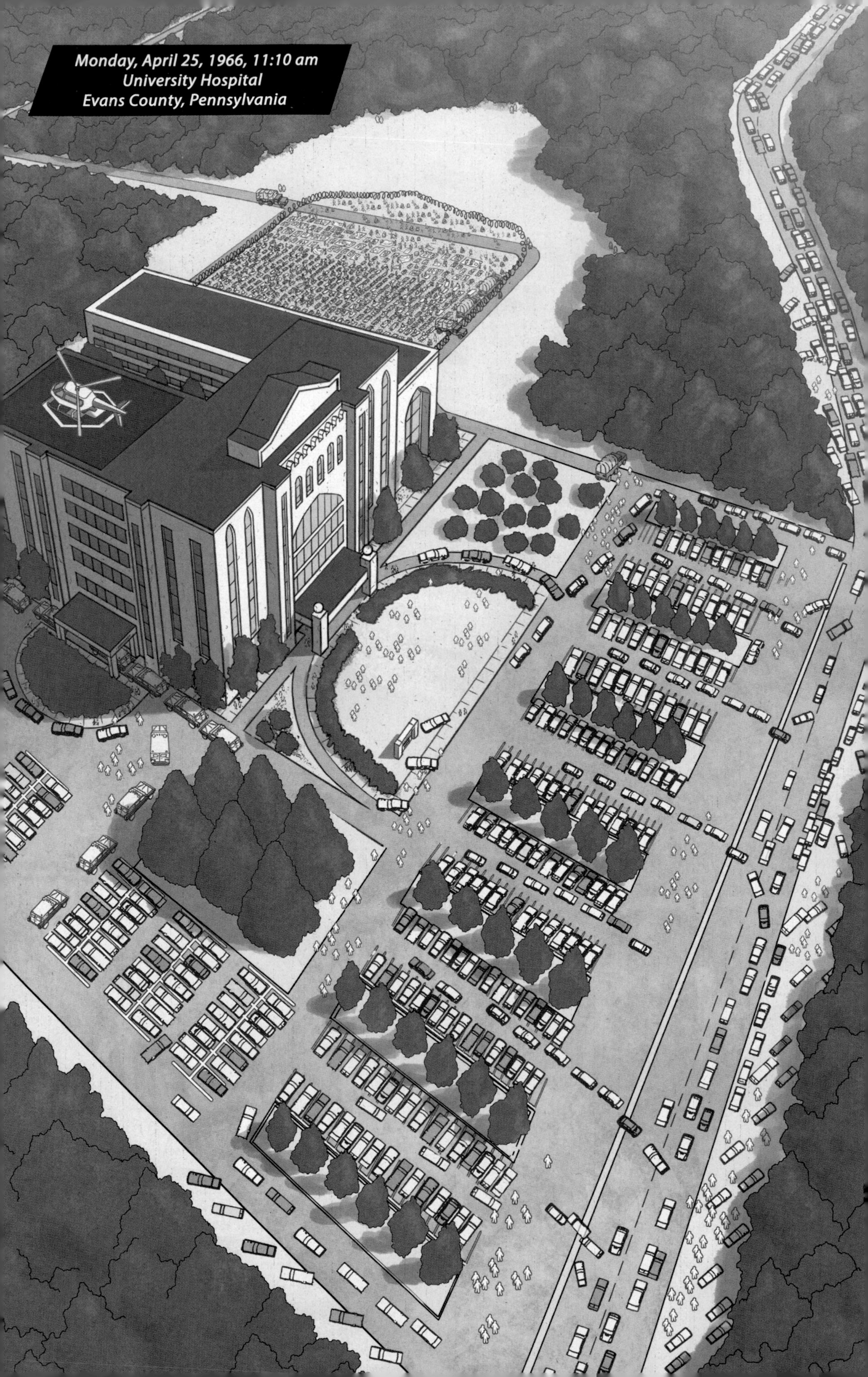
Monday, April 25, 1966, 11:10 am
University Hospital
Evans County, Pennsylvania

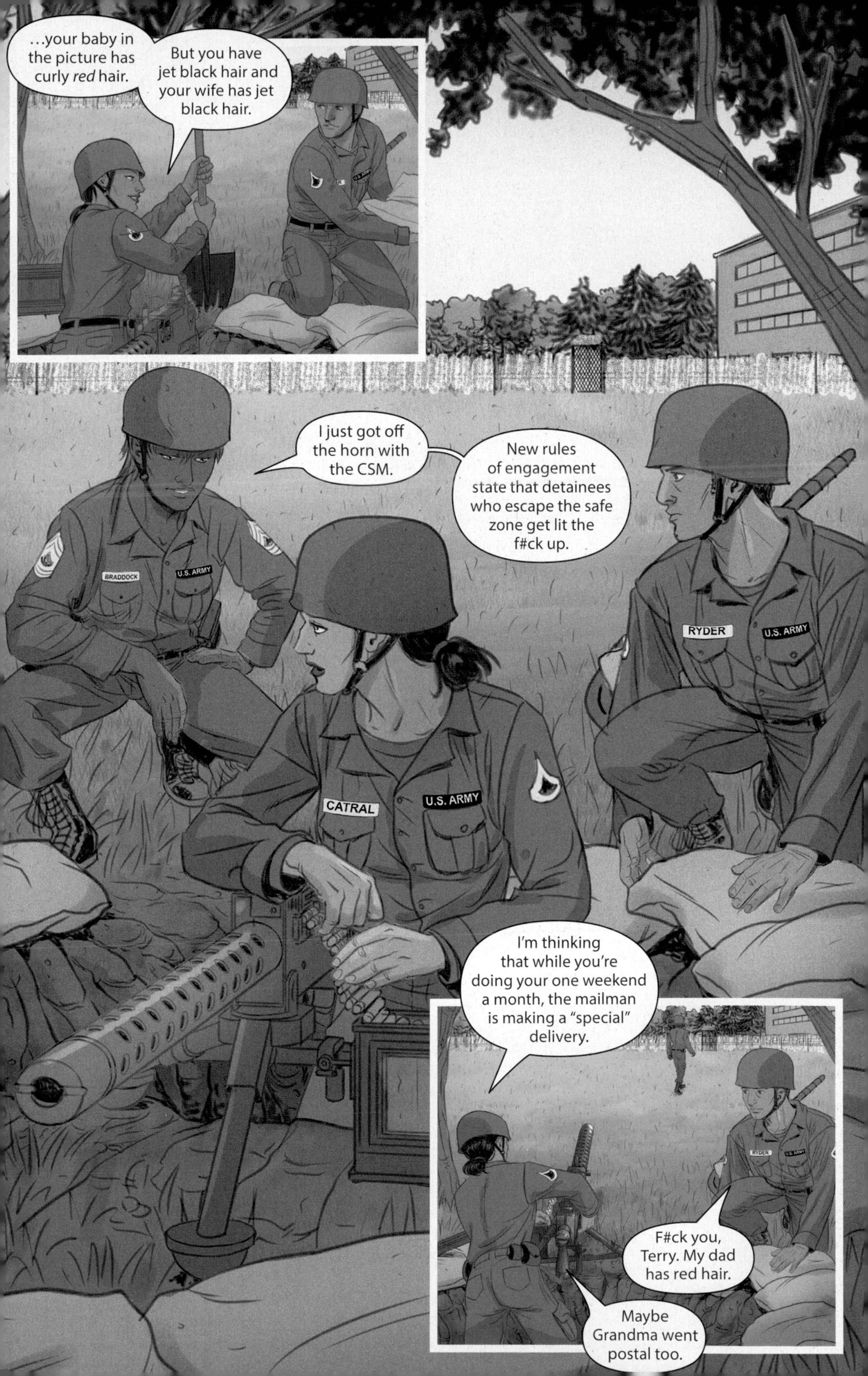

…your baby in the picture has curly *red* hair.
But you have jet black hair and your wife has jet black hair.
U.S. ARMY
BRADDOCK
U.S. ARMY
I just got off the horn with the CSM.
New rules of engagement state that detainees who escape the safe zone get lit the f#ck up.
RYDER
U.S. ARMY
CATRAL
U.S. ARMY
I'm thinking that while you're doing your one weekend a month, the mailman is making a "special" delivery.
RYDER
U.S. ARMY
F#ck you, Terry. My dad has red hair.
Maybe Grandma went postal too.

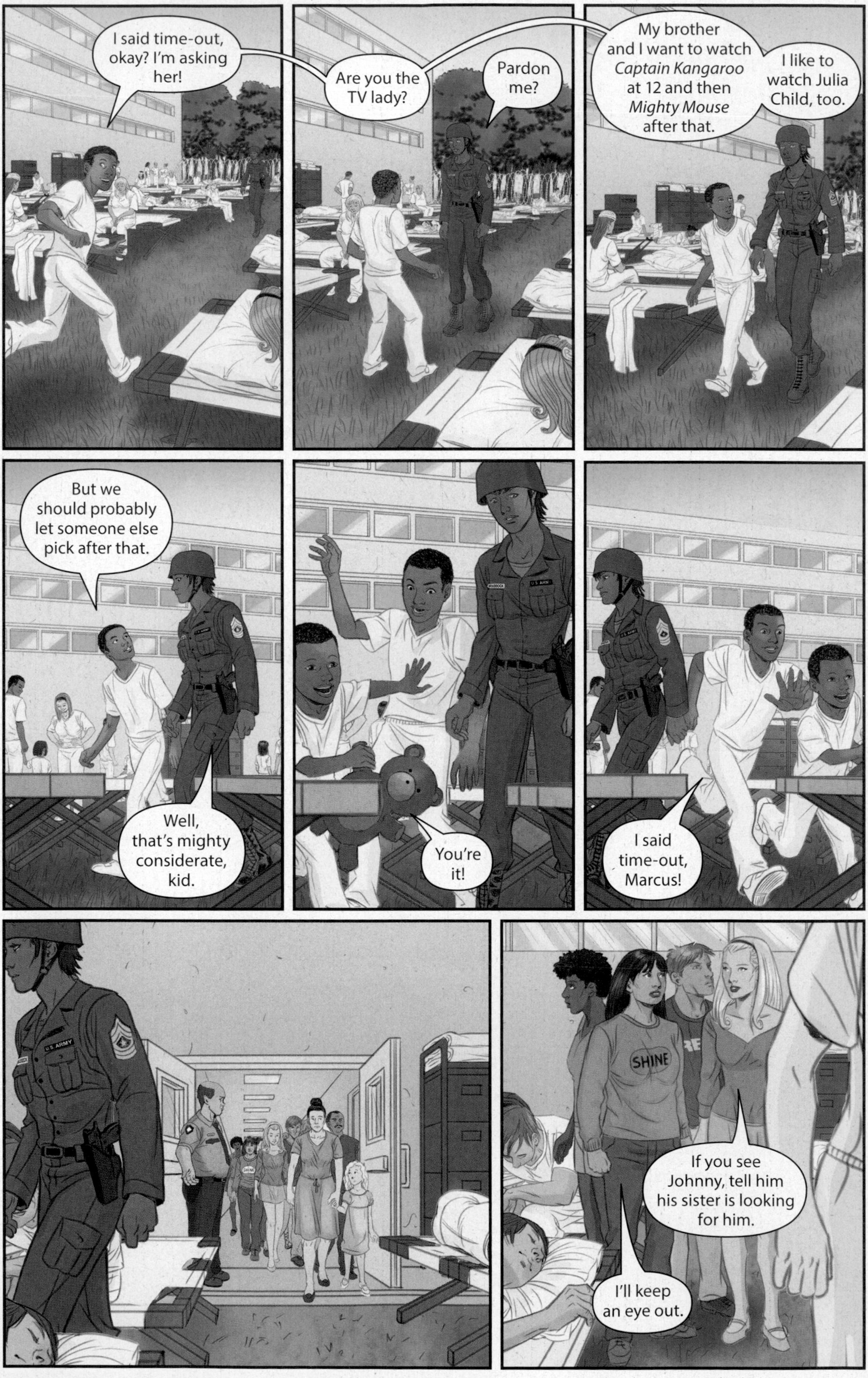
I said time-out, okay? I'm asking her!
Are you the TV lady?
Pardon me?
My brother and I want to watch *Captain Kangaroo* at 12 and then *Mighty Mouse* after that.
I like to watch Julia Child, too.
But we should probably let someone else pick after that.
Well, that's mighty considerate, kid.
You're it!
I said time-out, Marcus!
U.S. ARMY
SHINE
If you see Johnny, tell him his sister is looking for him.
I'll keep an eye out.

THE ★★ SKINNY

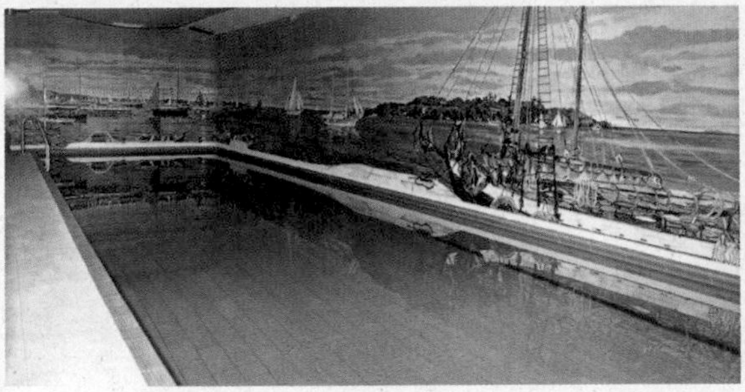

In 1668, Thomas Guidott set up the practice of nude swimming in the English town of Bath, believing in the curative properties of the waters. Doctors and quacks set up spa towns around mineral springs and guaranteed a cure by dipping naked in the cold mineral water.

In America, Benjamin Franklin and John Quincy Adams were also interested in nude swimming. Franklin was an avid swimmer and owned a book about the art of swimming, which had pictures of nude swimmers. As part of his morning ritual, John Quincy Adams would skinny-dip in the Potomac. A number of our presidents in the 20th century also spent time skinny-dipping. Sometimes for recreation—and sometimes, to break down political barriers.

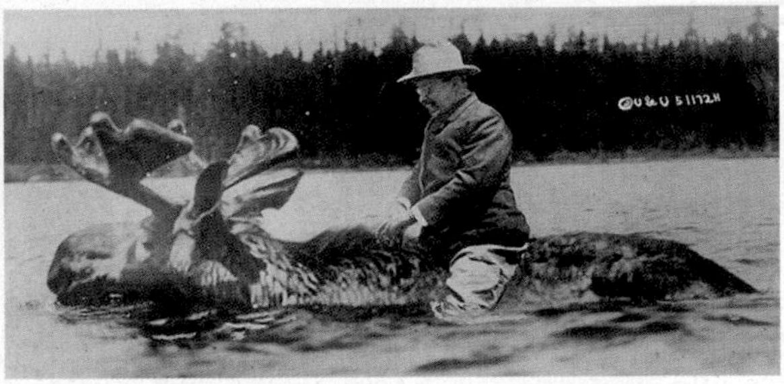
©U&U 51112H

THEODORE ROOSEVELT: Lifelong naturalist Teddy Roosevelt enjoyed recreational skinny-dipping. He also skinny-dipped for diplomacy. In 1903, Teddy Roosevelt invited the French Ambassador to a nude swim in the Potomac. The shy ambassador joined him but kept his gloves on in case they met ladies.

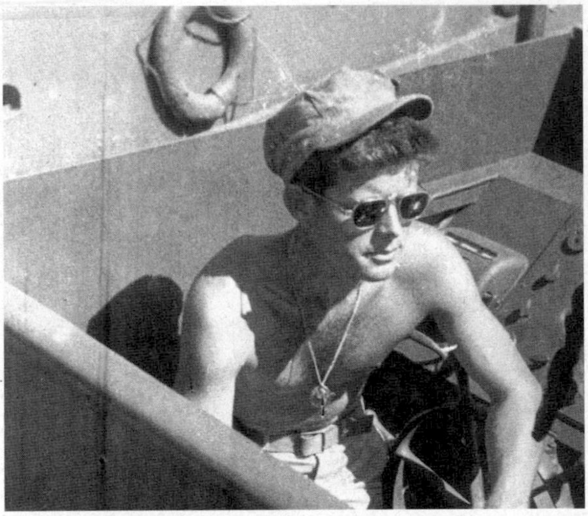

JOHN F. KENNEDY: JFK also enjoyed taking relaxing nude dips in the White House pool. Sometimes his brothers joined him. And on at least one occasion two young female assistants kept him company in the pool.

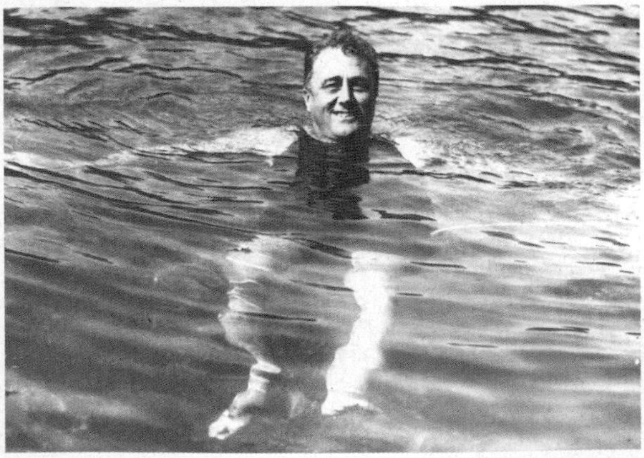

FRANKLIN DELANO ROOSEVELT: Taking a cue from his older cousin, FDR also stripped down to build political relationships. In 1937, he invited Congressional Democrats to a "stag party" to win over their good will. Activities included fishing, clay pigeon shooting, and skinny-dipping. The first White House pool was also built in 1933 for FDR's therapeutic use. It was located in the West Wing, enclosed, and easily accessible from the Oval Office.

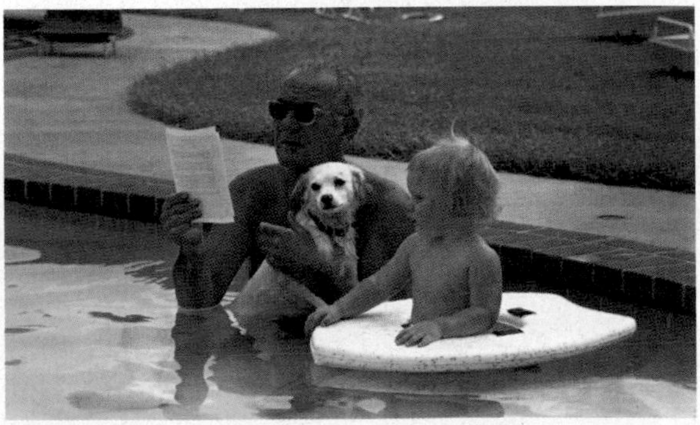

LYNDON B. JOHNSON: Shortly after being sworn in, LBJ invited Christian evangelist Billy Graham to skinny-dip in the White House pool. LBJ used the White House pool almost daily. He even sometimes held meetings with senior staff in the shallow end of the pool, while in the nude with his "Jumbo" out.

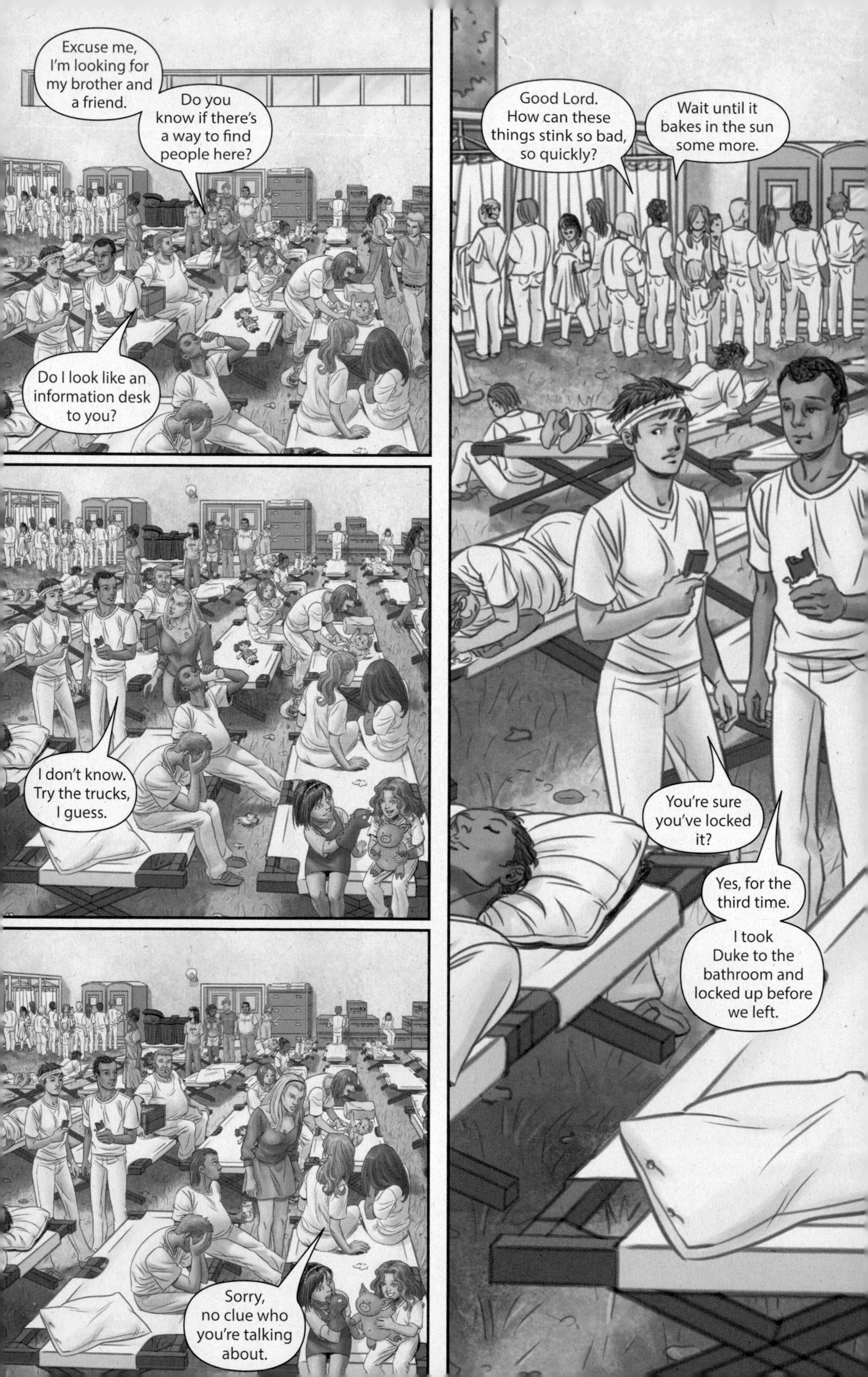

Excuse me, I'm looking for my brother and a friend.
Do you know if there's a way to find people here?
Do I look like an information desk to you?
I don't know. Try the trucks, I guess.
Sorry, no clue who you're talking about.
Good Lord. How can these things stink so bad, so quickly?
Wait until it bakes in the sun some more.
You're sure you've locked it?
Yes, for the third time.
I took Duke to the bathroom and locked up before we left.

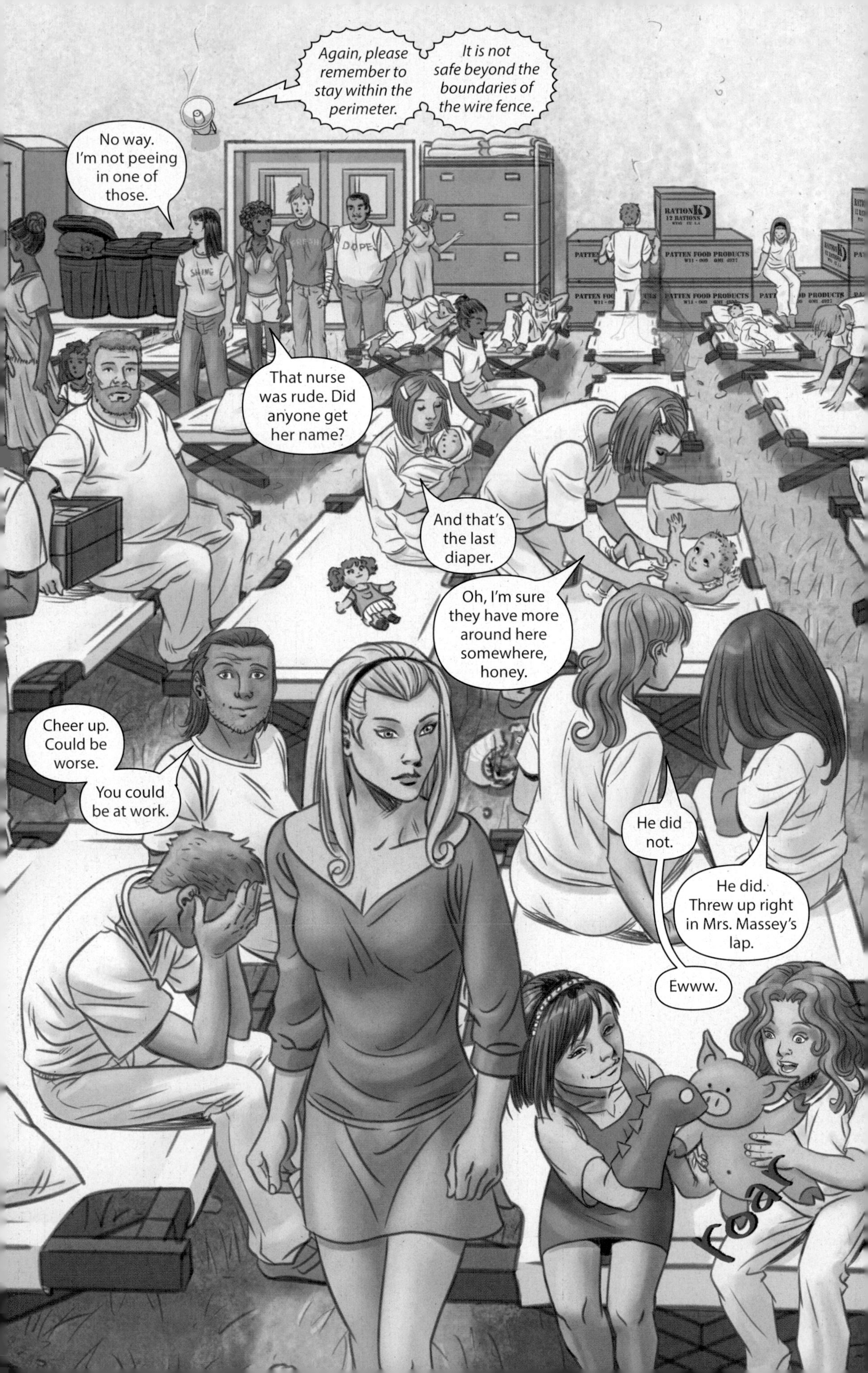

Again, please remember to stay within the perimeter.
It is not safe beyond the boundaries of the wire fence.
No way. I'm not peeing in one of those.
SHINE
FRESH
DOPE
RATION K 12 RATIONS
PATTEN FOOD PRODUCTS
That nurse was rude. Did anyone get her name?
And that's the last diaper.
Oh, I'm sure they have more around here somewhere, honey.
Cheer up. Could be worse.
You could be at work.
He did not.
He did. Threw up right in Mrs. Massey's lap.
Ewww.
roar

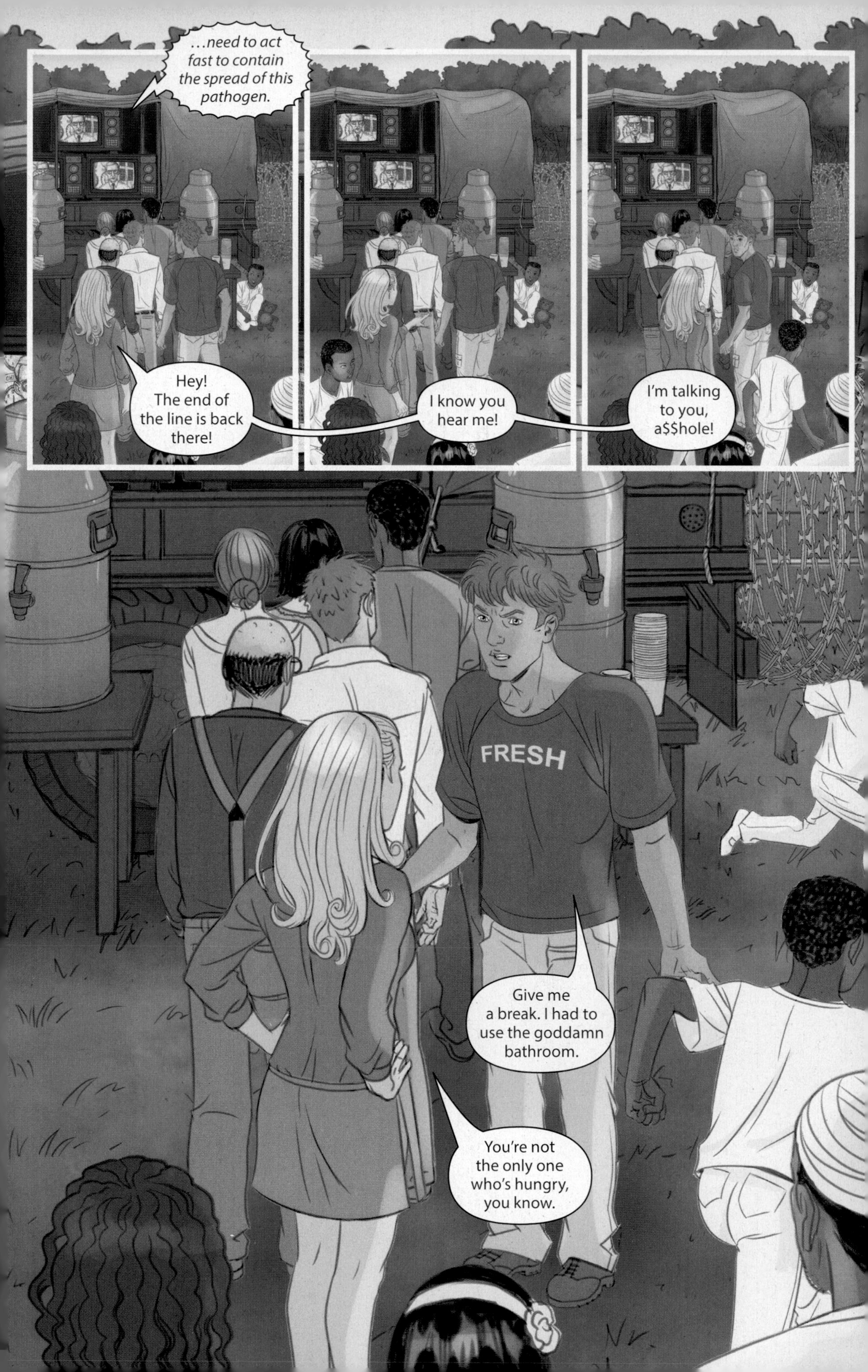
…need to act fast to contain the spread of this pathogen.
Hey! The end of the line is back there!
I know you hear me!
I'm talking to you, a$$hole!
FRESH
Give me a break. I had to use the goddamn bathroom.
You're not the only one who's hungry, you know.

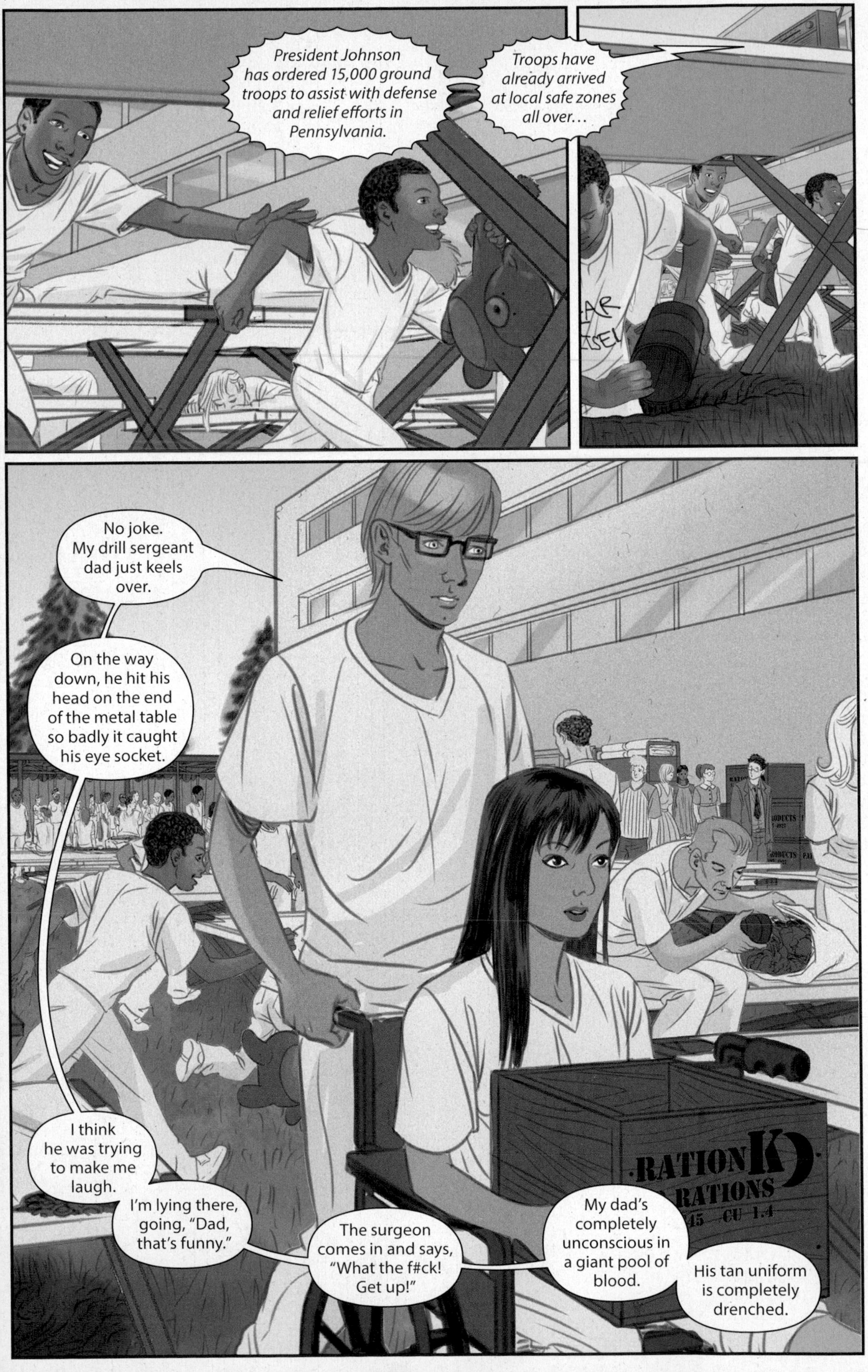
President Johnson has ordered 15,000 ground troops to assist with defense and relief efforts in Pennsylvania.
Troops have already arrived at local safe zones all over…
No joke. My drill sergeant dad just keels over.
On the way down, he hit his head on the end of the metal table so badly it caught his eye socket.
I think he was trying to make me laugh.
I'm lying there, going, "Dad, that's funny."
The surgeon comes in and says, "What the f#ck! Get up!"
My dad's completely unconscious in a giant pool of blood.
His tan uniform is completely drenched.
RATION K
RATIONS

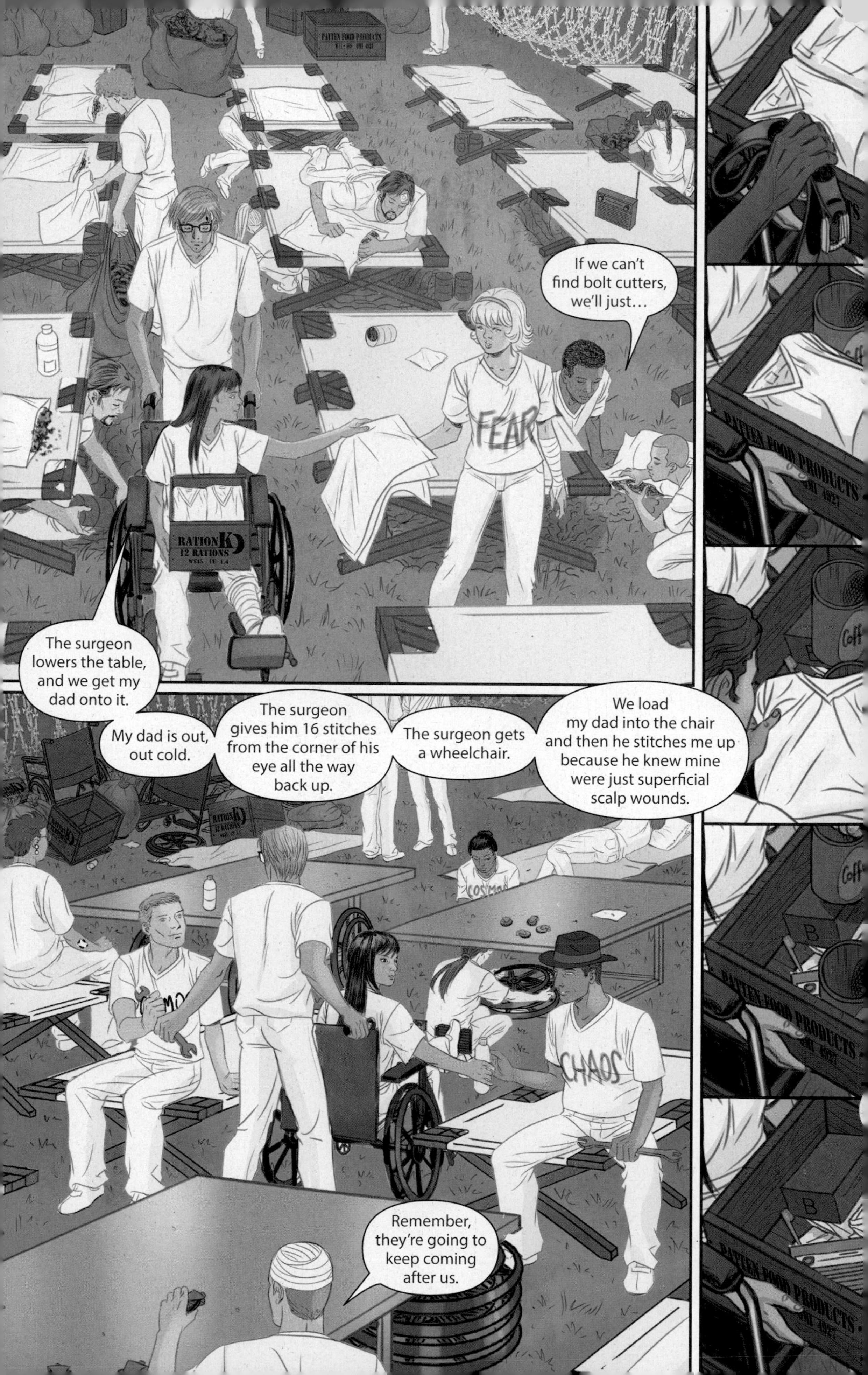

If we can't find bolt cutters, we'll just…
The surgeon lowers the table, and we get my dad onto it.
My dad is out, out cold.
The surgeon gives him 16 stitches from the corner of his eye all the way back up.
The surgeon gets a wheelchair.
We load my dad into the chair and then he stitches me up because he knew mine were just superficial scalp wounds.
Remember, they're going to keep coming after us.

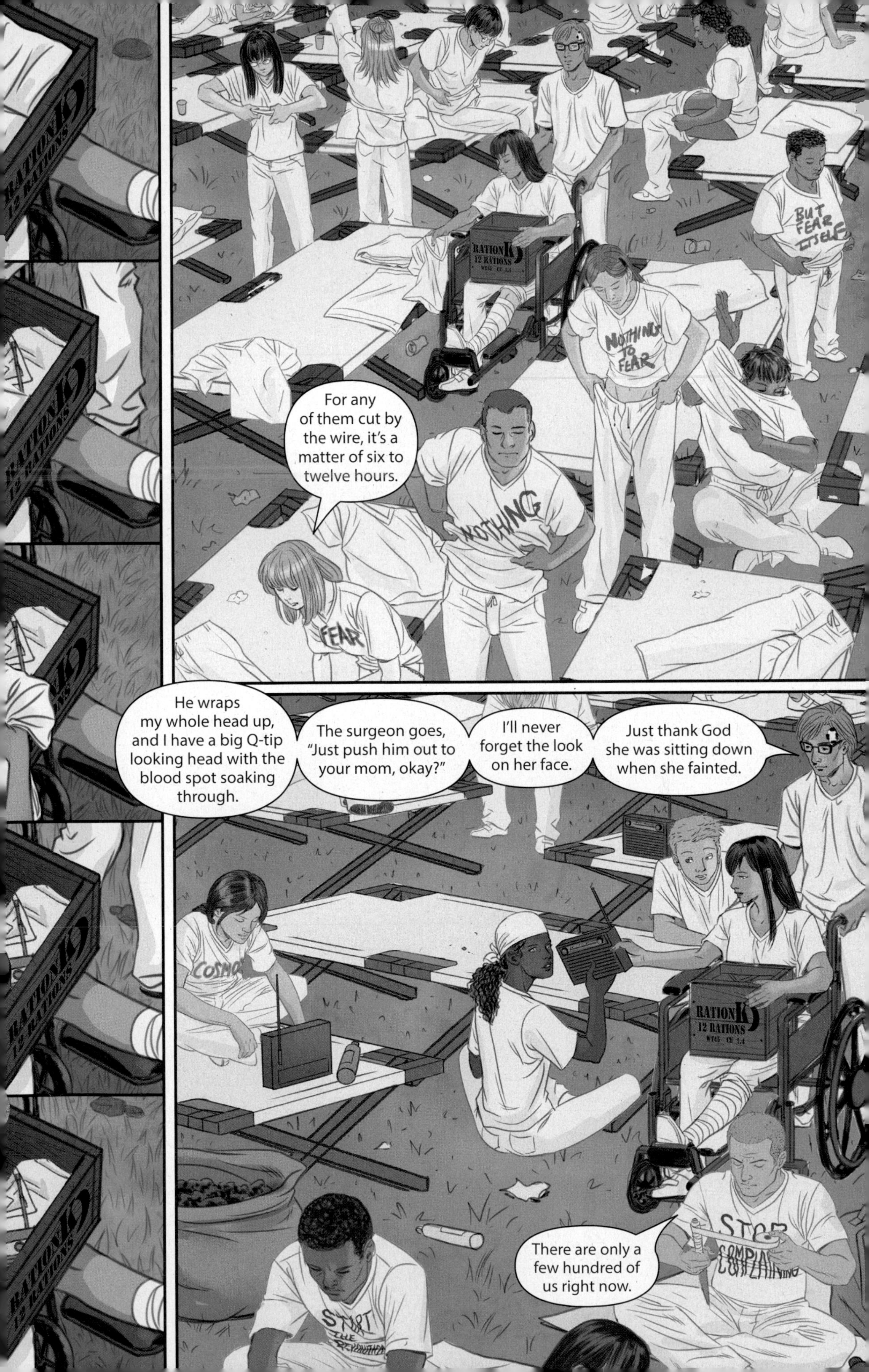

RATION K 12 RATIONS
BUT FEAR ITSELF
NOTHING TO FEAR
For any of them cut by the wire, it's a matter of six to twelve hours.
NOTHING
FEAR
He wraps my whole head up, and I have a big Q-tip looking head with the blood spot soaking through.
The surgeon goes, "Just push him out to your mom, okay?"
I'll never forget the look on her face.
Just thank God she was sitting down when she fainted.
COSMO
There are only a few hundred of us right now.
STOP COMPLAINING
START

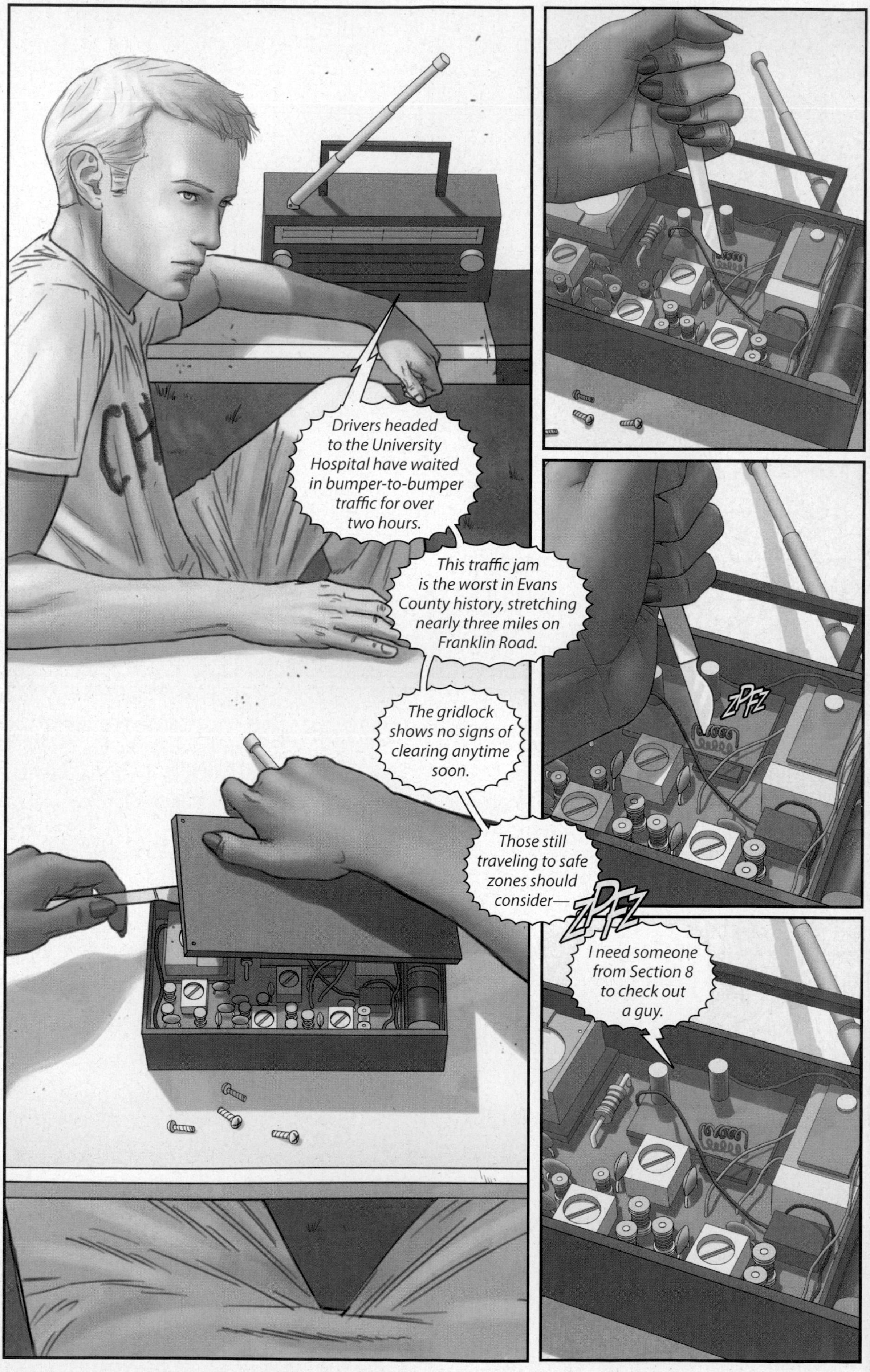
Drivers headed to the University Hospital have waited in bumper-to-bumper traffic for over two hours.
This traffic jam is the worst in Evans County history, stretching nearly three miles on Franklin Road.
The gridlock shows no signs of clearing anytime soon.
Those still traveling to safe zones should consider—
ZPFZ
ZPFZ
I need someone from Section 8 to check out a guy.

THEN NOW

	1966	2015
WORLD POPULATION	3,400,000,000	7,200,000,000
McDonald's		
LOCATIONS	850	36,000
COUNTRIES	1	118
BIGGEST BURGER	1.6oz	5.4oz
AVERAGE MEAL CALORIES	590	1,500
Walmart		
LOCATIONS	24	11,495
COUNTRIES	1	28
PERCENTAGE OF PRODUCTS MADE IN CHINA	0%	70%
NFL		
SUPER BOWL VIEWERS	50,000,000	114,000,000
AVERAGE SALARY	$15,000	$1,900,000
Apple		
LOCATIONS	0	453
iOS DEVICES SOLD	0	1,000,000,000
Prison Industry		
STATE AND FEDERAL PRISON POPULATION	200,000	2,300,000
PERCENTAGE OF FEDERAL PRISON POPULATION: DRUG VIOLATIONS	11%–16%	50%
Health Industry		
COST OF HEALTH CARE	$201 PER CAPITA	$10,000 PER CAPITA
COST OF MEDICARE	$3,000,000,000	$634,300,000,000
Political Industry		
COST OF PRESIDENTIAL CAMPAIGN	$8,800,000	$5,000,000,000

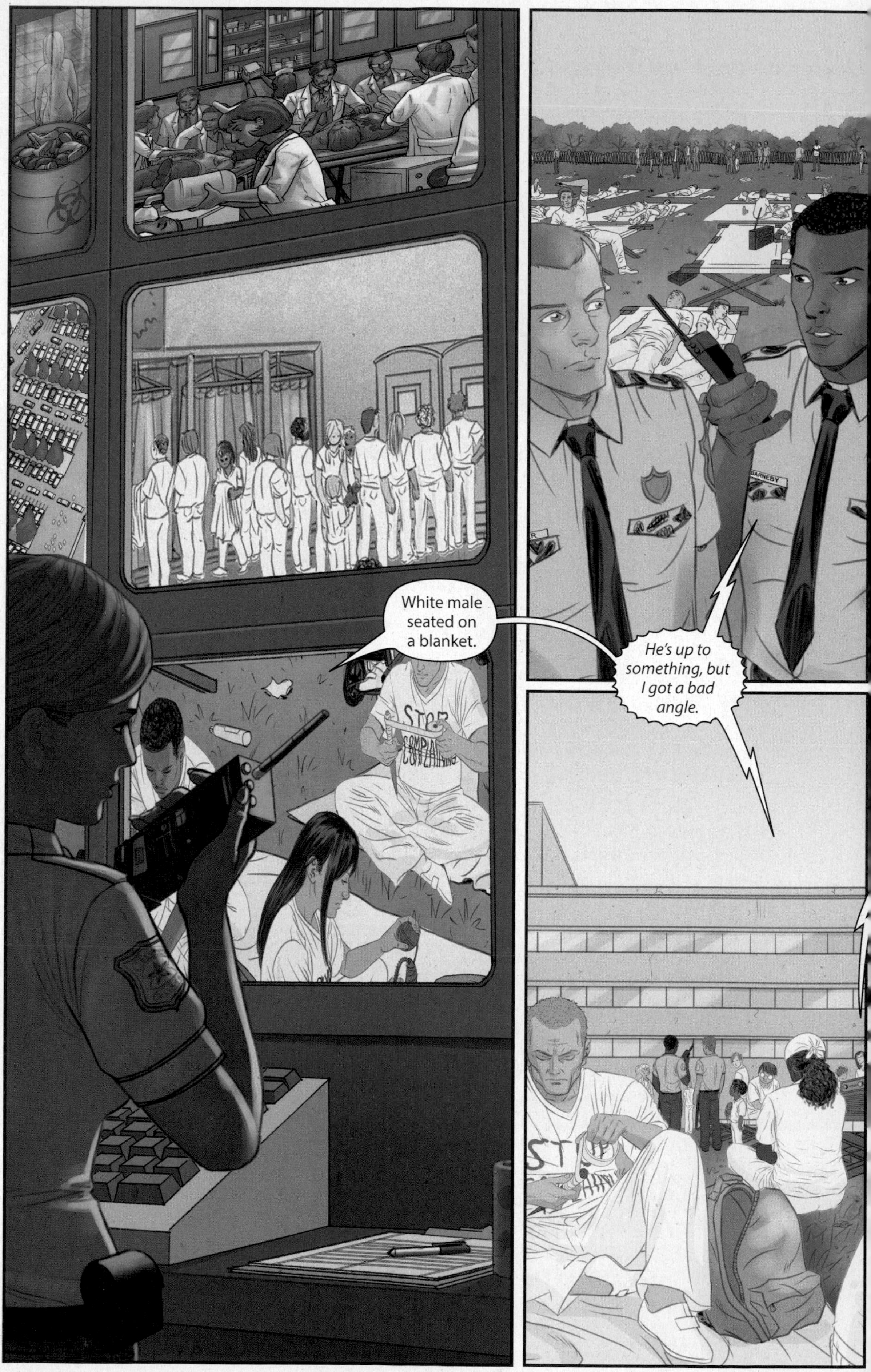
White male seated on a blanket.
He's up to something, but I got a bad angle.

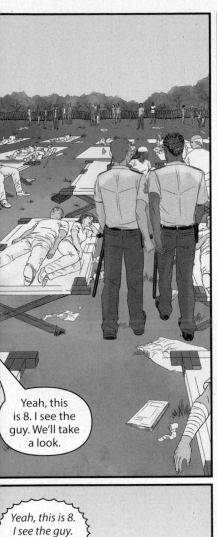

Yeah, this is 8. I see the guy. We'll take a look.

Yeah, this is 8. I see the guy. We'll take a look.

Look out.

He's clean, Bridget.

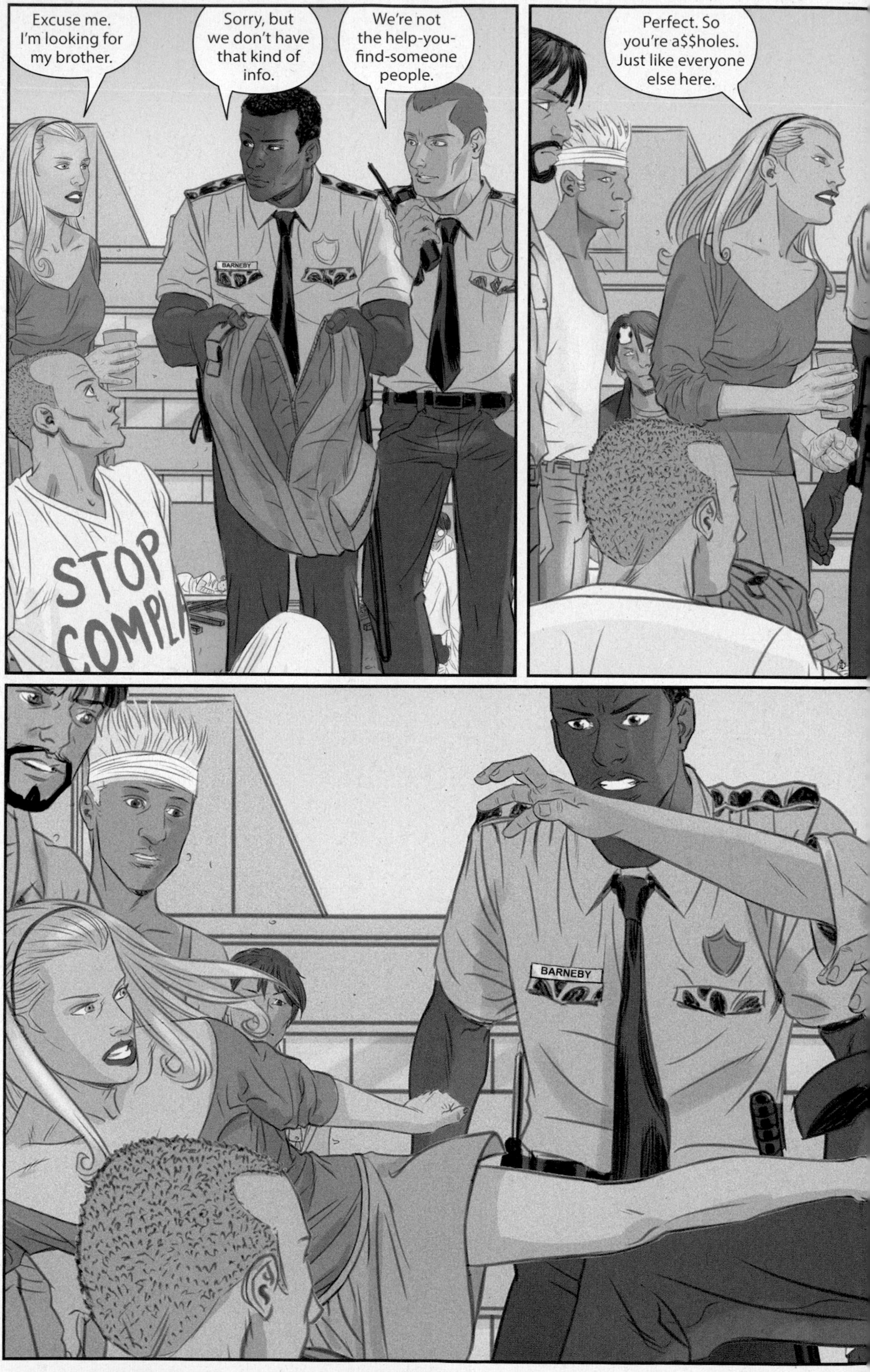
Excuse me. I'm looking for my brother.
Sorry, but we don't have that kind of info.
We're not the help-you-find-someone people.
Perfect. So you're a$$holes. Just like everyone else here.
BARNEBY
STOP COMPLA
BARNEBY

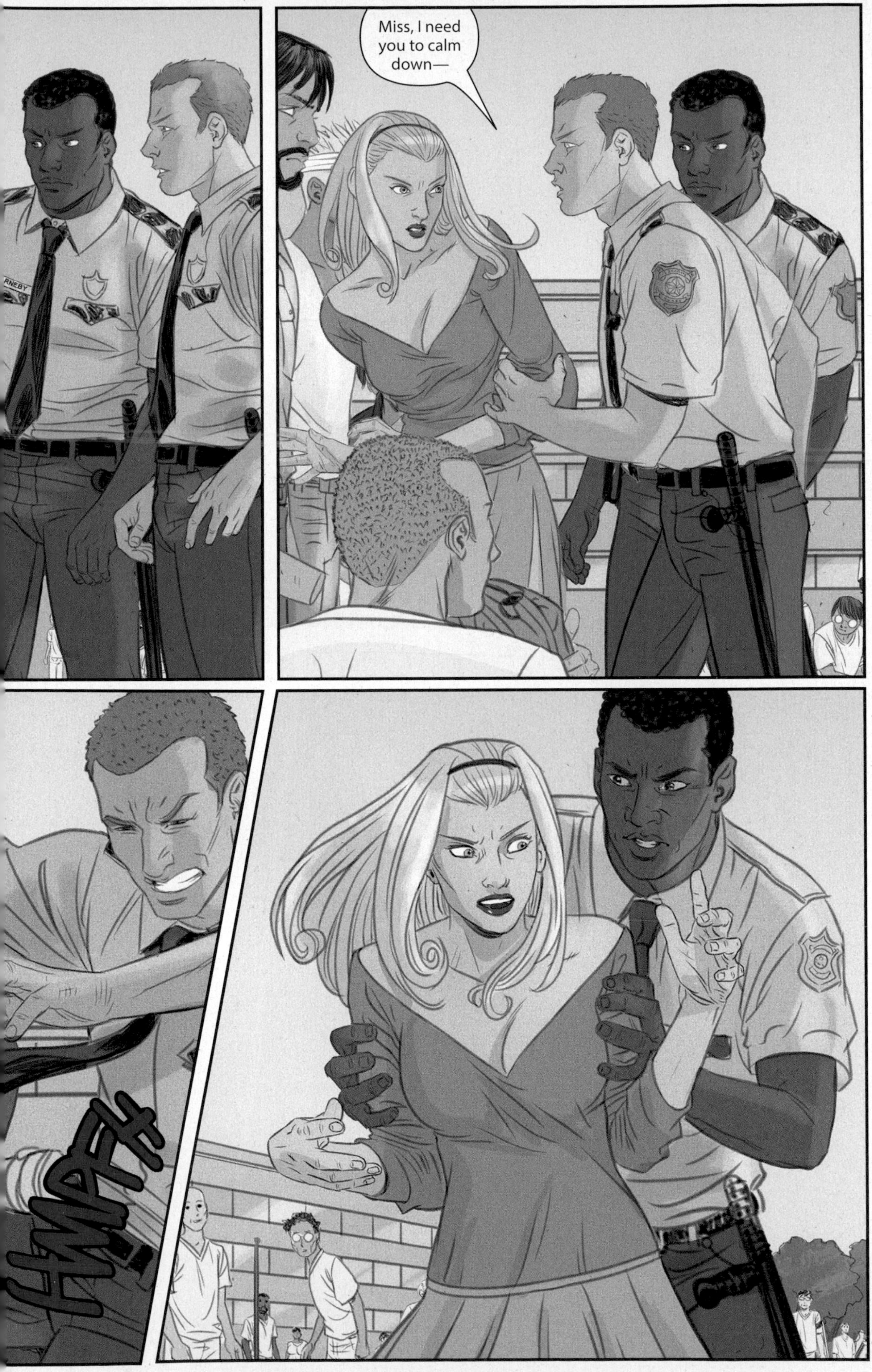
Miss, I need you to calm down—
HMPFH

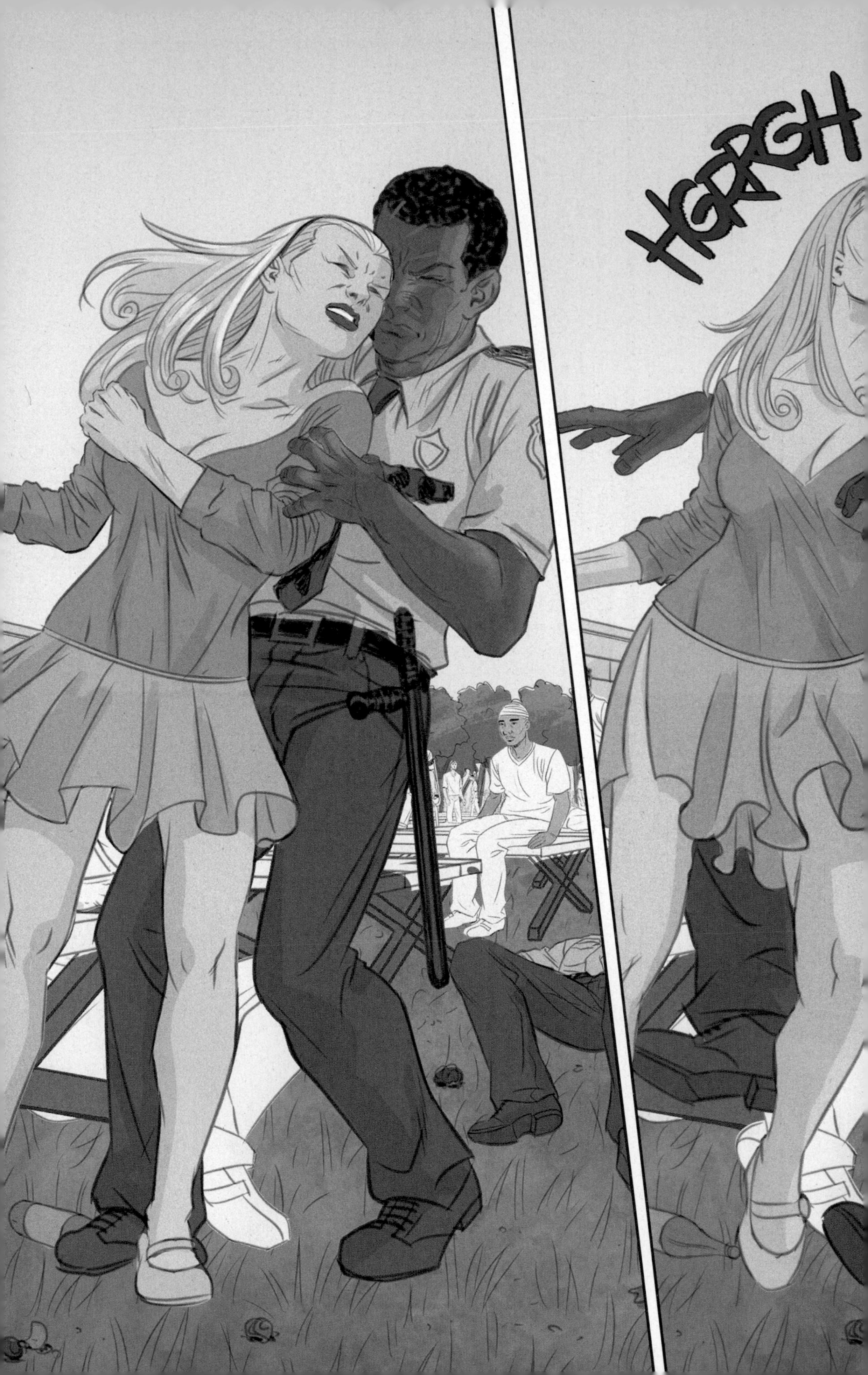
HGRGH

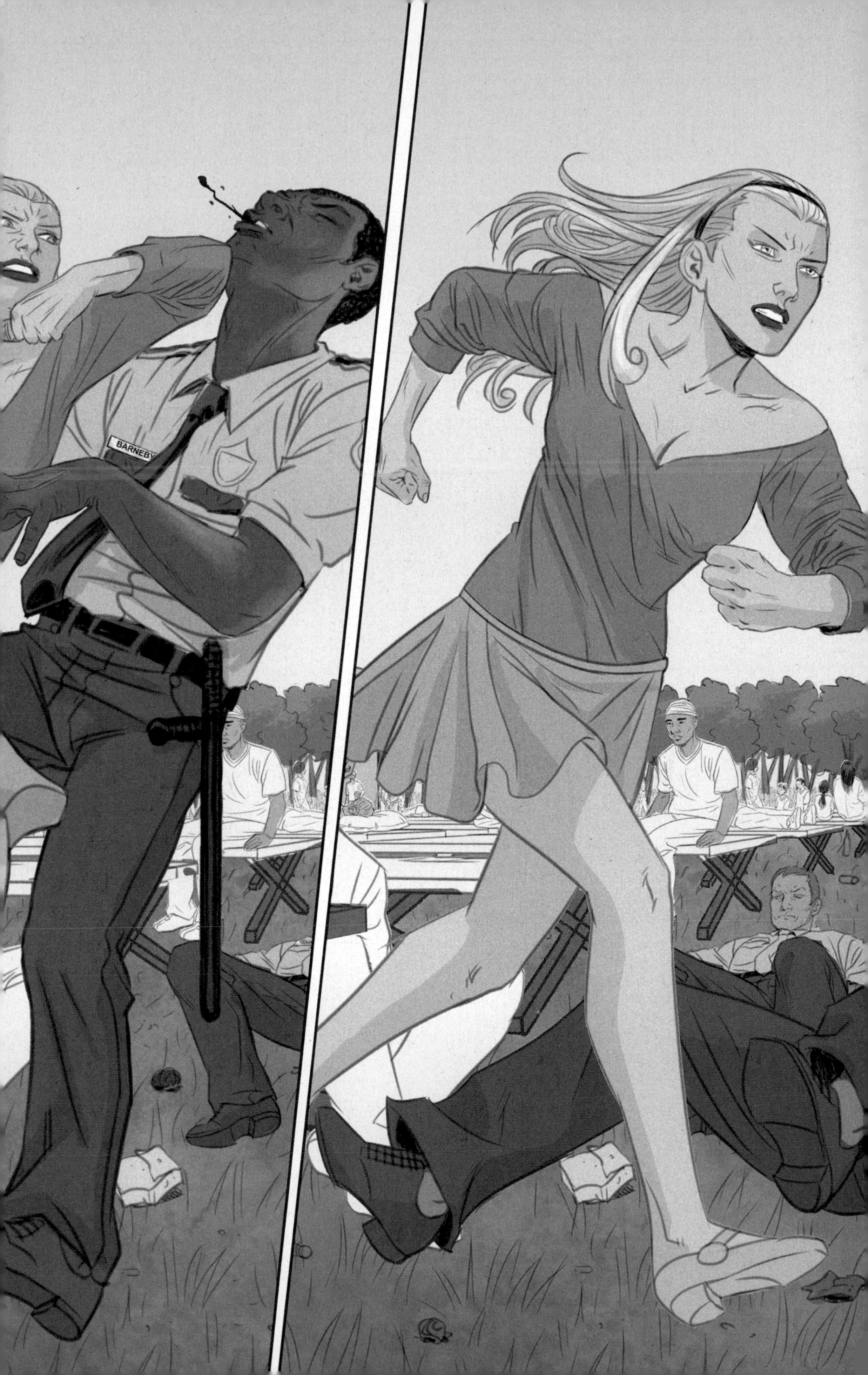
BARNEBY

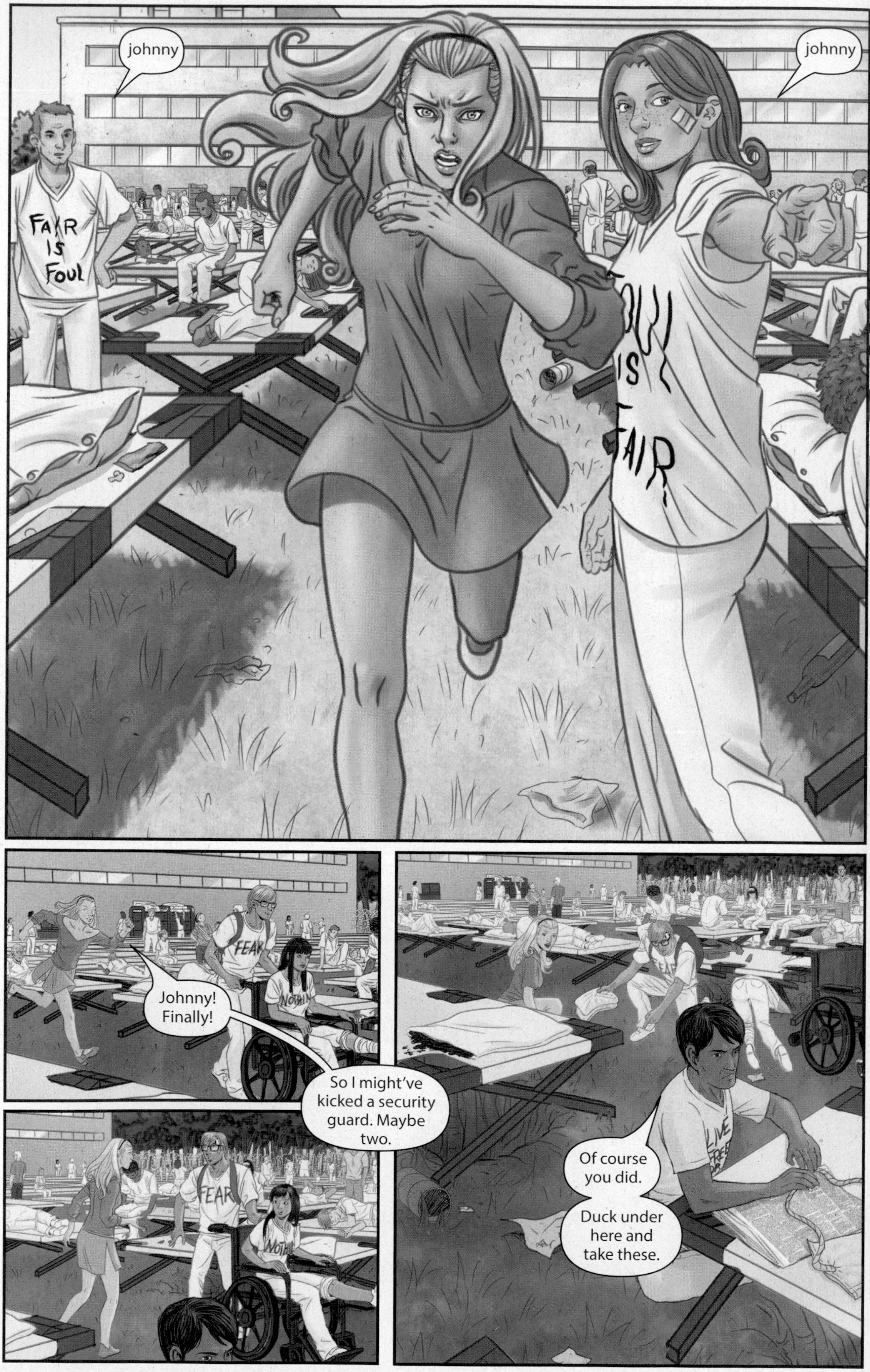
johnny
FAIR IS FOUL
johnny
Johnny! Finally!
FEAR
So I might've kicked a security guard. Maybe two.
Of course you did.
Duck under here and take these.

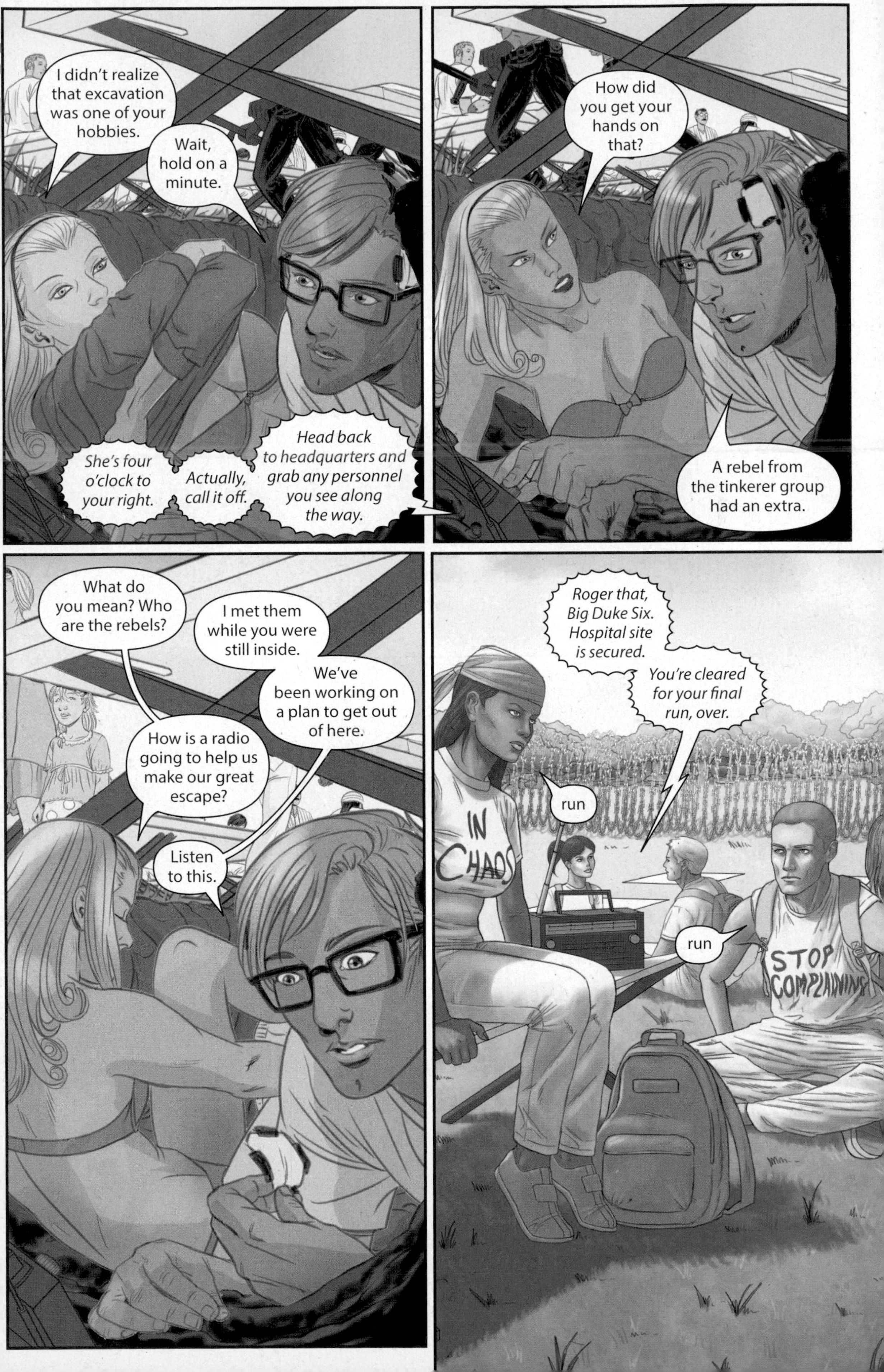
I didn't realize that excavation was one of your hobbies.
Wait, hold on a minute.
She's four o'clock to your right.
Actually, call it off.
Head back to headquarters and grab any personnel you see along the way.
How did you get your hands on that?
A rebel from the tinkerer group had an extra.
What do you mean? Who are the rebels?
I met them while you were still inside.
We've been working on a plan to get out of here.
How is a radio going to help us make our great escape?
Listen to this.
Roger that, Big Duke Six. Hospital site is secured.
You're cleared for your final run, over.
run
IN CHAOS
run
STOP COMPLAINING

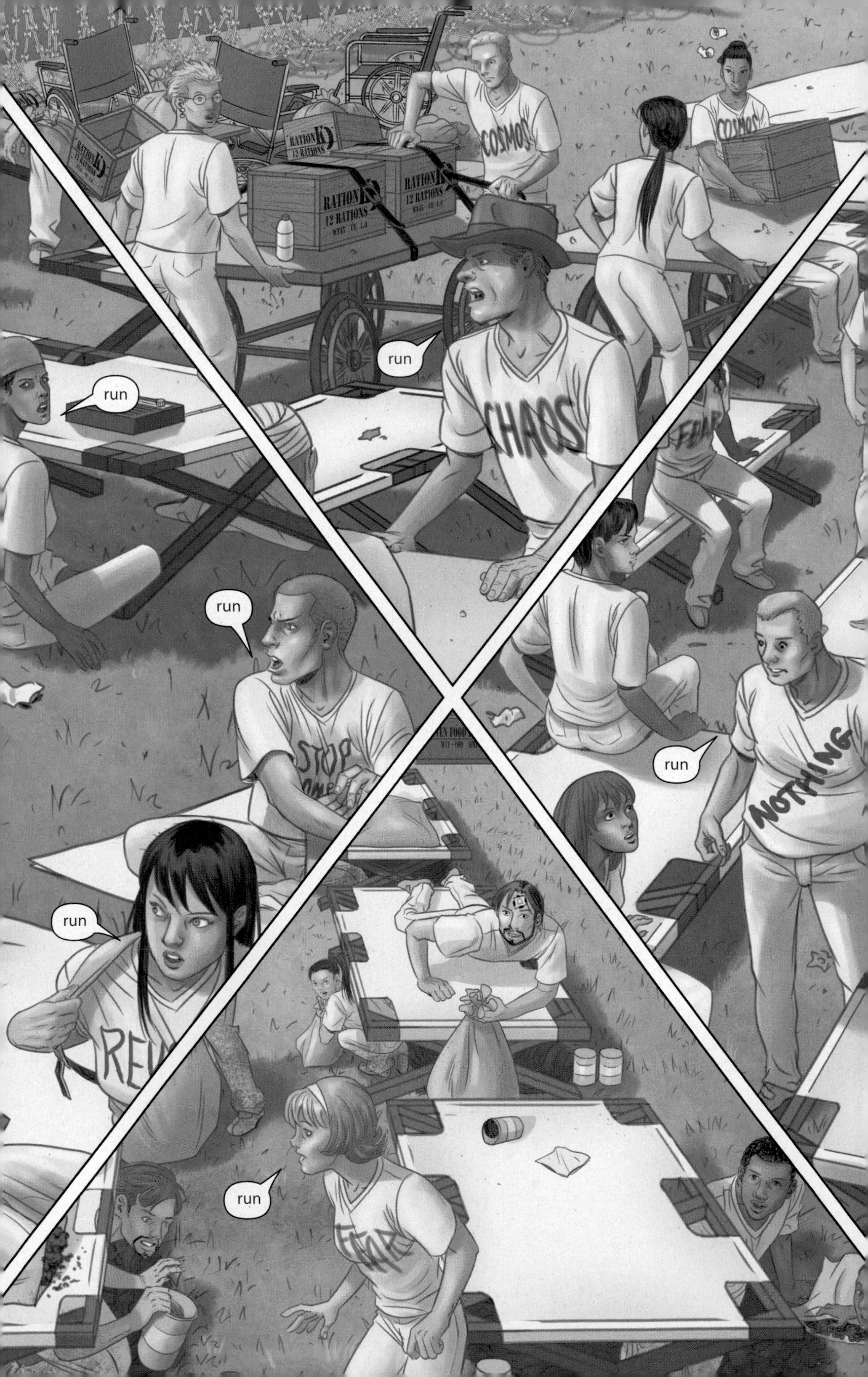

run
run
run
run
run
run

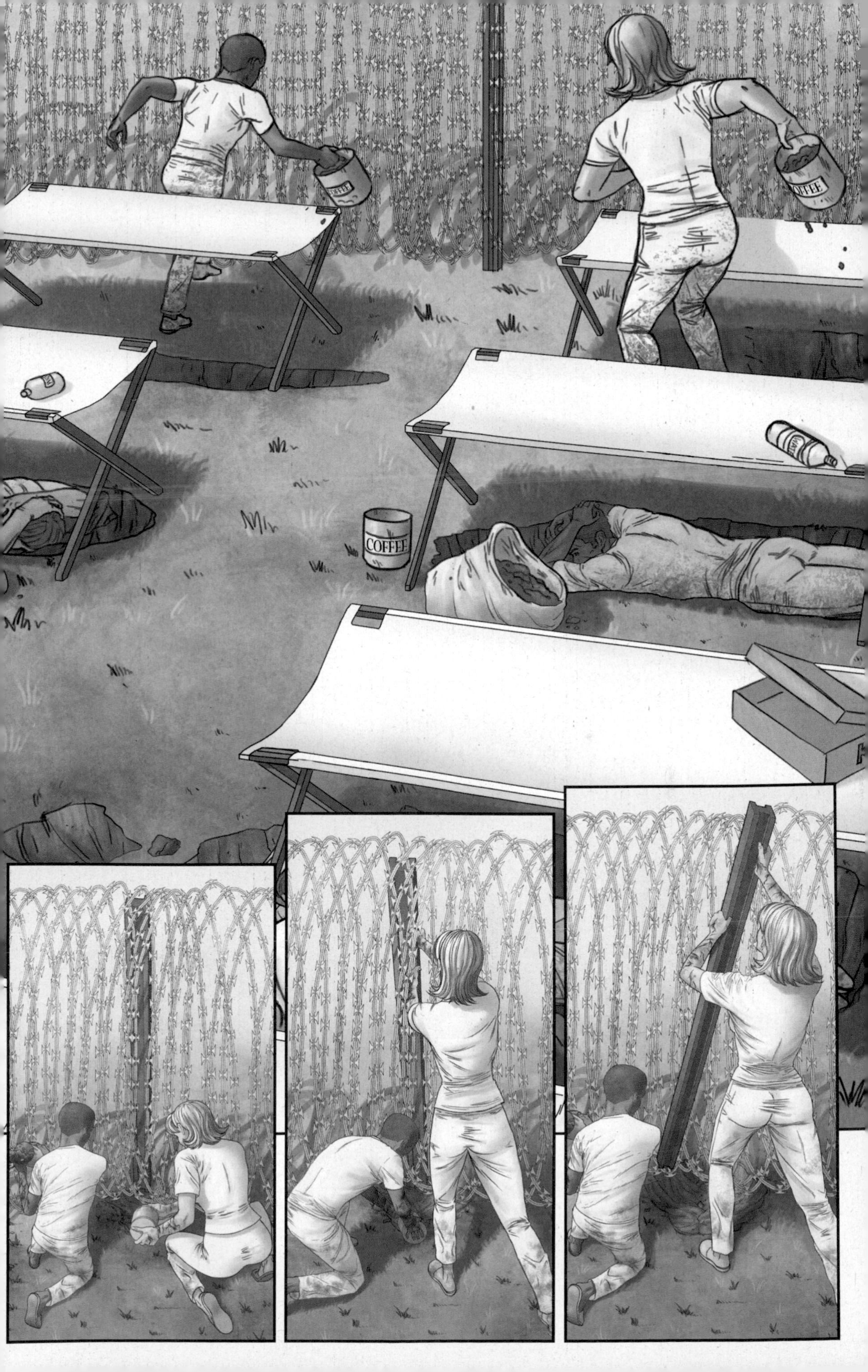
COFFEE
COFFEE
COFFEE

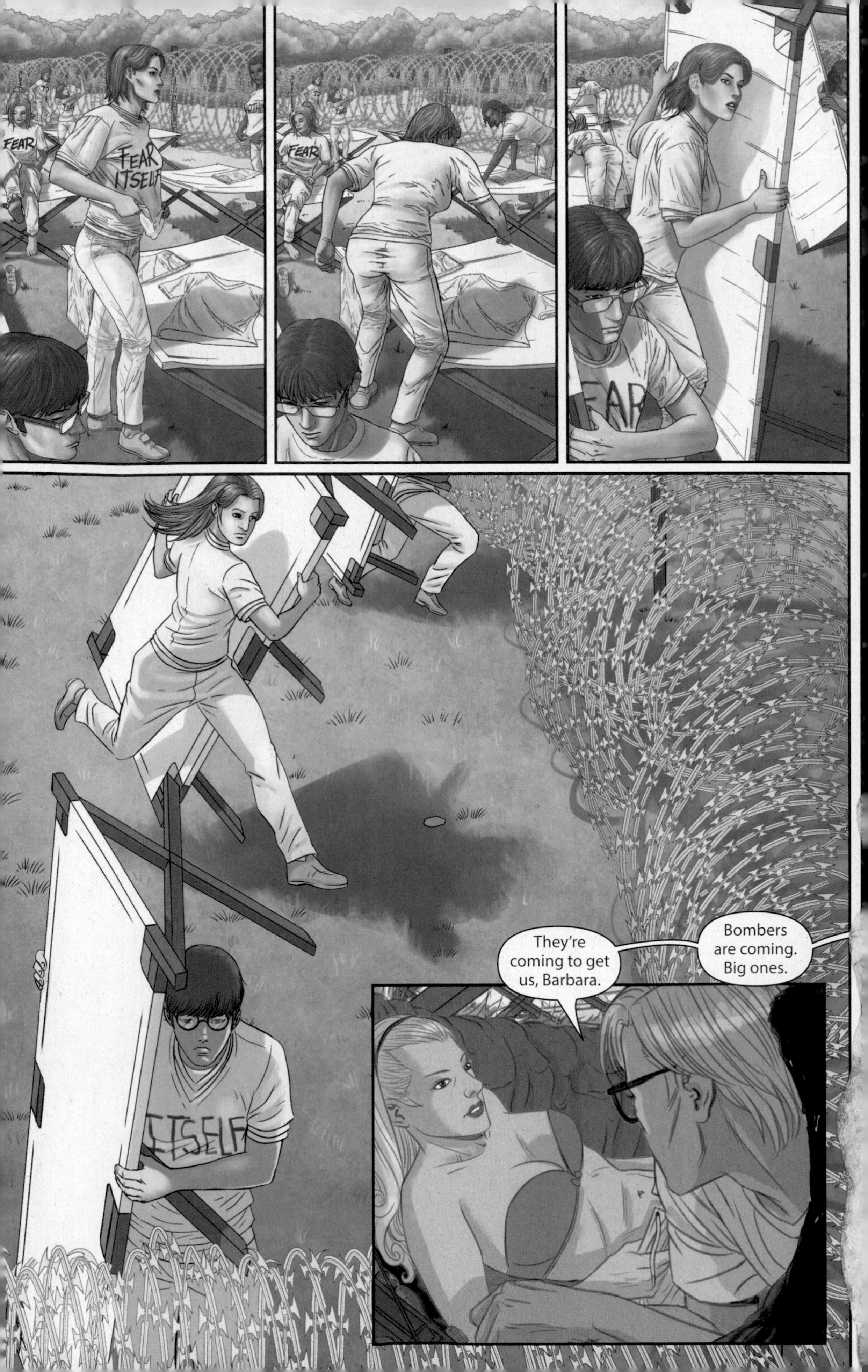
FEAR
FEAR ITSELF
NOTHIN
FEAR
FEAR
ITSELF
Bombers are coming. Big ones.
They're coming to get us, Barbara.

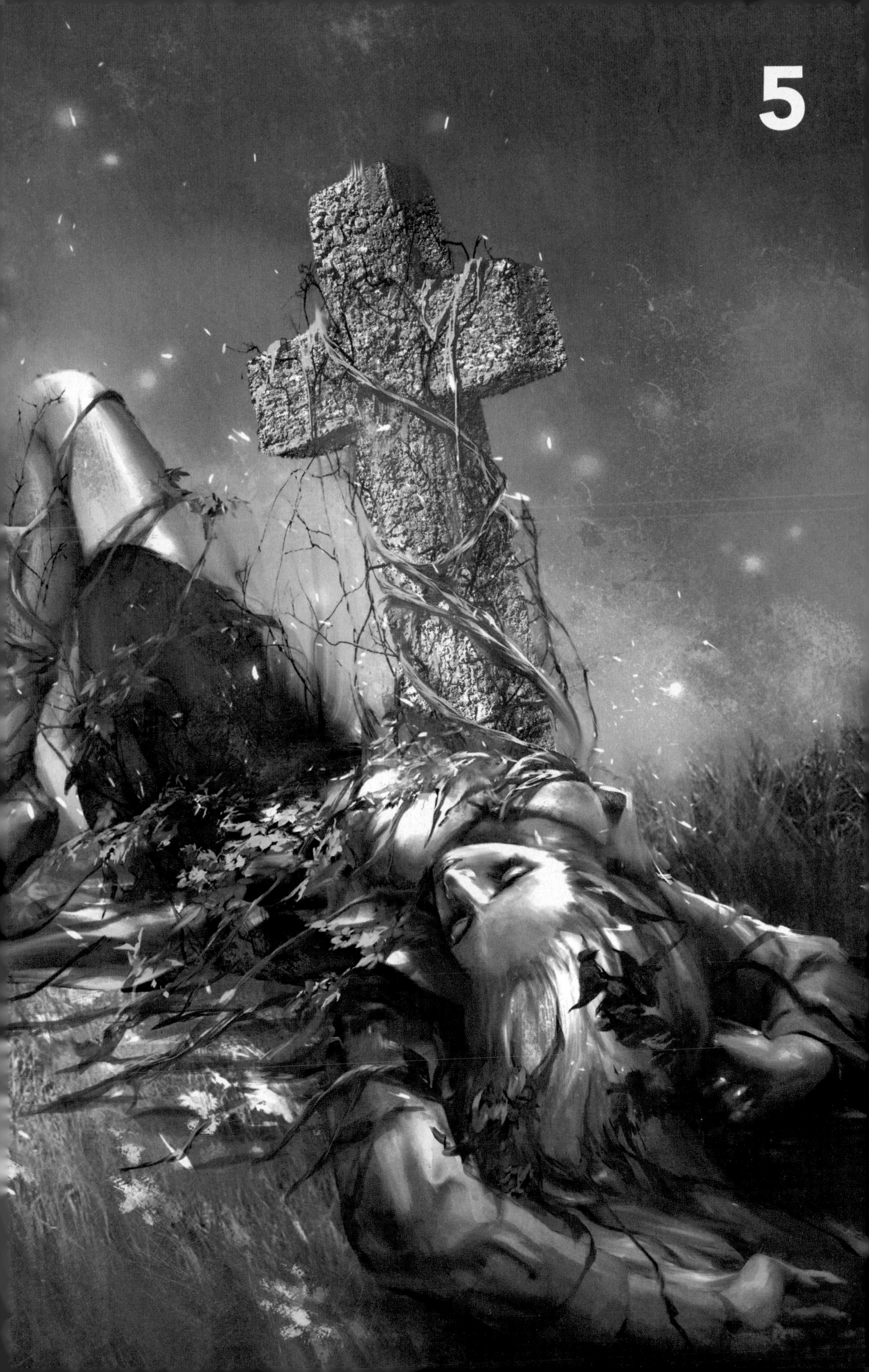
5

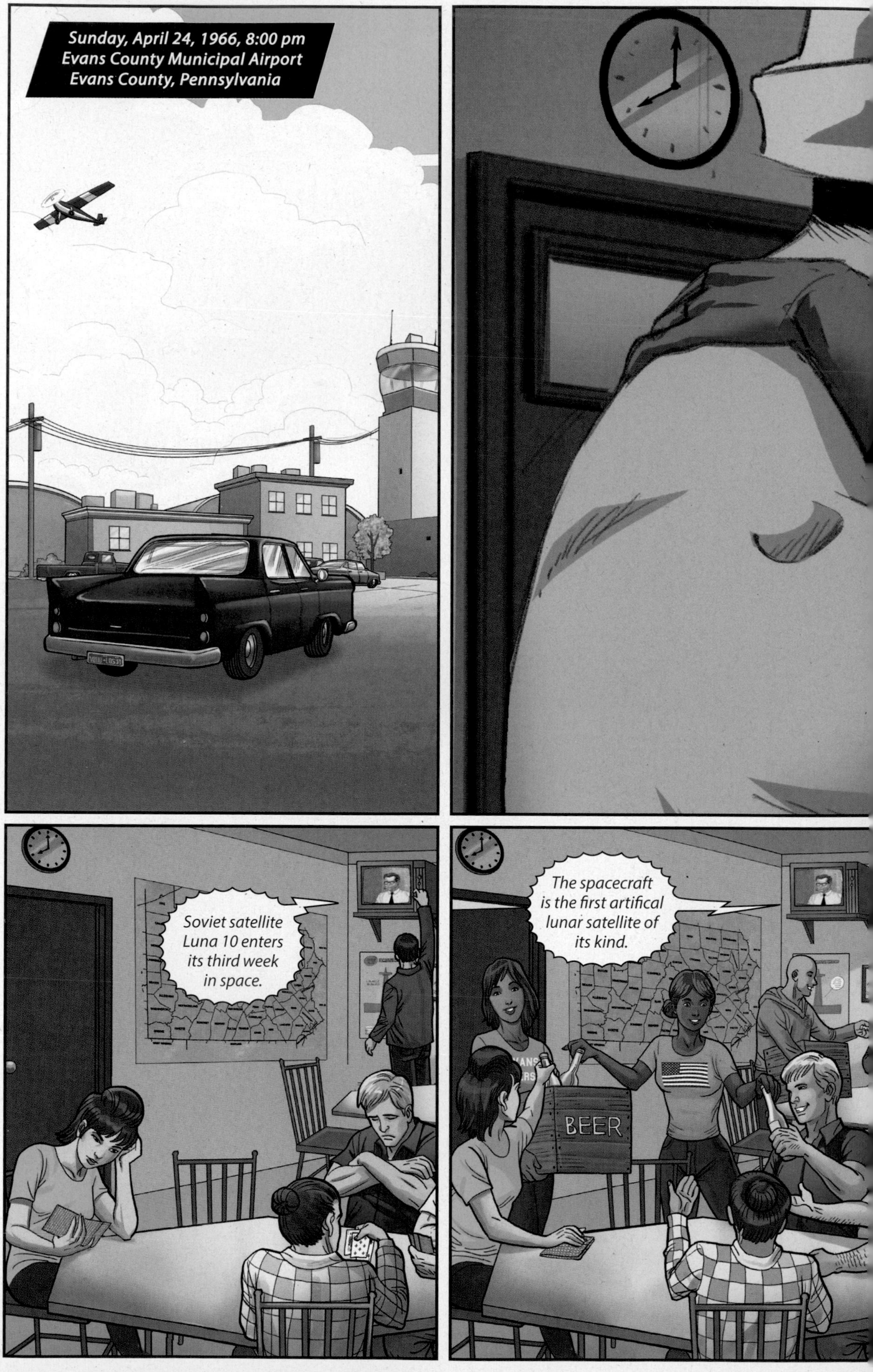
Sunday, April 24, 1966, 8:00 pm
Evans County Municipal Airport
Evans County, Pennsylvania
Soviet satellite Luna 10 enters its third week in space.
The spacecraft is the first artifical lunar satellite of its kind.
BEER

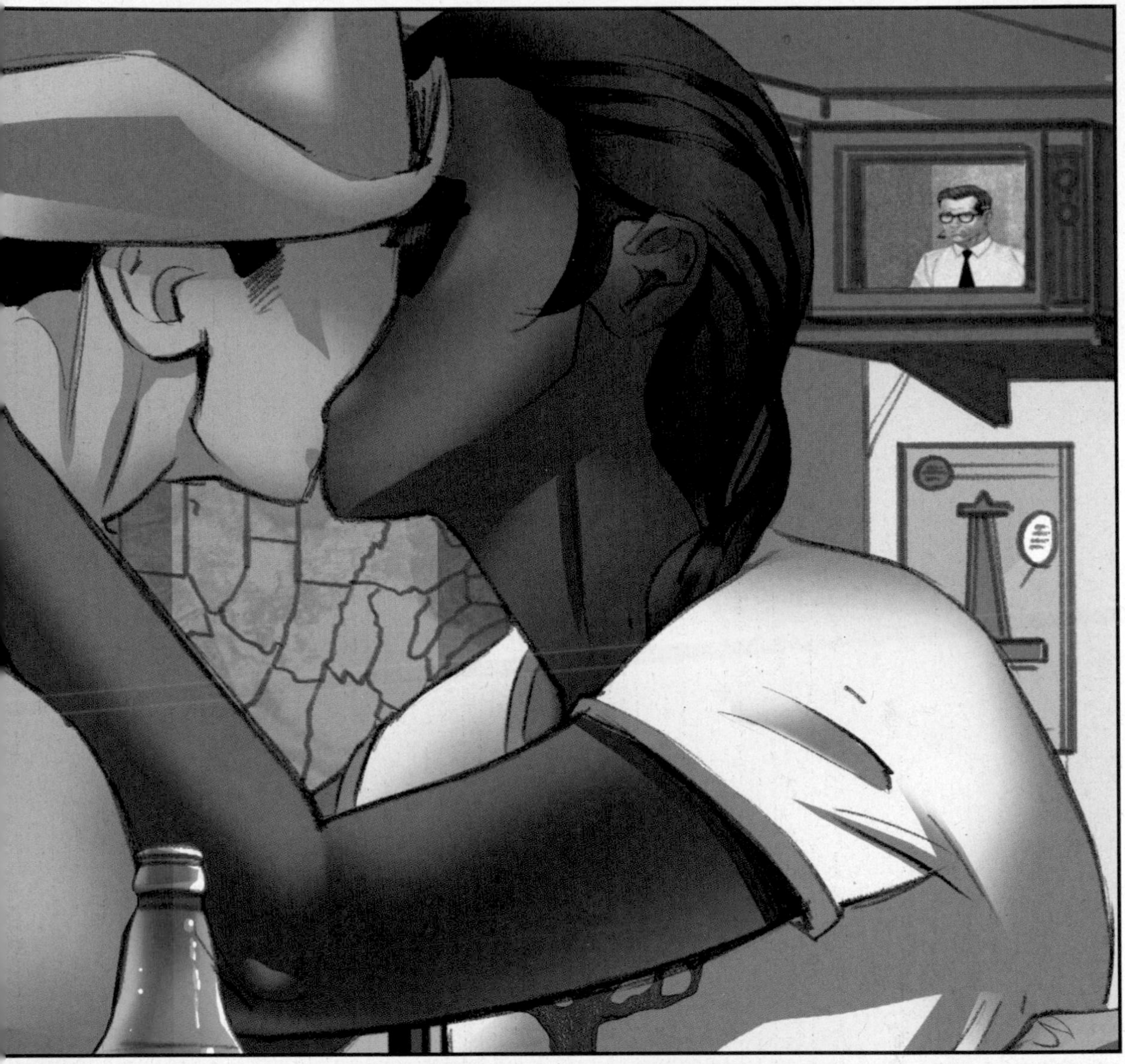

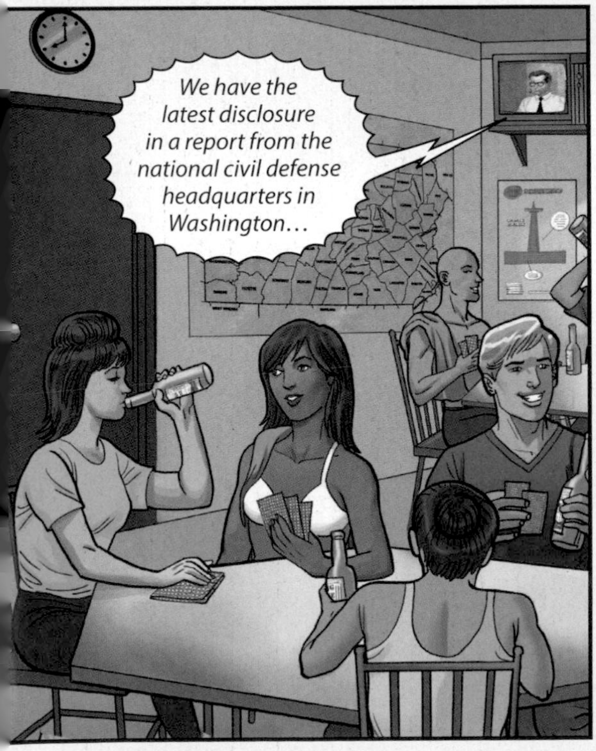
We have the latest disclosure in a report from the national civil defense headquarters in Washington…

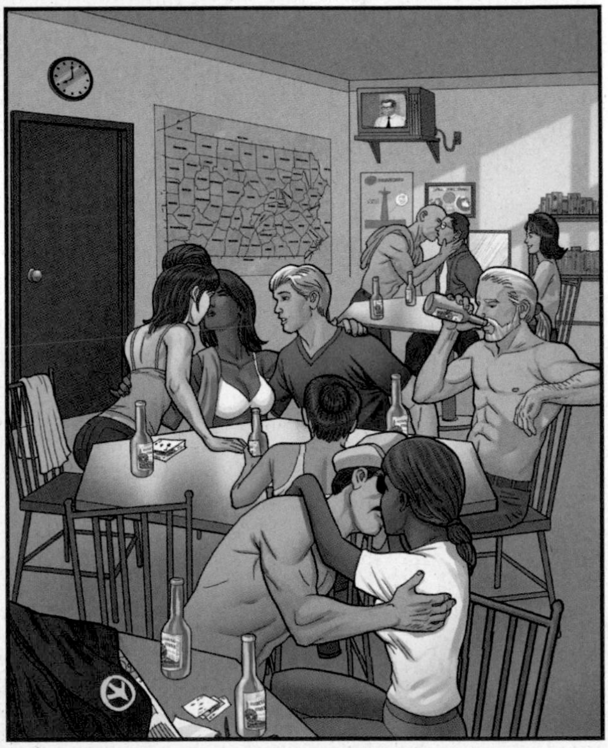

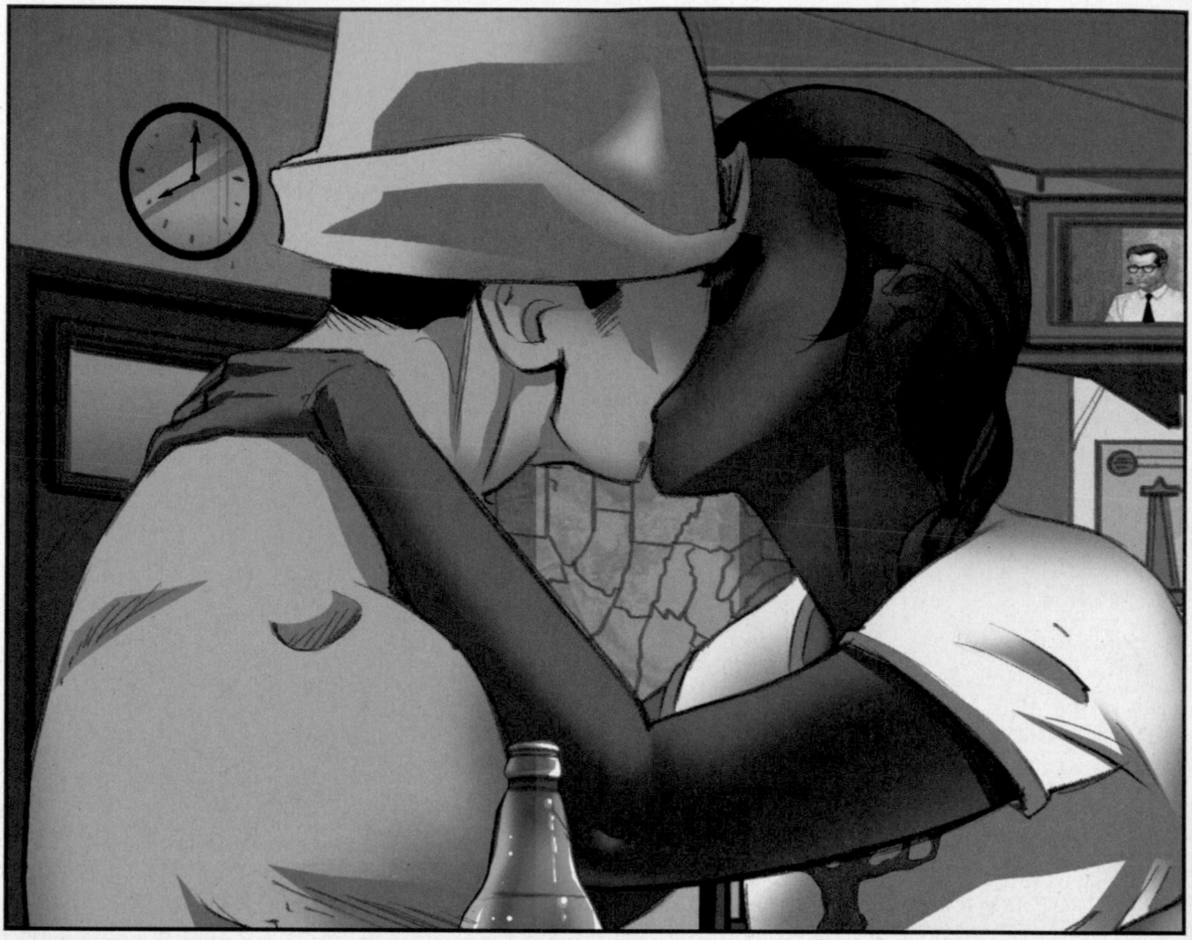

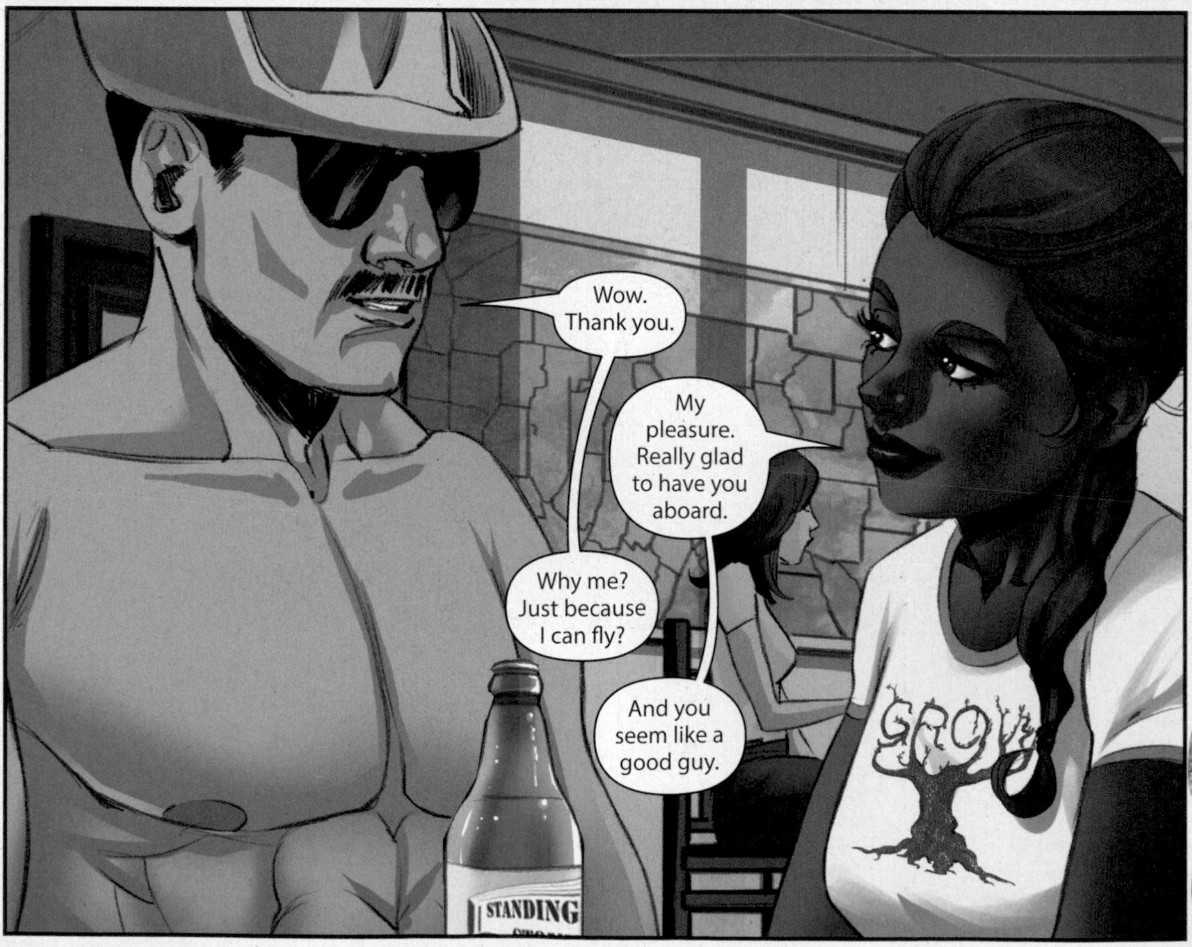
Wow.
Thank you.
My pleasure. Really glad to have you aboard.
Why me? Just because I can fly?
And you seem like a good guy.
GROW
STANDING

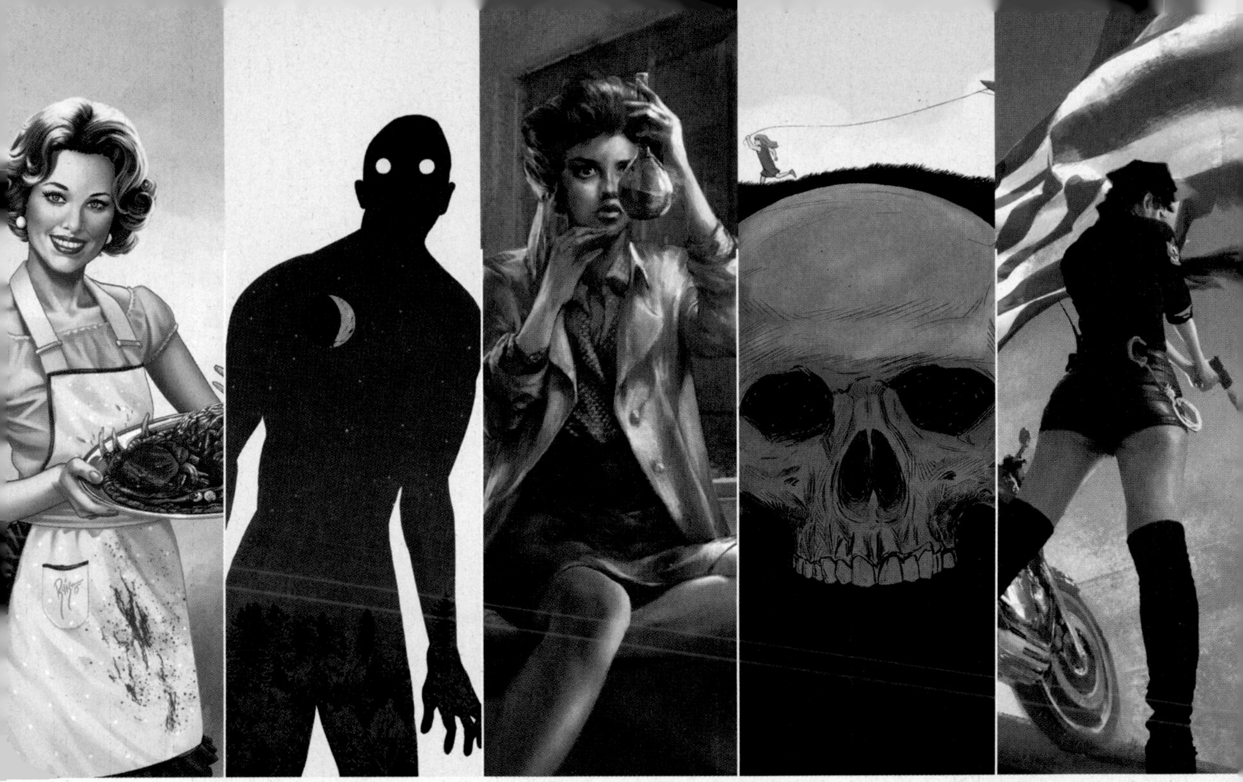

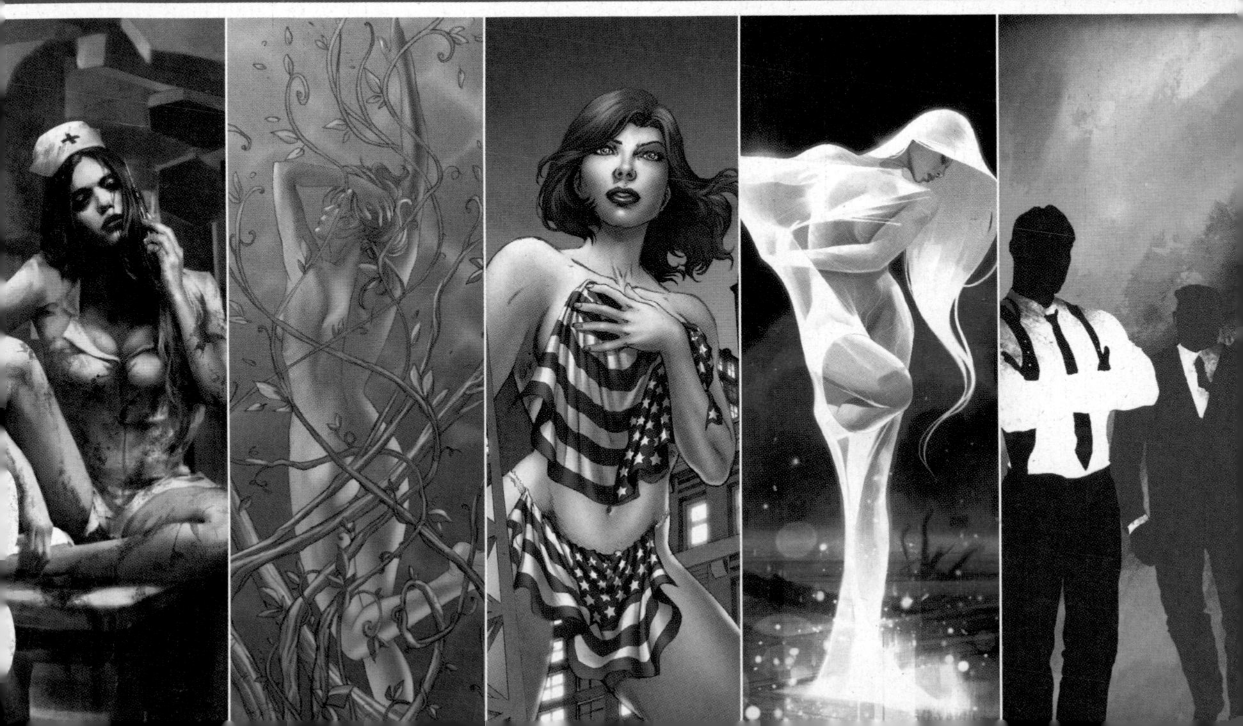

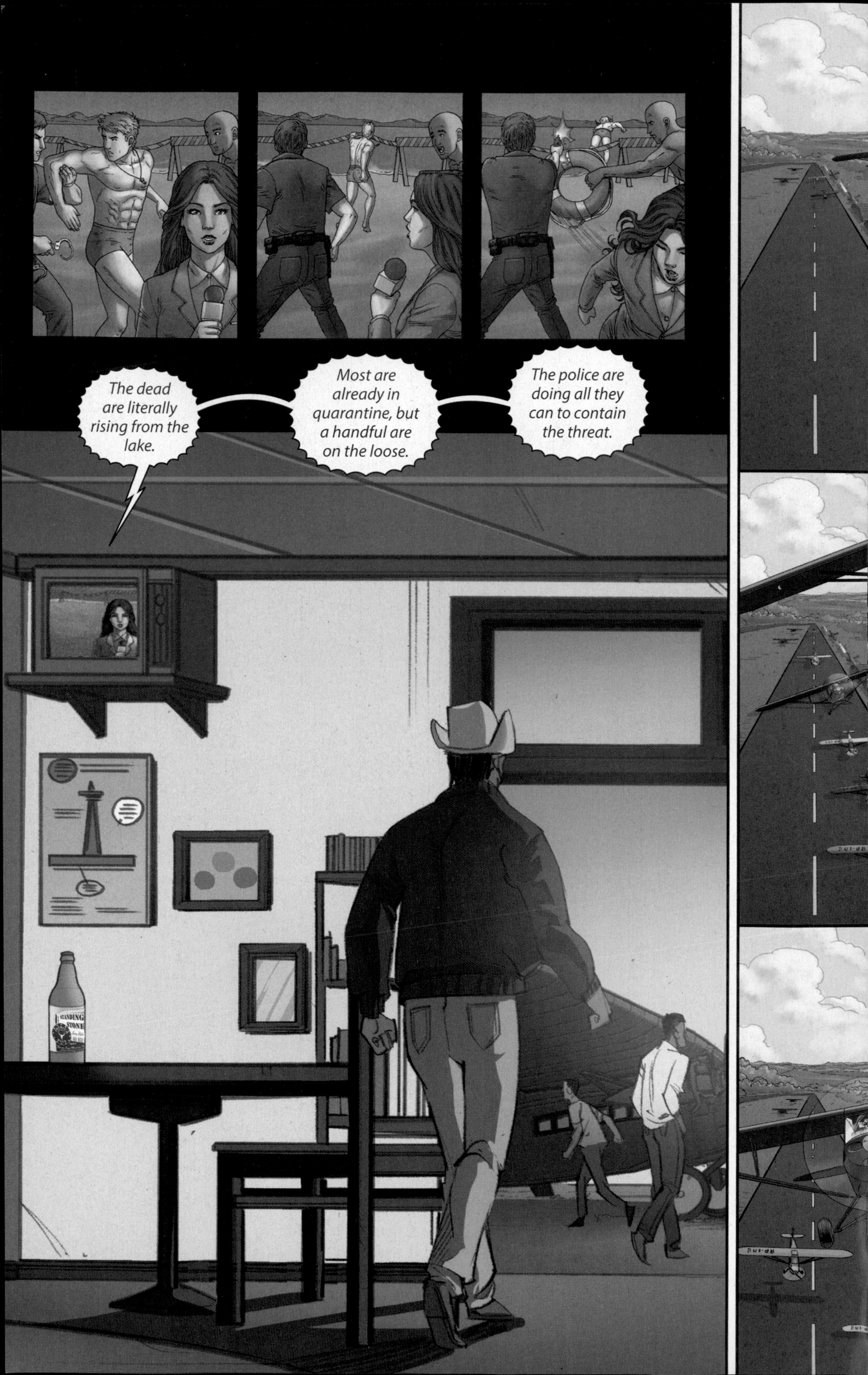
The dead are literally rising from the lake.
Most are already in quarantine, but a handful are on the loose.
The police are doing all they can to contain the threat.
STANDING STONE

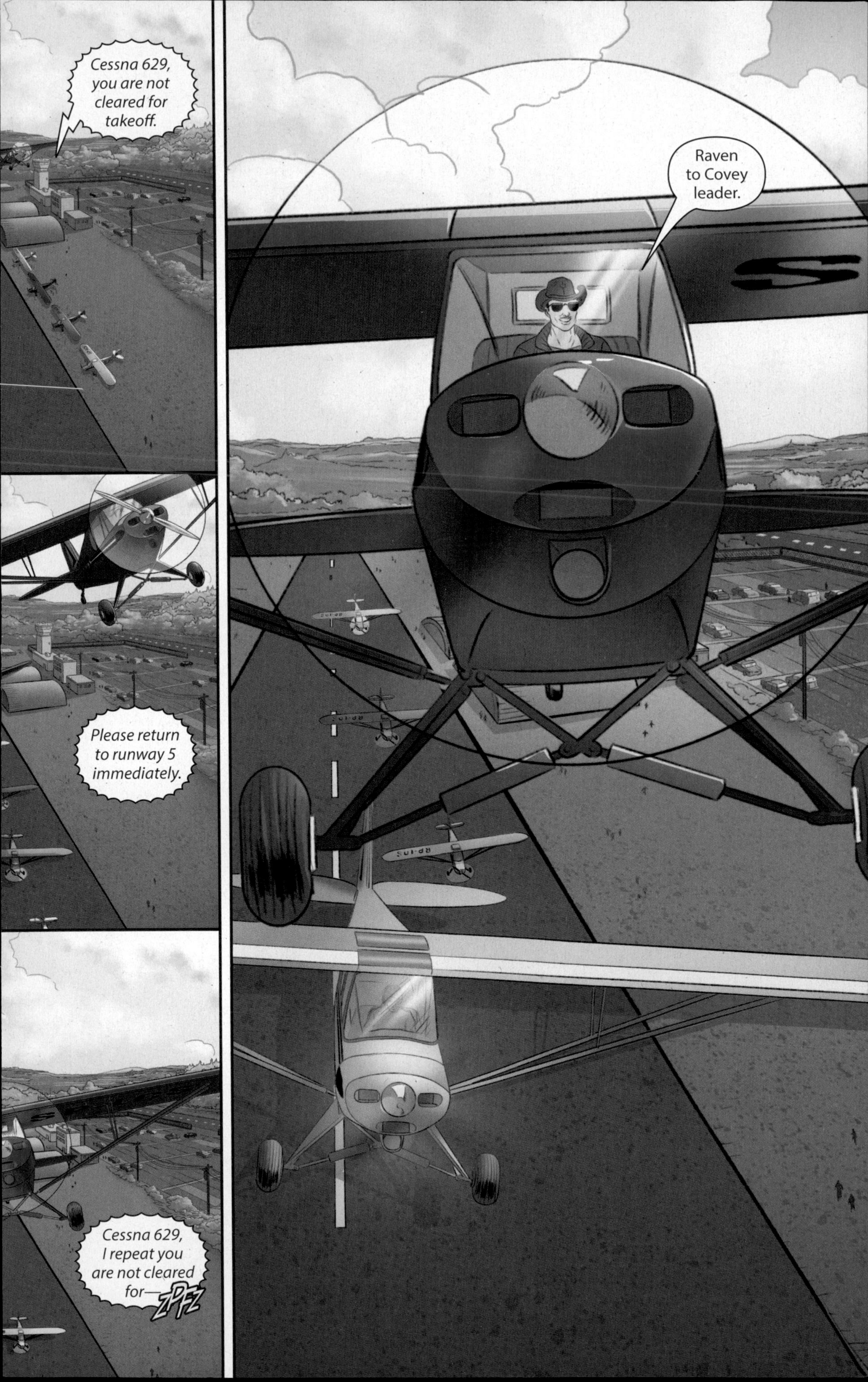
Cessna 629, you are not cleared for takeoff.
Raven to Covey leader.
Please return to runway 5 immediately.
Cessna 629, I repeat you are not cleared for—
ZPFZ

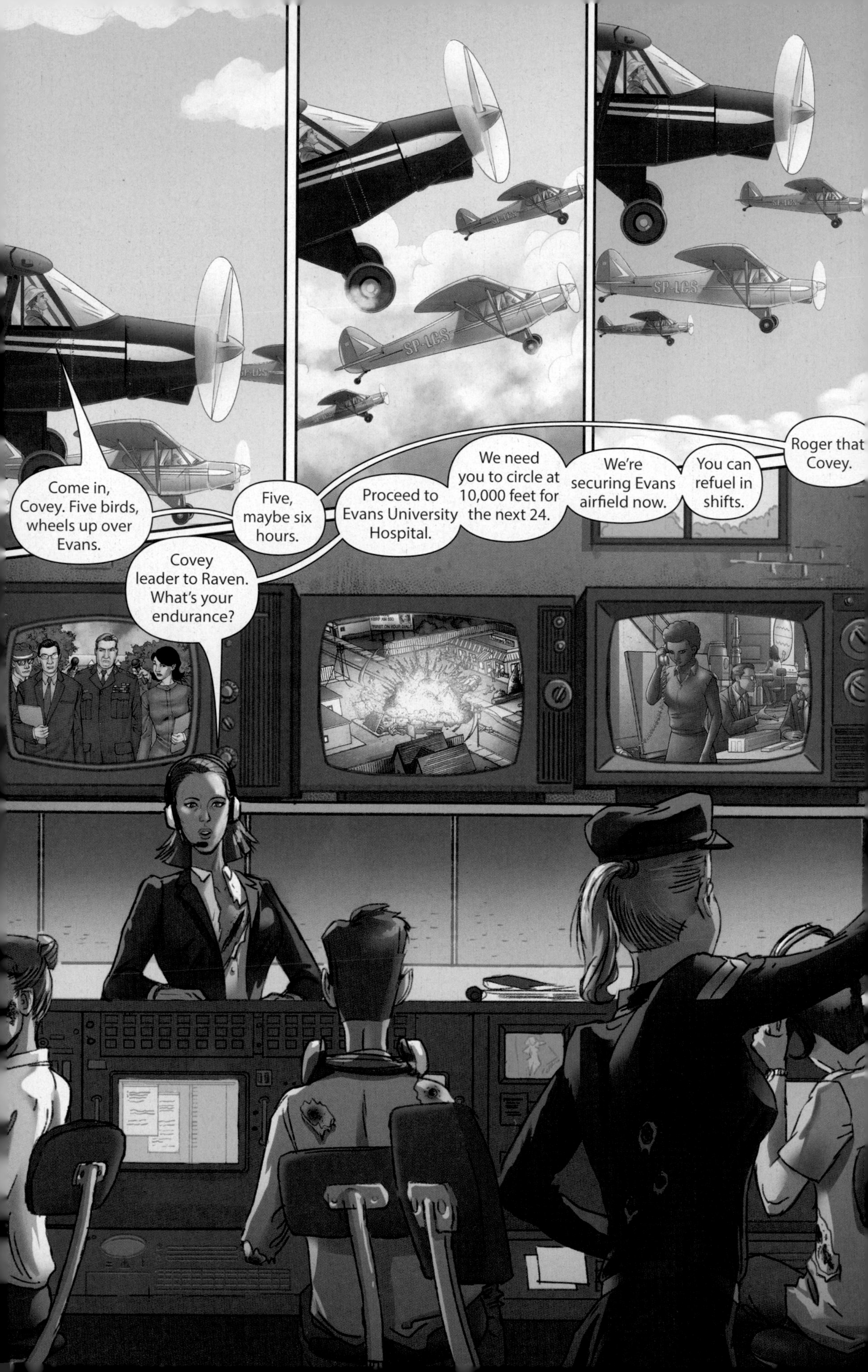
Come in, Covey. Five birds, wheels up over Evans.
Covey leader to Raven. What's your endurance?
Five, maybe six hours.
Proceed to Evans University Hospital.
We need you to circle at 10,000 feet for the next 24.
We're securing Evans airfield now.
You can refuel in shifts.
Roger that Covey.

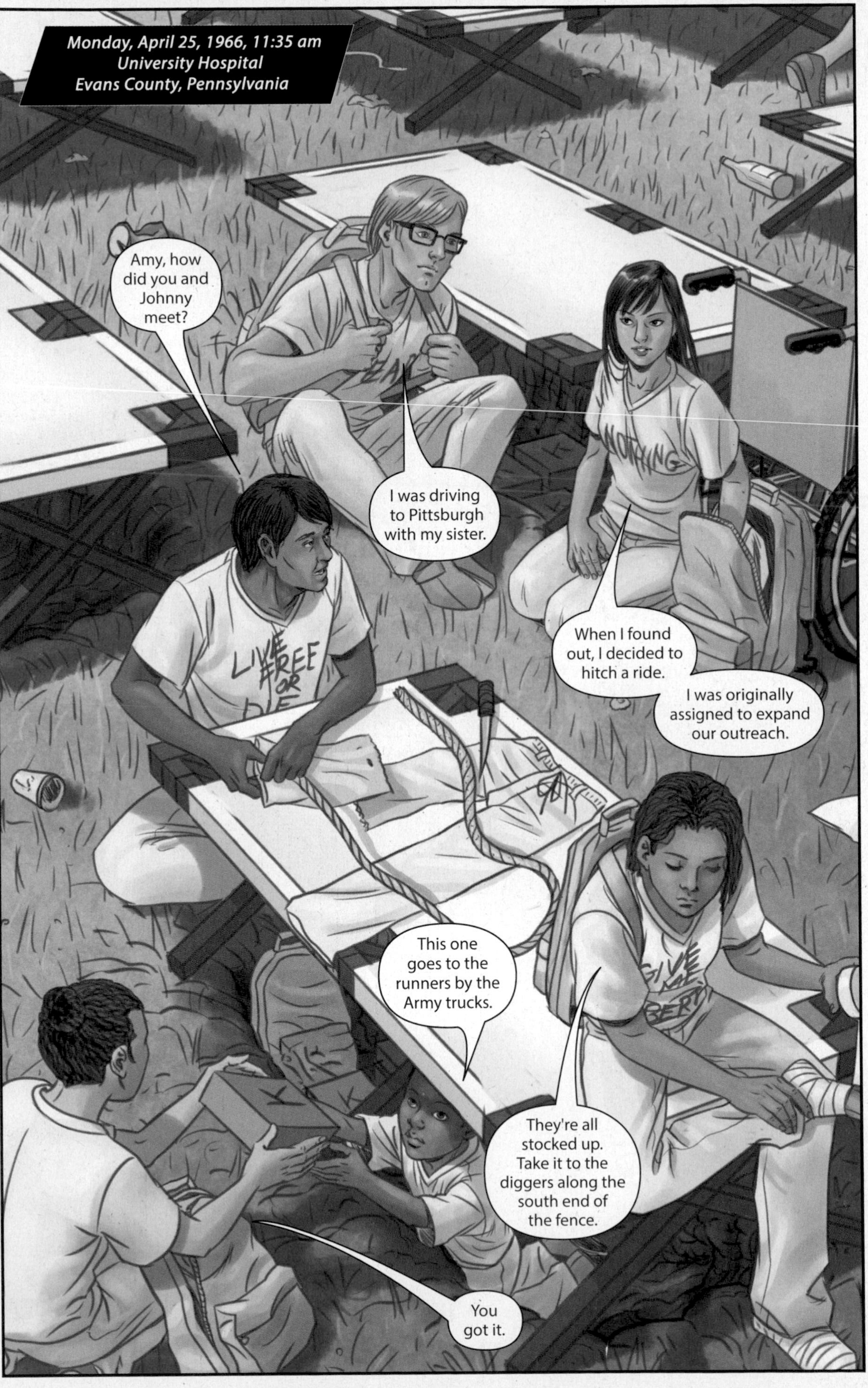

Monday, April 25, 1966, 11:35 am
University Hospital
Evans County, Pennsylvania
Amy, how did you and Johnny meet?
I was driving to Pittsburgh with my sister.
When I found out, I decided to hitch a ride.
I was originally assigned to expand our outreach.
This one goes to the runners by the Army trucks.
They're all stocked up. Take it to the diggers along the south end of the fence.
You got it.

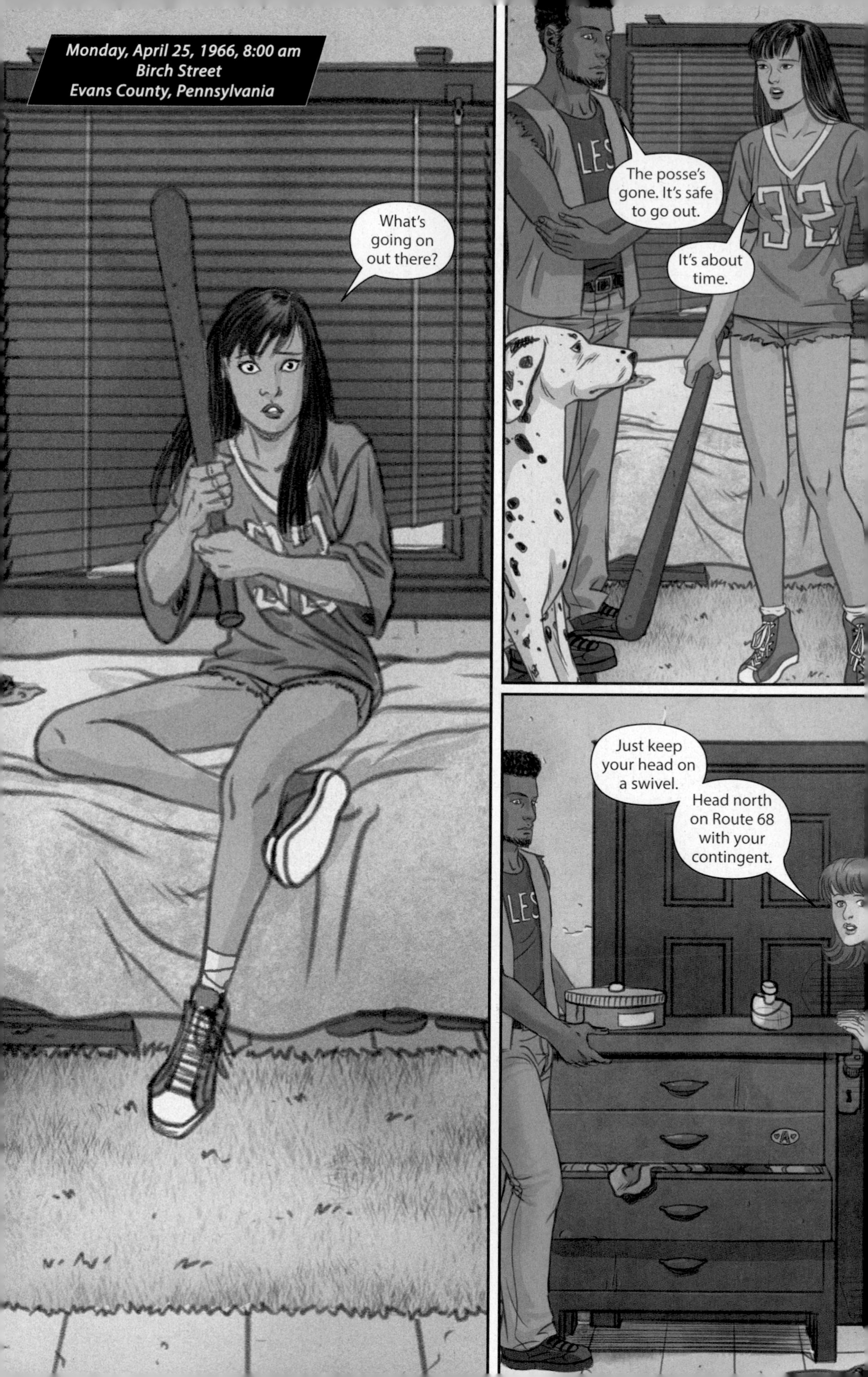

Monday, April 25, 1966, 8:00 am
Birch Street
Evans County, Pennsylvania
What's going on out there?
The posse's gone. It's safe to go out.
It's about time.
Just keep your head on a swivel.
Head north on Route 68 with your contingent.

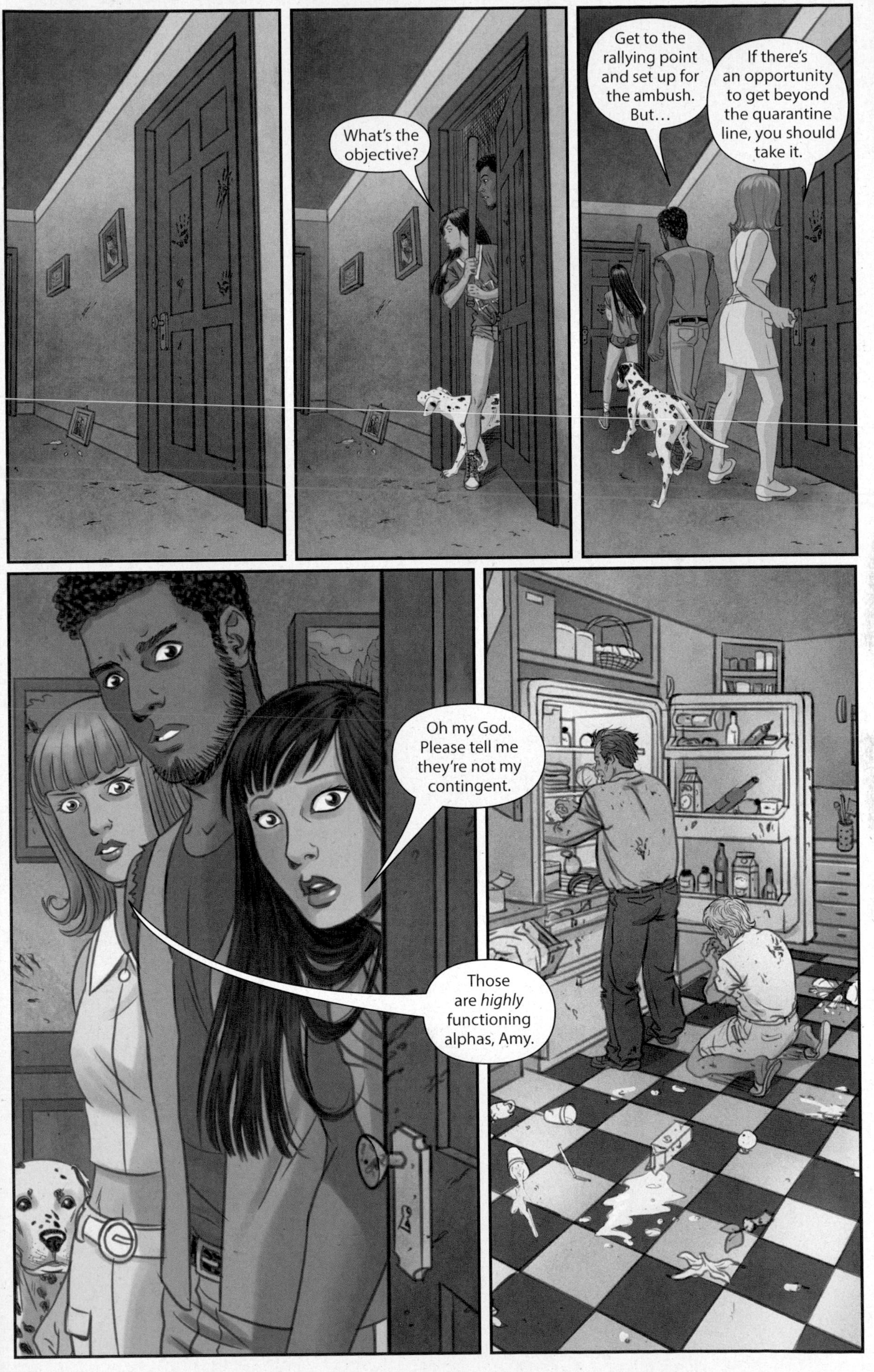
What's the objective?
Get to the rallying point and set up for the ambush. But…
If there's an opportunity to get beyond the quarantine line, you should take it.
Oh my God. Please tell me they're not my contingent.
Those are *highly* functioning alphas, Amy.

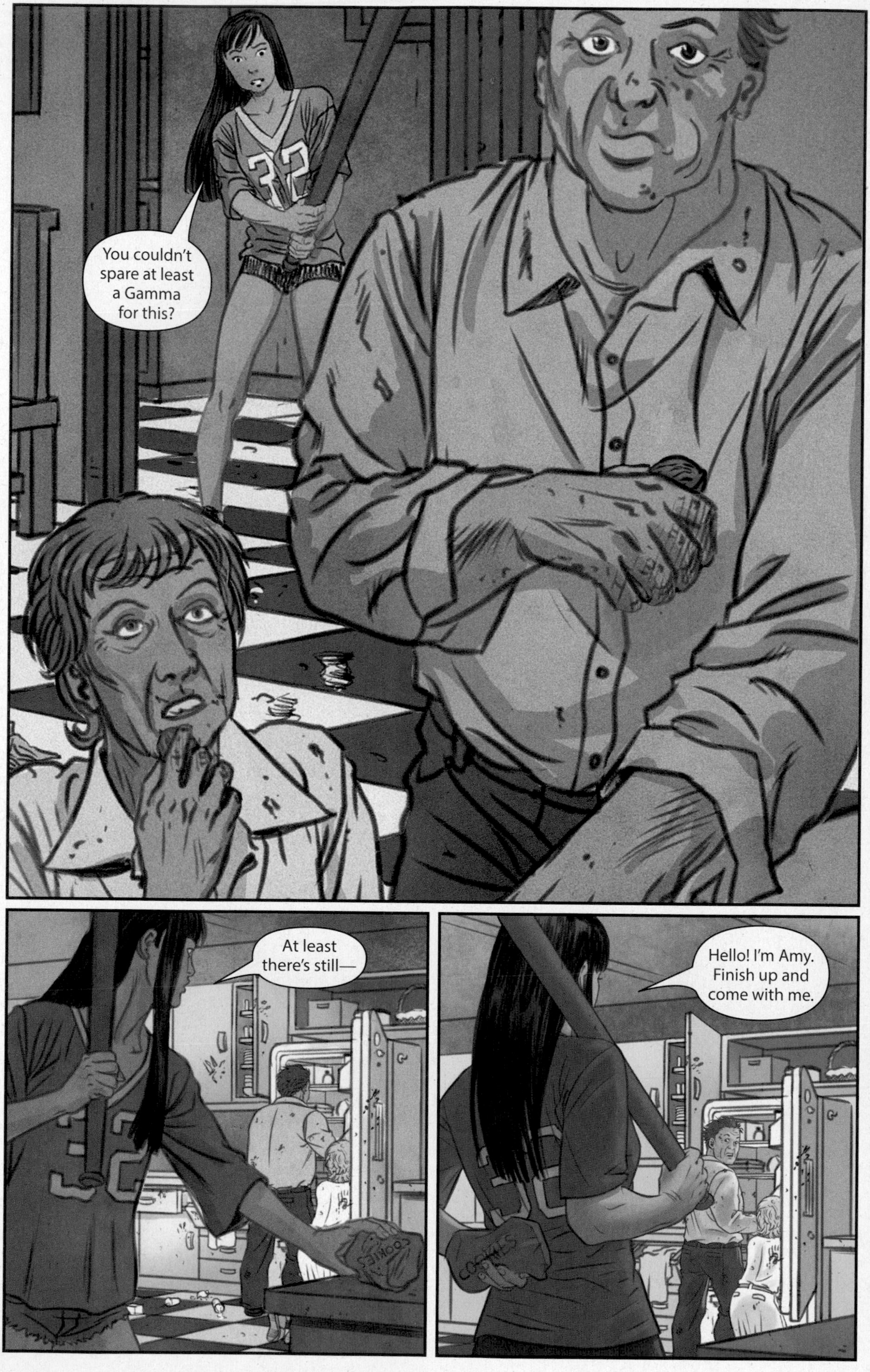
You couldn't spare at least a Gamma for this?
At least there's still—
Hello! I'm Amy. Finish up and come with me.

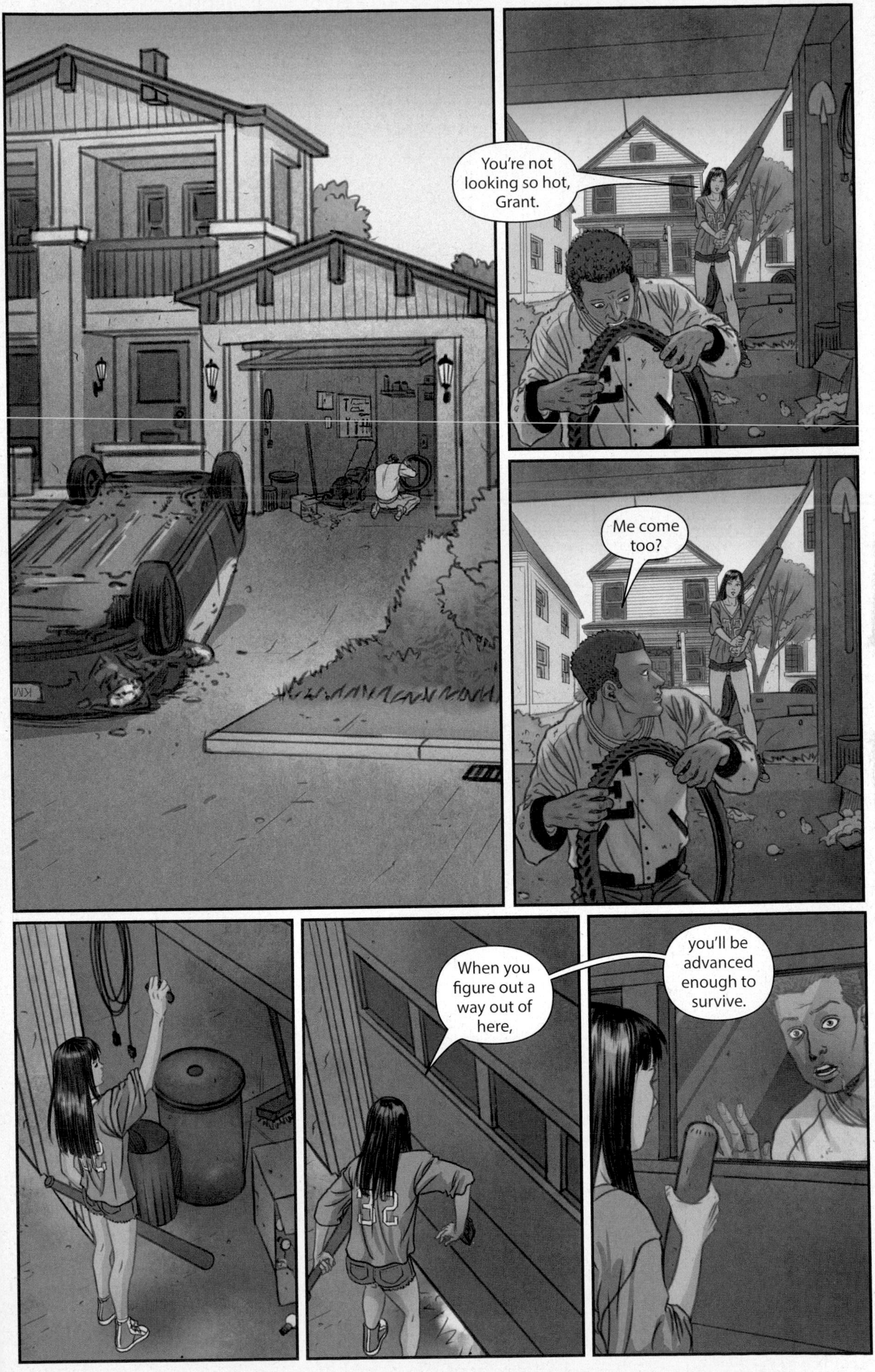
You're not looking so hot, Grant.
Me come too?
When you figure out a way out of here,
you'll be advanced enough to survive.

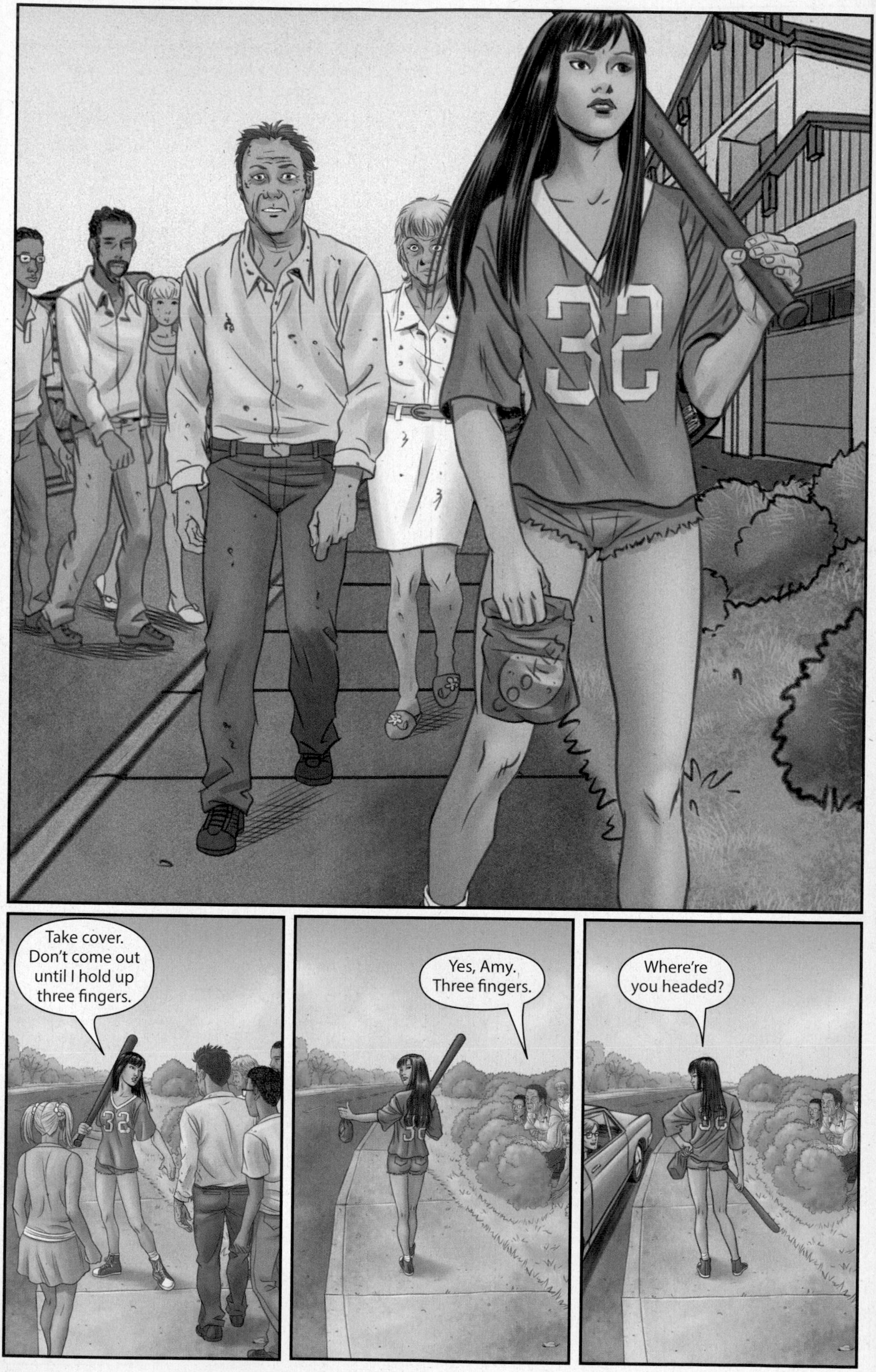
Take cover. Don't come out until I hold up three fingers.
Yes, Amy. Three fingers.
Where're you headed?

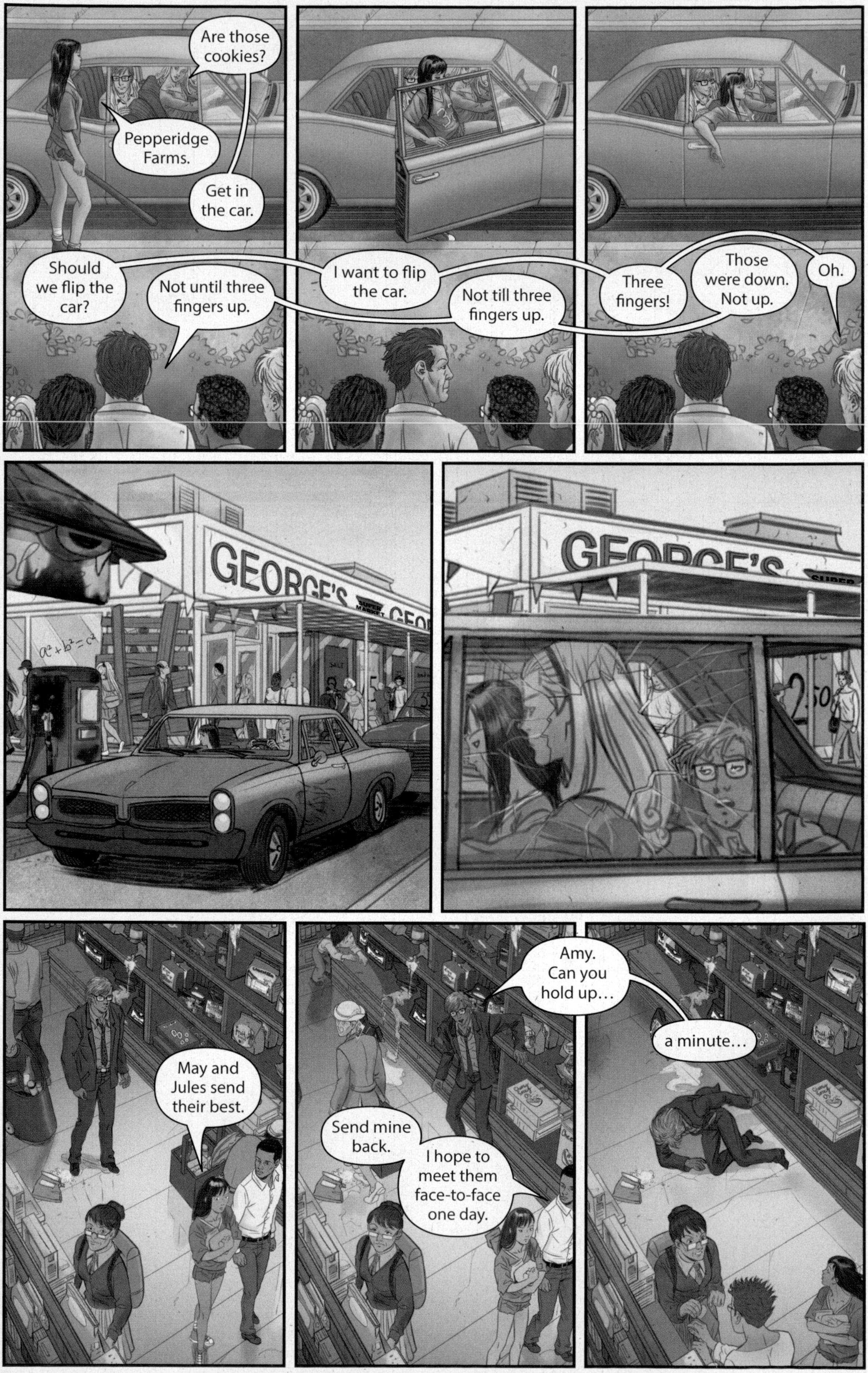
Are those cookies?
Pepperidge Farms.
Get in the car.
Should we flip the car?
Not until three fingers up.
I want to flip the car.
Not till three fingers up.
Three fingers!
Those were down. Not up.
Oh.
GEORGE'S
SUPER MARKET
GEORGE'S
May and Jules send their best.
Amy. Can you hold up…
Send mine back.
I hope to meet them face-to-face one day.
a minute…

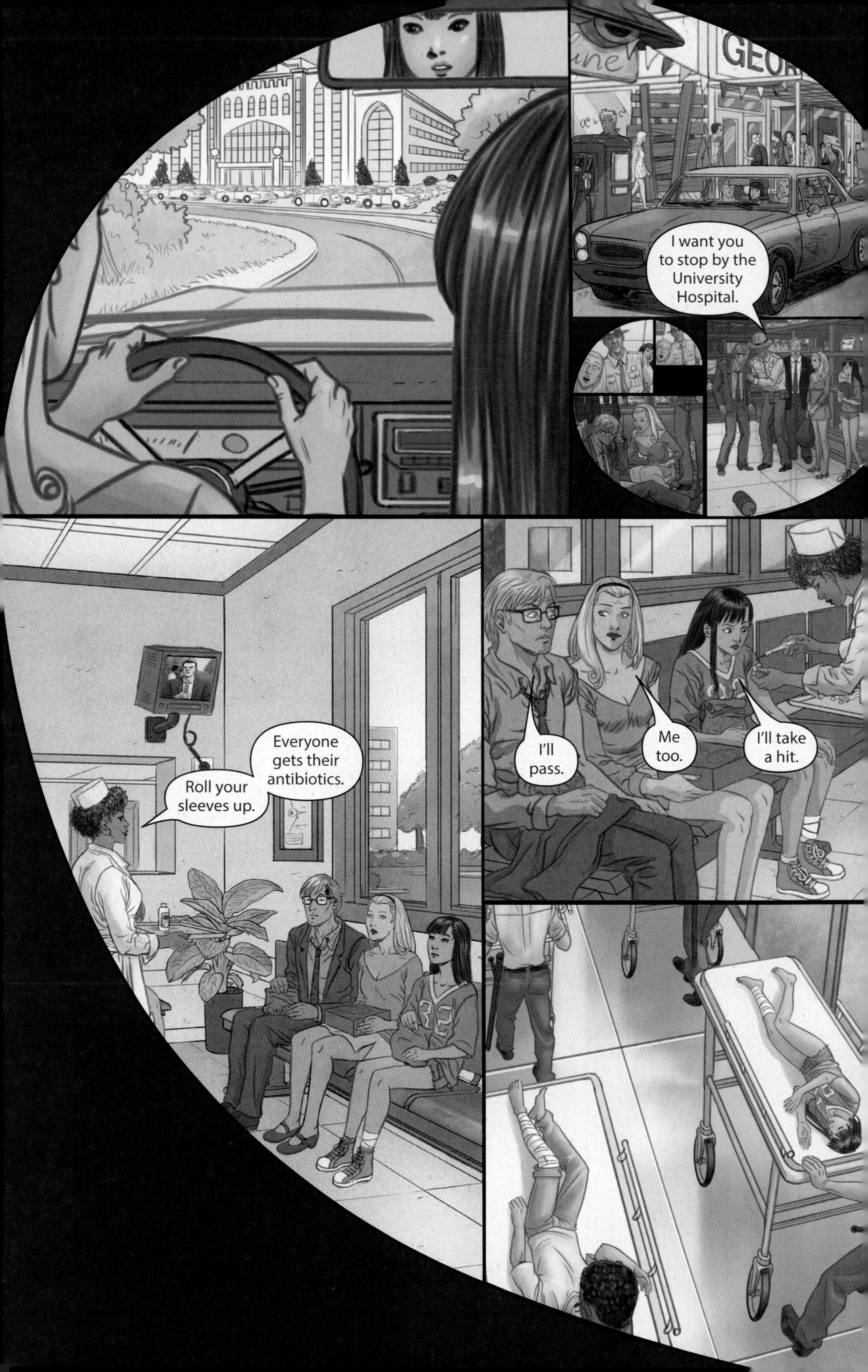

I want you to stop by the University Hospital.
Everyone gets their antibiotics.
Roll your sleeves up.
I'll pass.
Me too.
I'll take a hit.

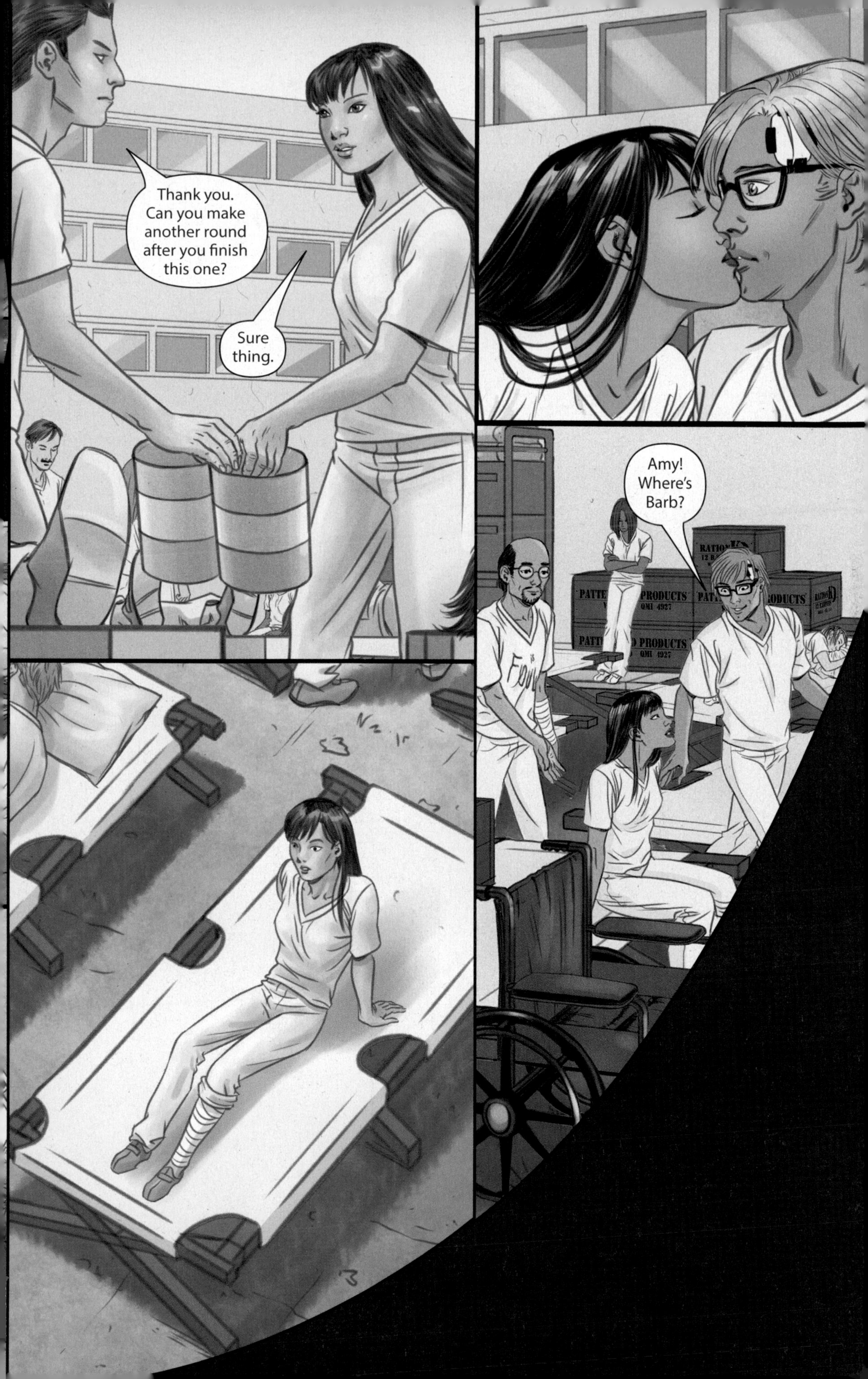
Thank you. Can you make another round after you finish this one?
Sure thing.
Amy! Where's Barb?

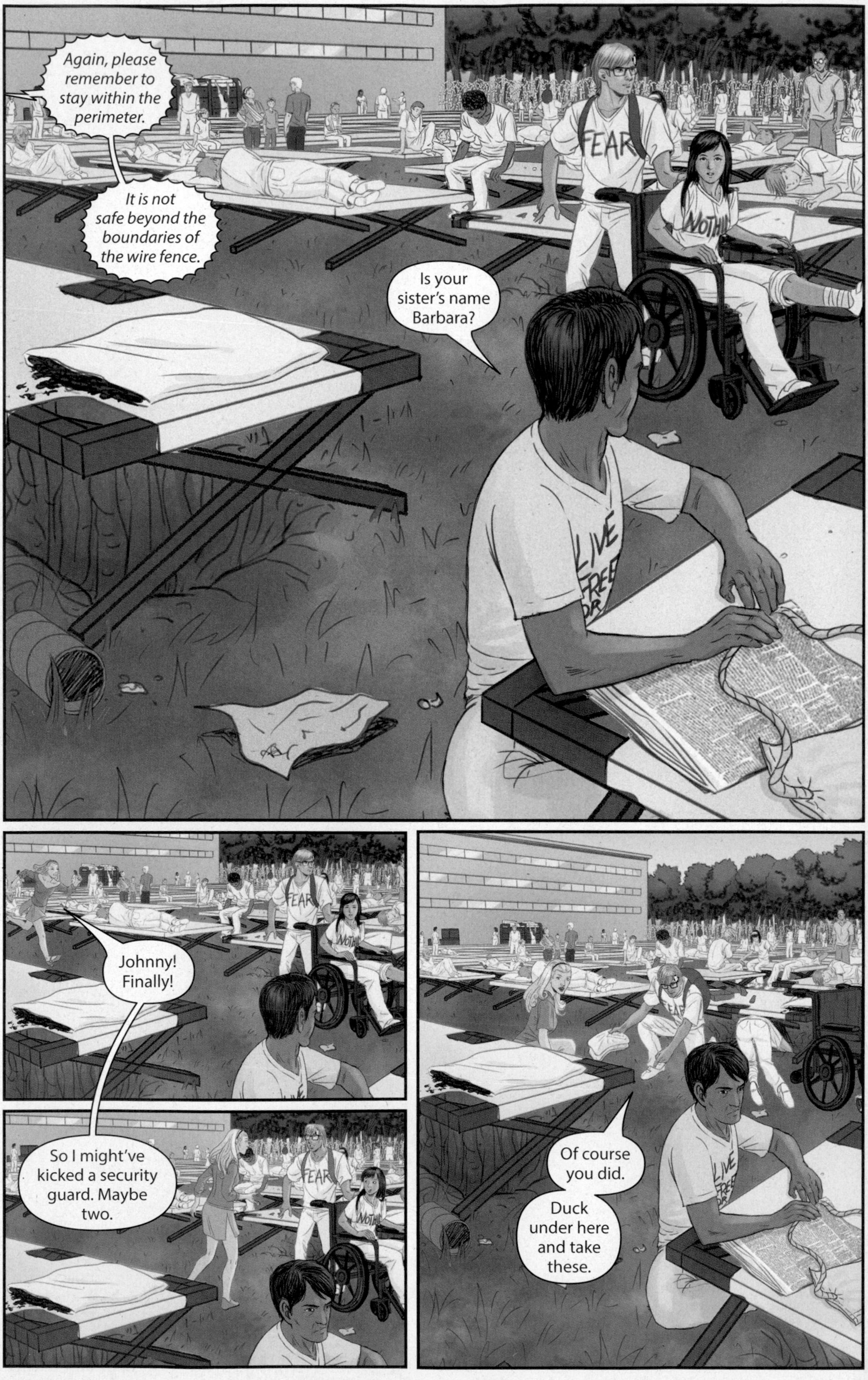
Again, please remember to stay within the perimeter.
It is not safe beyond the boundaries of the wire fence.
Is your sister's name Barbara?
Johnny! Finally!
So I might've kicked a security guard. Maybe two.
Of course you did.
Duck under here and take these.

Monday, April 25, 1966, 11:30 am
White House
Washington, DC

Almost all good news.

90 percent of known enemy forces have been eliminated.

90 percent of pandemic victims are in quarantine.

We're ready for mass vaccination in concentric circles around Evans County.

Good work, Curtis.

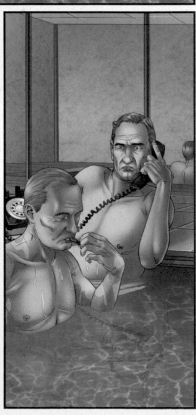

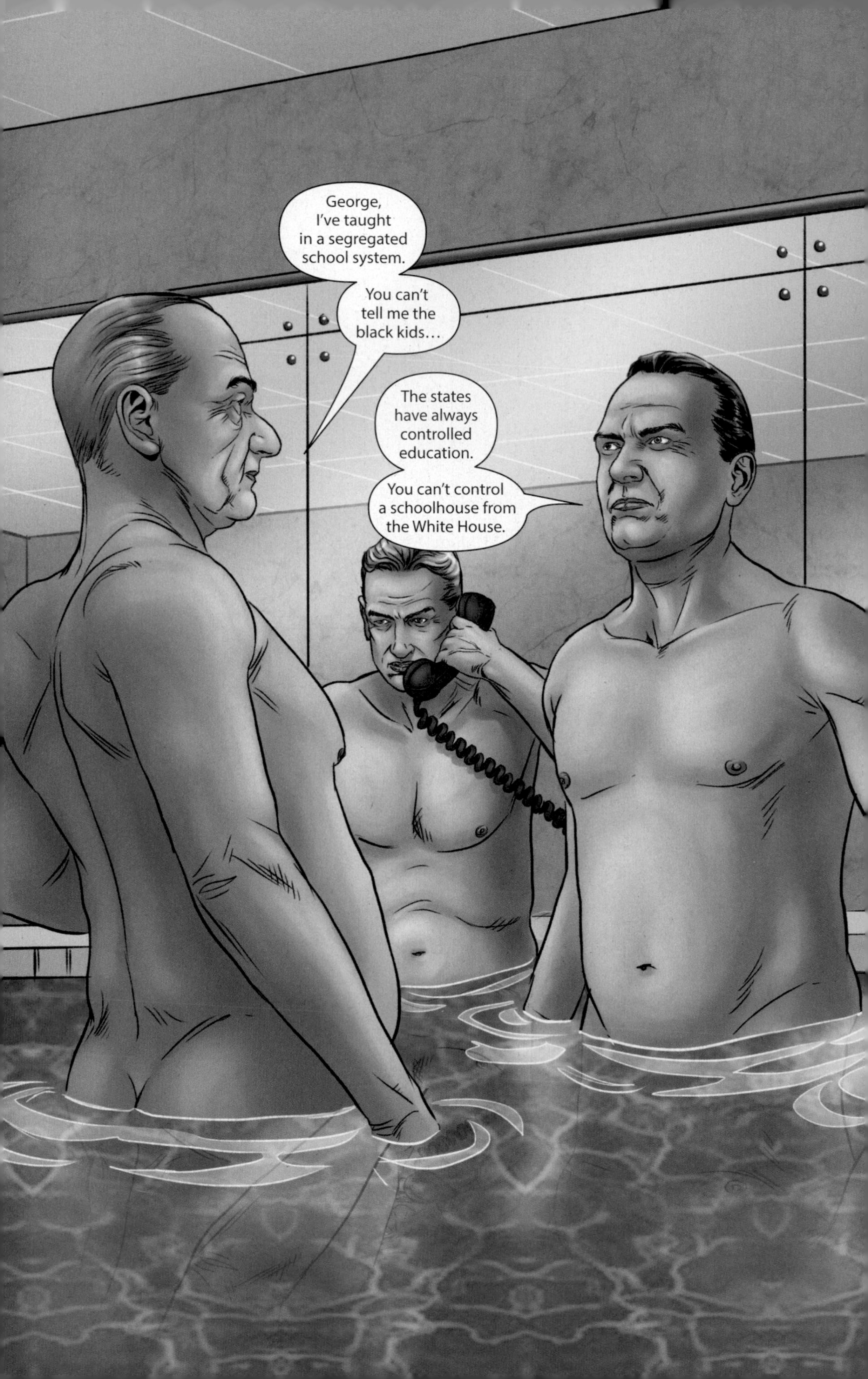
George, I've taught in a segregated school system.
You can't tell me the black kids…
The states have always controlled education.
You can't control a schoolhouse from the White House.

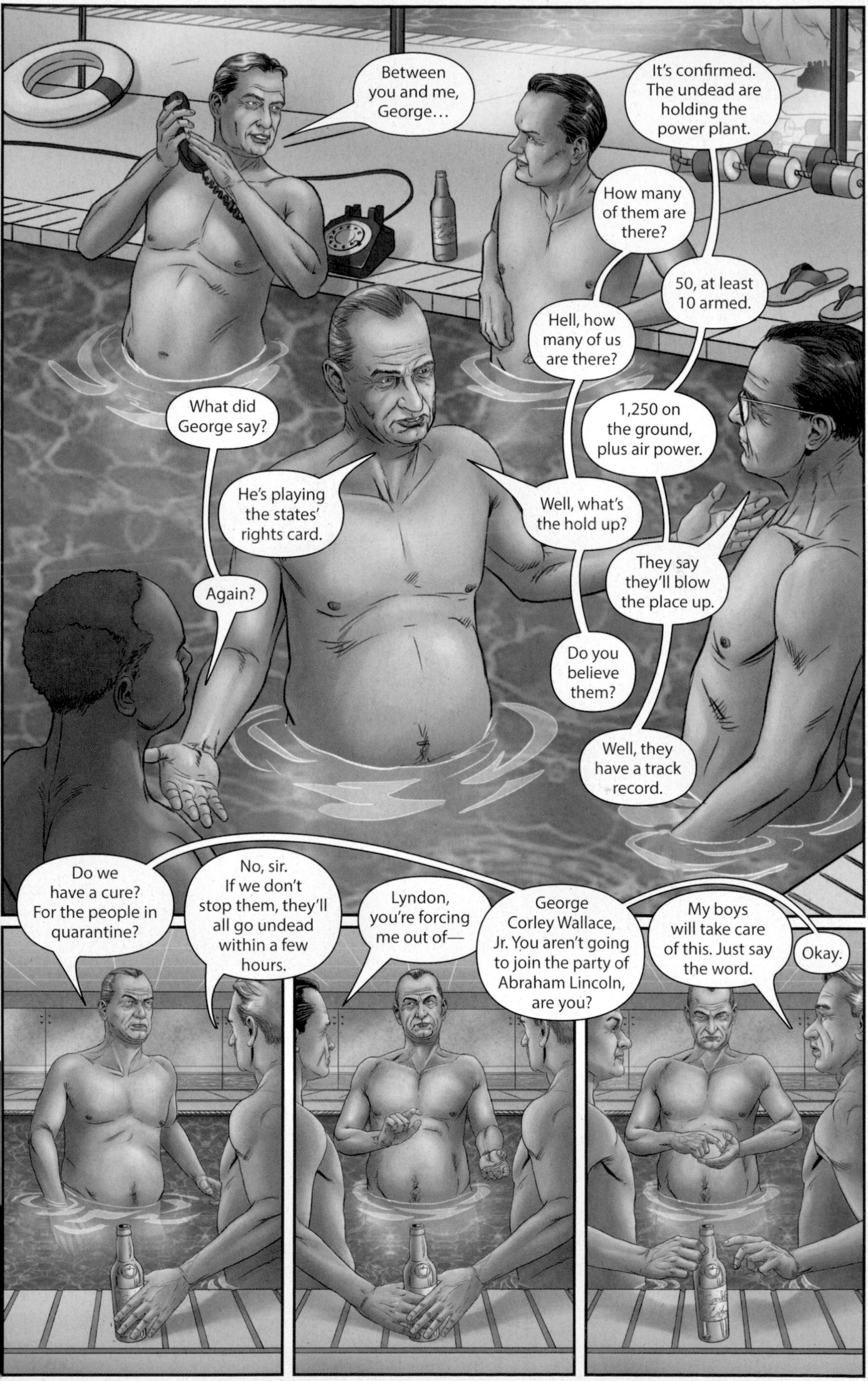
Between you and me, George…
It's confirmed. The undead are holding the power plant.
How many of them are there?
50, at least 10 armed.
Hell, how many of us are there?
1,250 on the ground, plus air power.
What did George say?
He's playing the states' rights card.
Again?
Well, what's the hold up?
They say they'll blow the place up.
Do you believe them?
Well, they have a track record.
Do we have a cure? For the people in quarantine?
No, sir. If we don't stop them, they'll all go undead within a few hours.
Lyndon, you're forcing me out of—
George Corley Wallace, Jr. You aren't going to join the party of Abraham Lincoln, are you?
My boys will take care of this. Just say the word.
Okay.

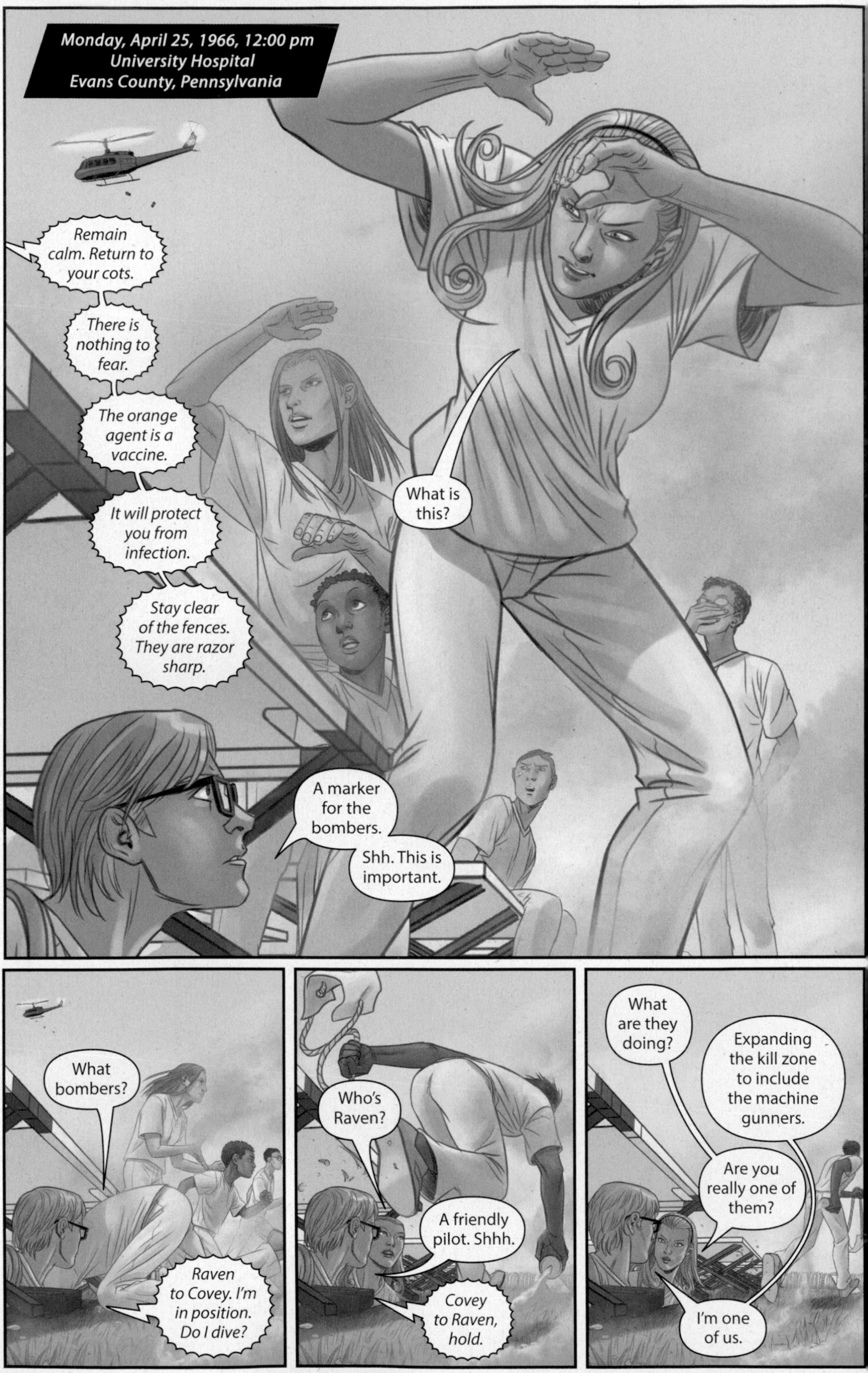
Monday, April 25, 1966, 12:00 pm
University Hospital
Evans County, Pennsylvania
Remain calm. Return to your cots.
There is nothing to fear.
The orange agent is a vaccine.
It will protect you from infection.
Stay clear of the fences. They are razor sharp.
What is this?
A marker for the bombers.
Shh. This is important.
What bombers?
Raven to Covey. I'm in position. Do I dive?
Who's Raven?
A friendly pilot. Shhh.
Covey to Raven, hold.
What are they doing?
Expanding the kill zone to include the machine gunners.
Are you really one of them?
I'm one of us.

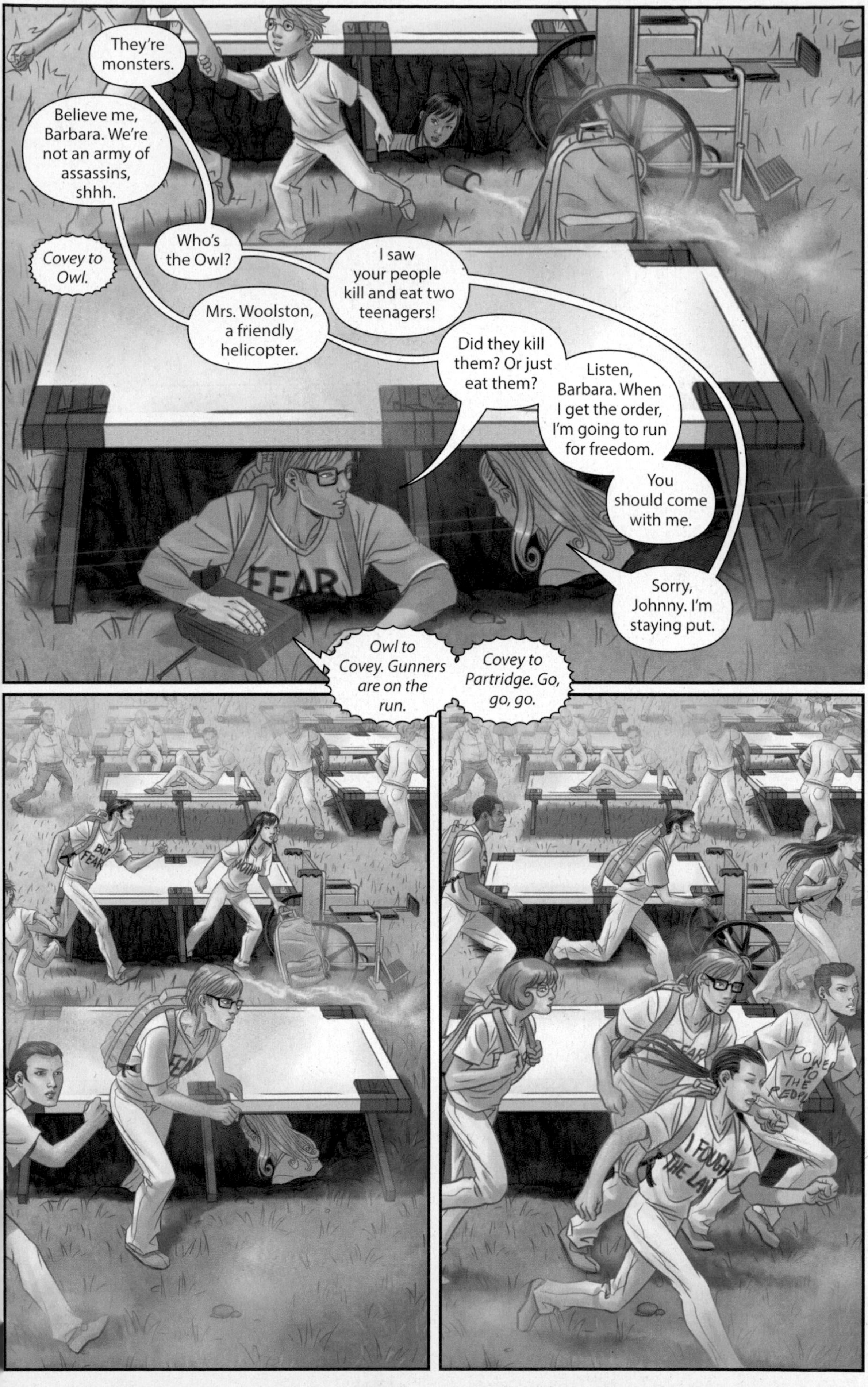
They're monsters.
Believe me, Barbara. We're not an army of assassins, shhh.
Who's the Owl?
Covey to Owl.
I saw your people kill and eat two teenagers!
Mrs. Woolston, a friendly helicopter.
Did they kill them? Or just eat them?
Listen, Barbara. When I get the order, I'm going to run for freedom.
You should come with me.
Sorry, Johnny. I'm staying put.
FEAR
Owl to Covey. Gunners are on the run.
Covey to Partridge. Go, go, go.
POWER TO THE PEOPLE

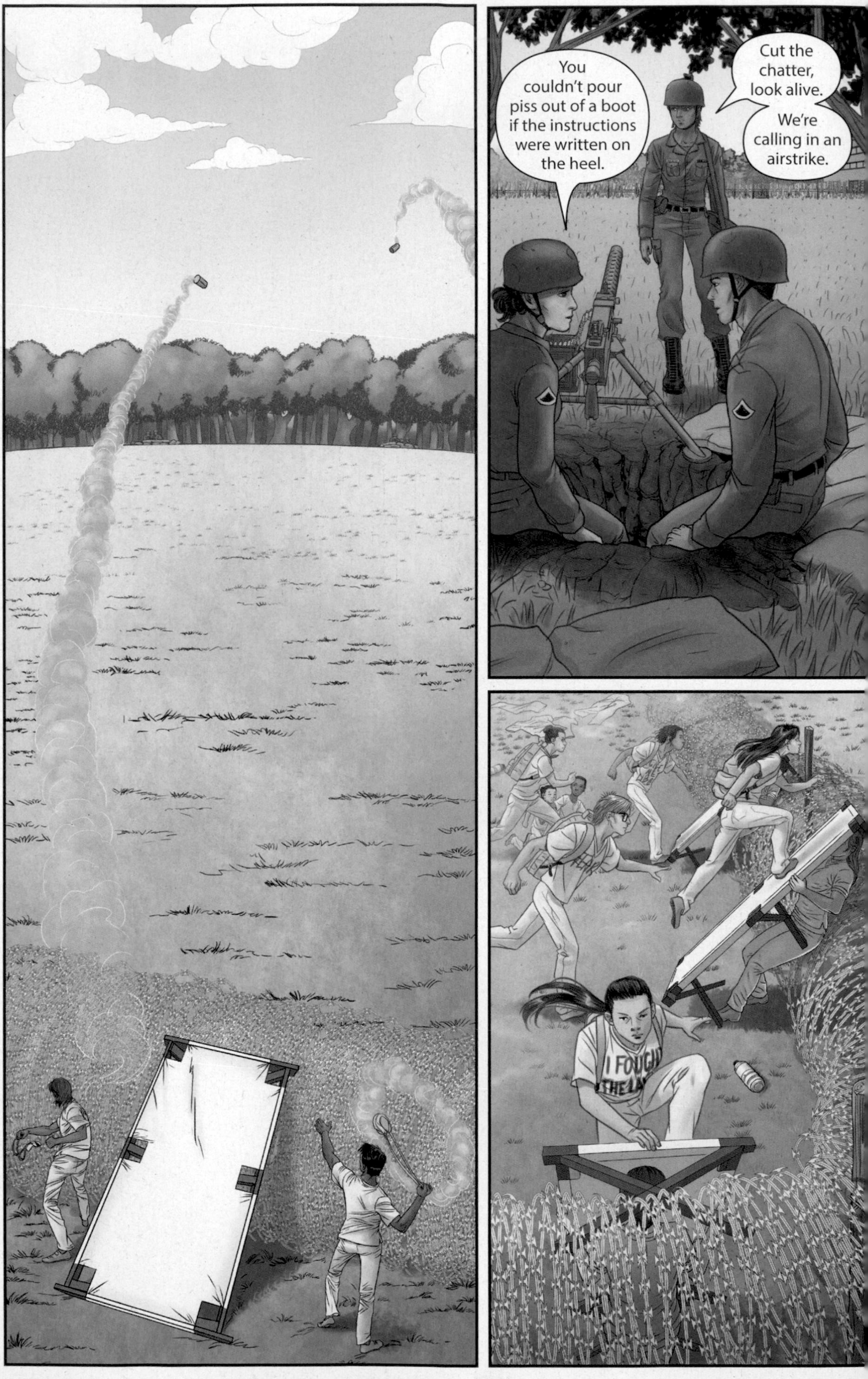
You couldn't pour piss out of a boot if the instructions were written on the heel.
Cut the chatter, look alive.
We're calling in an airstrike.

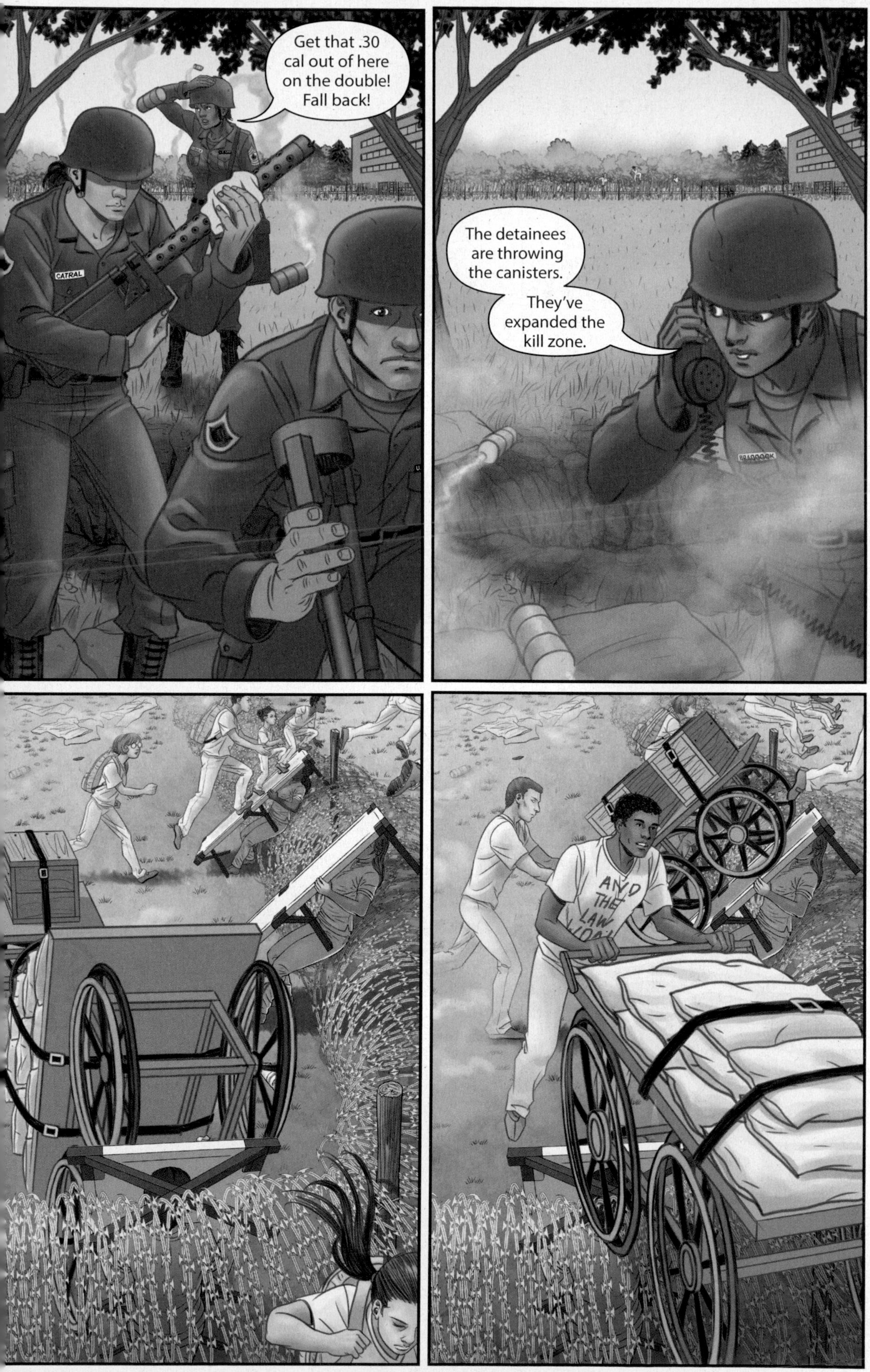

Get that .30 cal out of here on the double! Fall back!
CATRAL
The detainees are throwing the canisters.
They've expanded the kill zone.

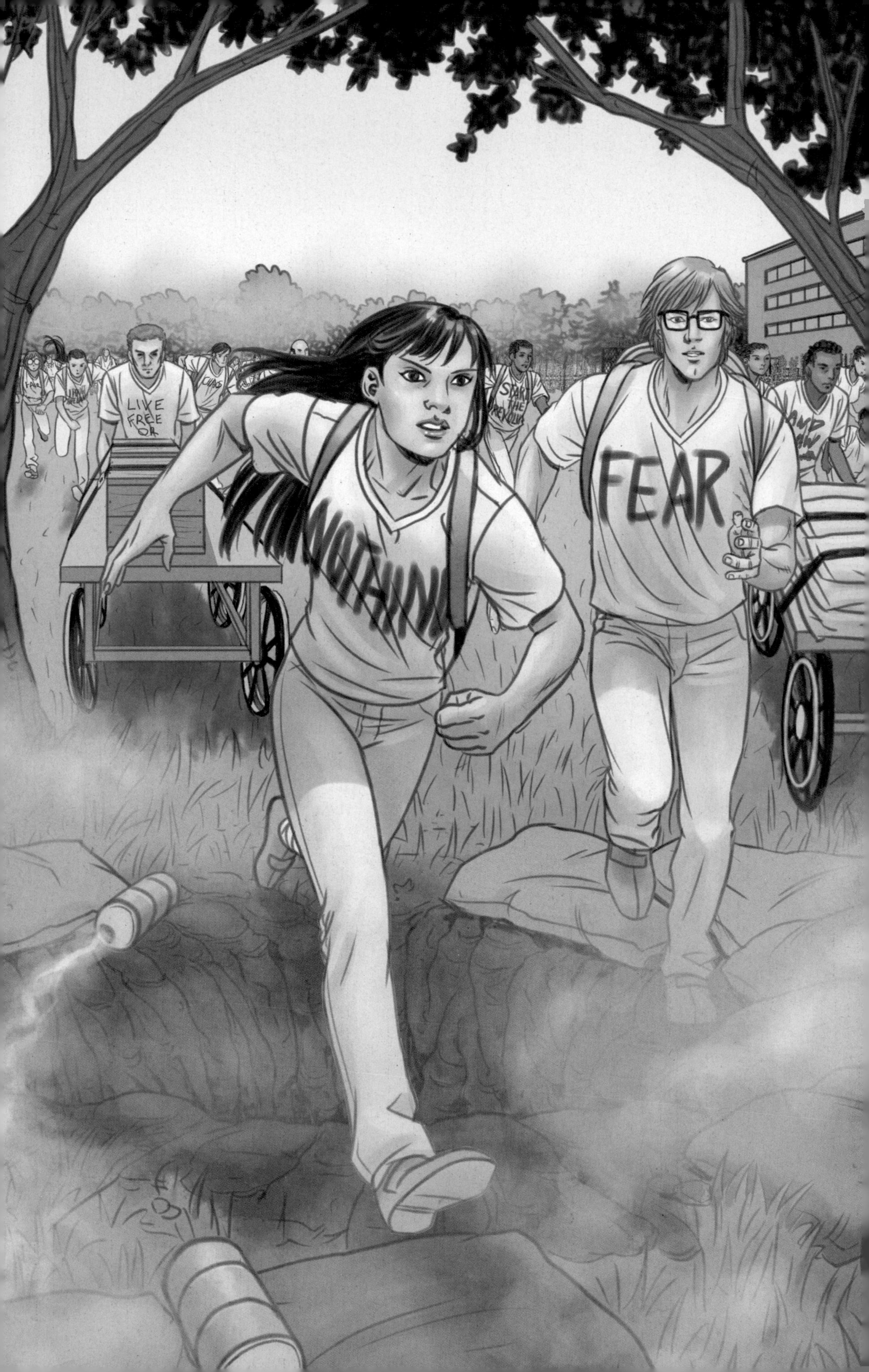
LIVE FREE OR
FEAR

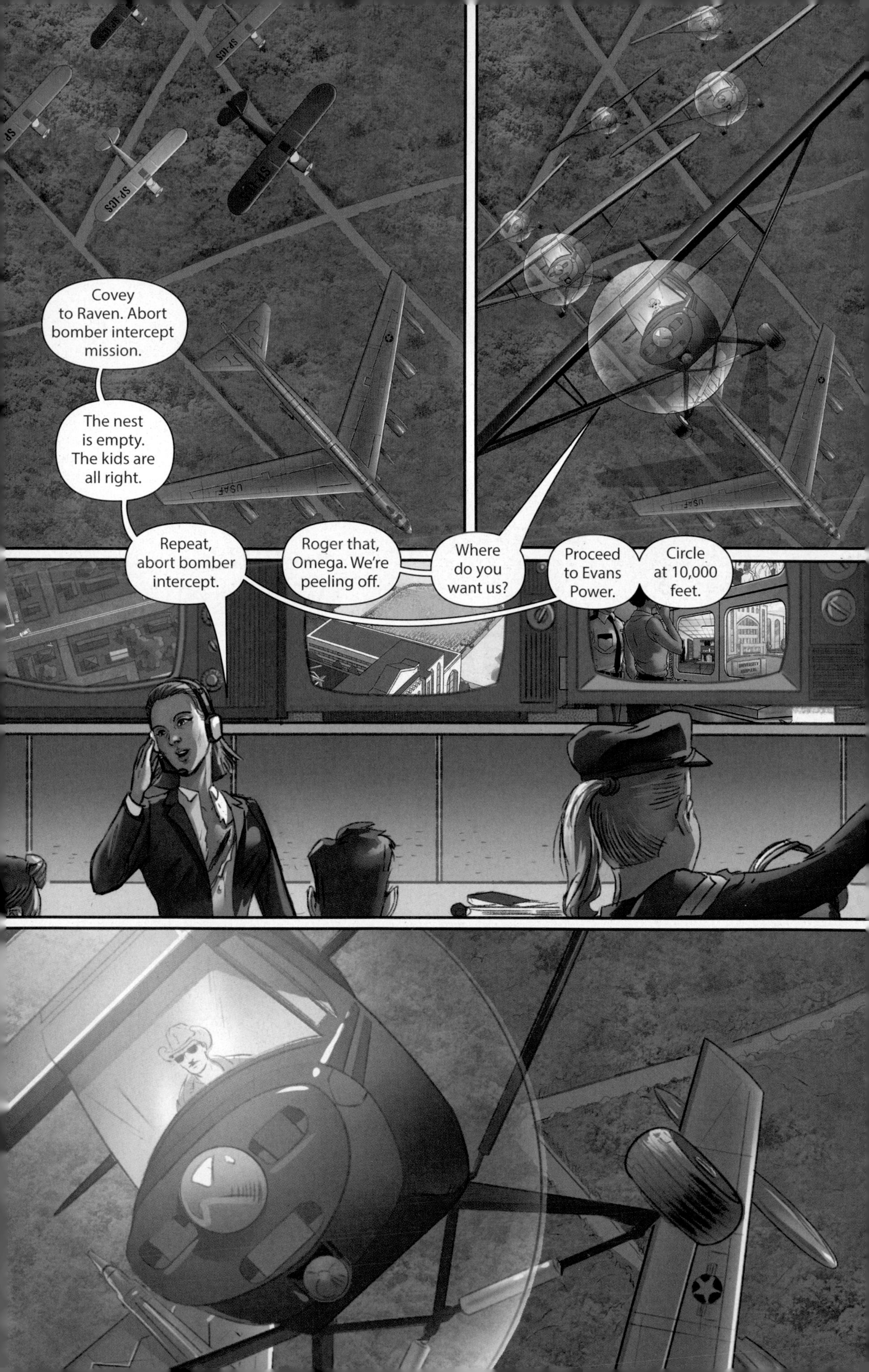
Covey to Raven. Abort bomber intercept mission.
The nest is empty. The kids are all right.
Repeat, abort bomber intercept.
Roger that, Omega. We're peeling off.
Where do you want us?
Proceed to Evans Power.
Circle at 10,000 feet.

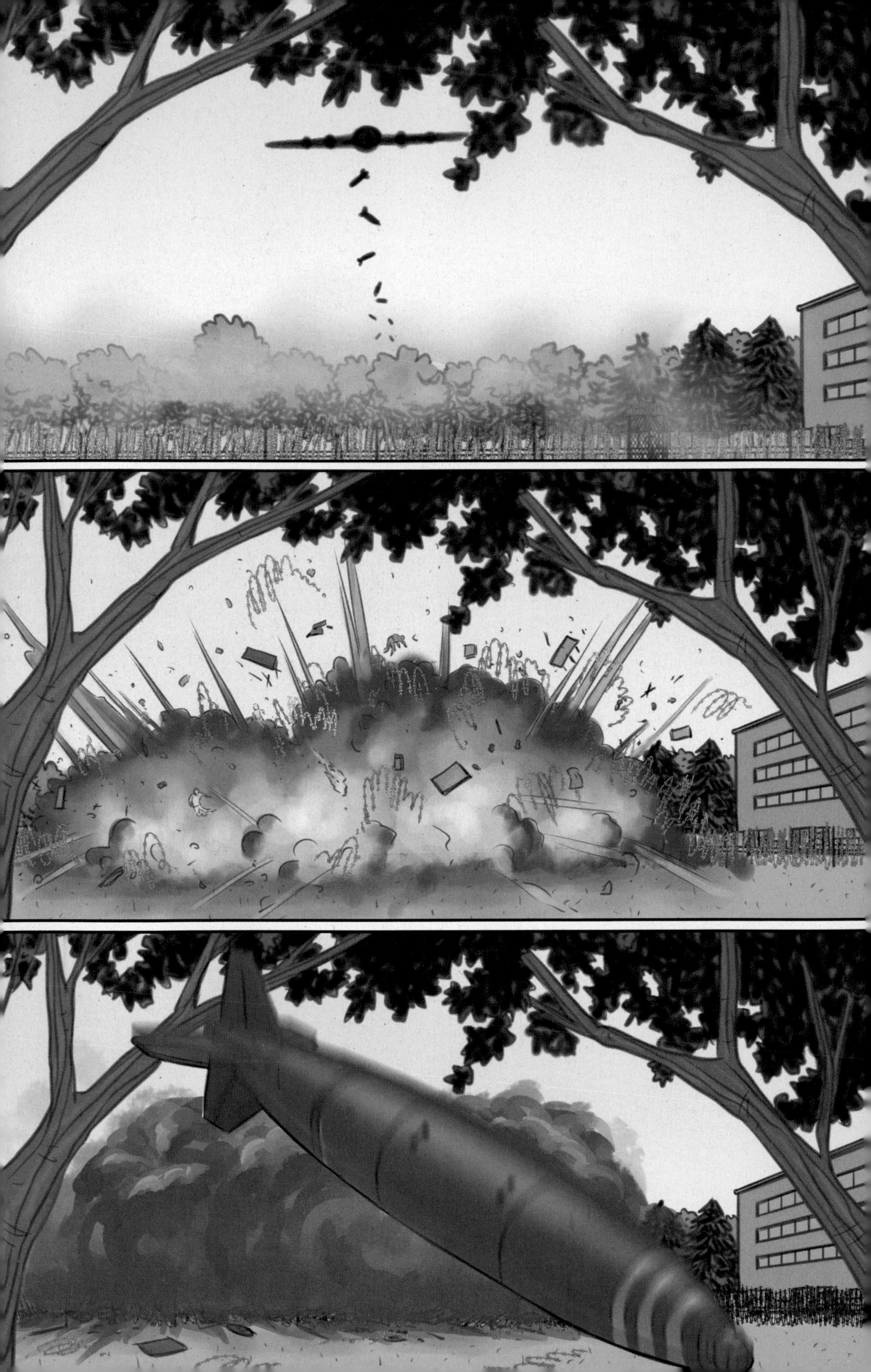

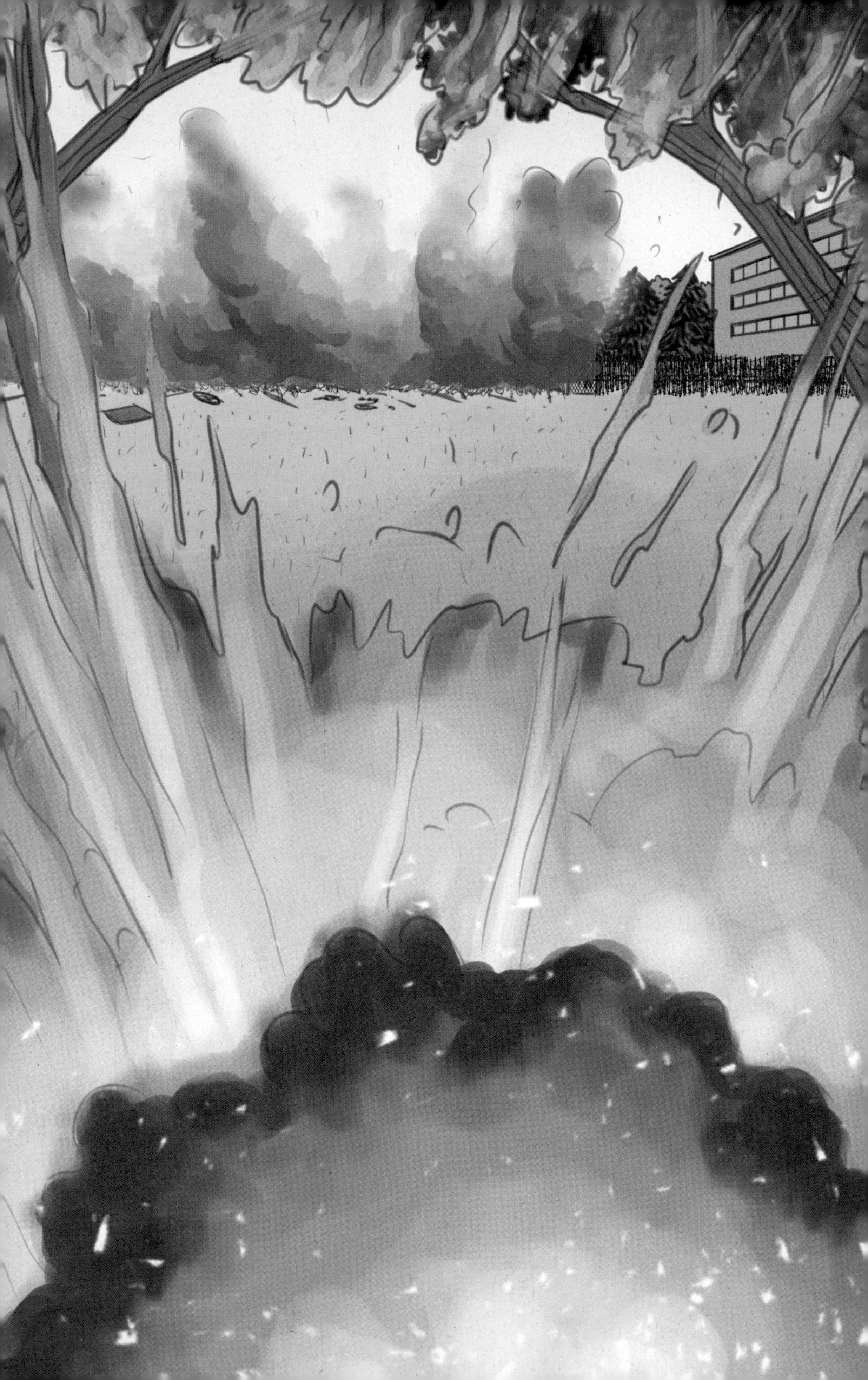

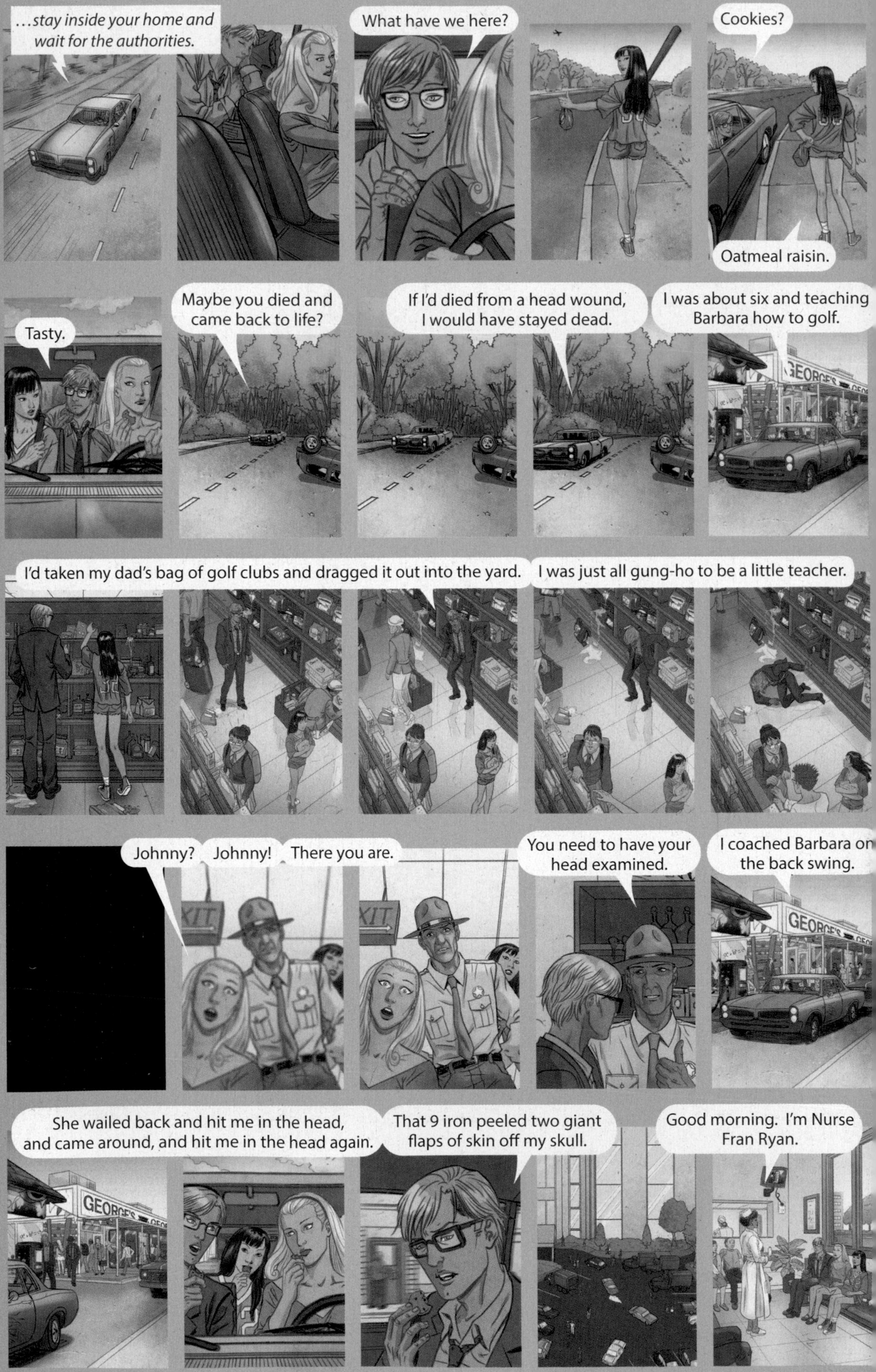
…stay inside your home and wait for the authorities.
What have we here?
Cookies?
Oatmeal raisin.
Tasty.
Maybe you died and came back to life?
If I'd died from a head wound, I would have stayed dead.
I was about six and teaching Barbara how to golf.
GEORGE'S
I'd taken my dad's bag of golf clubs and dragged it out into the yard.
I was just all gung-ho to be a little teacher.
Johnny?
Johnny!
There you are.
XIT
You need to have your head examined.
I coached Barbara on the back swing.
GEORGE'S
She wailed back and hit me in the head, and came around, and hit me in the head again.
GEORGE'S
That 9 iron peeled two giant flaps of skin off my skull.
Good morning. I'm Nurse Fran Ryan.